STARTING
FROM
SCRATCH

STARTING FROM SCRATCH

50 PROFITABLE BUSINESS OPPORTUNITIES

JOE SUTHERLAND GOULD

John Wiley & Sons

New York   Chichester   Brisbane   Toronto   Singapore

Library of Congress Cataloging in Publication Data:

Gould, J. Sutherland.
  Starting from scratch.

  Bibliography: p
  Includes index.
  1. New business enterprises.   I. Title.

HD62.5.G68   1987   658.1′1   86-28136
ISBN 0-471-85024-1
ISBN 0-471-01190-8 (pbk)

Printed in the United States of America

10 9 8 7 6 5 4 3 2 1

To my brother, Mac, a brilliant attorney whose logical guidance has helped me function intelligently instead of reacting emotionally

PREFACE

One of the great American fantasies for people locked into nine-to-five jobs is to have a business of their own where the strain of survival is replaced by a welcome freedom from authority. If successful, the profit and psychological benefits are bountiful.

Instead of that always impending agony of a call from your boss who might reproach you for some innocent error or press you to heighten your performance, or the fear of dismissal that concerns everyone who is employed, you are free to suffer your own blunders or to enjoy the exhilaration of your success.

It is indeed one of the American dreams. It is also an option over the years that more people in the work force have converted from a fantasy into a reality. Paycheck comfort is tougher to surrender than a spouse. However, today more people are taking the breakaway option. More often than ever you now hear, "Hell, I'd rather get ulcers or heart attacks being my own boss."

The entrepreneurial boom has been fueled by the wave of acquisitions, mergers, and reorganizations that has swept through American business in recent years. People in their 40s and 50s, many of whom had never worked for any other company, have lost their jobs.

Shortly after the American Broadcasting Company was in the hands of its new owners in 1986, a substantial number of employees were let go. To cut overhead costs after spending several millions of dollars to keep Ted Turner from taking over the network, the Columbia Broadcasting System embarked on a job slashing program, as well as selling its wholly owned subsidiaries.

Of course, increased automation has reduced the number of workers needed in many industries. Automated newspaper production and robots used to assemble cars has trimmed the number of jobs available in these fields.

Job Disappointment

One of the reasons many top executives break away from six figure salaries is job disappointment. Thomas Watson, a vice president of Olin Corporation supervising 4000 people, left when he failed to be appointed the president of the company. Today, he and his wife operate Miller Press, a successful printing firm in Jacksonville, Florida, employing 65 people.

Frank Morgan, 47, had held several different marketing posts during his 18 years with the Sun Company, finally becoming president of the overseas operation. Failing to get the promotion he wanted after the company reorganized in 1982, he left. After a short search for a new position, Morgan decided, "I wanted to be my own boss and have the freedom to make my own decisions."

As a result, he converted a hobby into a profitable business. For over a dozen years, Morgan had enjoyed recreational sailing. During a visit to St. Michaels, Maryland, he learned that the St. Michaels Town Dock Marina situated on Chesapeake Bay was for sale. He bought it and now employs eight people during the peak season. Morgan said that the business is able to support him completely.

Kay Redditt, after establishing an office-automation training program for the Katharine Gibbs national chain of secretarial schools, found that just supervising the operation was a boring, unchallenging job.

She left to start a consulting firm, the Cognitech Services Corporation, using her home in Easton, Connecticut as her office. She is the advisor to many businesses on automation and financial planning.

Career Switch or Business

Increasing numbers of people are going into business for themselves for various reasons from personal satisfaction to sheer necessity. Teachers, police officers, and other civic employees often exercise their options to retire with pension after 20 years of service. They are then faced with the decision to make a career switch from their mid-forties upward or to use their savings to start businesses of their own.

There is little doubt that the combination of factors such as promotional setbacks, job burnout, and the desire to shed the stress of being accountable to an authority figure every day has prompted people to try the entrepreneurial route.

According to Dr. Adela Oliver, president of Human Resources Consultants, Inc., New York, 10 percent of the hundreds of executives she counsels each year opt to start a business rather than take another job. Five years ago only two percent of her clients made the move to be on their own.

The Young Entrepreneurs

Youth, too, has been attracted to the virtues and pleasures of becoming an entrepreneur. In fact, there has been a swell of students who view entering a structured work routine as psychologically suffocating and start making it on their own before they are out of college.

While the enchantment of being your own boss is indeed attractive, the most practical motivation for owning a business is that this is how the truly big bucks are made. Verne Harnish, national chairman of the Association of Collegiate Entrepreneurs in 1985, observed, "When the business goes over $100,000 in gross revenues, it reaches a point where you either turn in your term paper or your tax forms."

As a junior at the University of Michigan, Bobby Kotick discovered creative and profitable satisfaction after founding the Arktronics Corporation with his friend, Howard Marks. After three years of designing and marketing software that they sold to such computer companies as Apple and Commodore, they grossed nearly $2 million in 1985.

"I never wanted to work for anyone else," Mark David McKee declared when he was a junior at the University of Kansas in 1985. "I'd rather be in charge of my own destiny. My goal is to be a millionaire by the time I am 25."

McKee is well on his way toward his monetary objective. When only into his third year at the university he was already president of two companies: Pyramid Pizza, a franchise operating on three campuses that earned $700,000 in sales revenue in 1985; and Waddles Active Wear, a fashion design company specializing in Hawaiian clothes. In 1986 McKee anticipated gross earnings of $2 million.

At every level of life, today more people are earning their livings doing it their way.

JOE SUTHERLAND GOULD

Yorktown Heights, New York
January 1987

CONTENTS

STARTING
FROM
SCRATCH

1

Introduction

What better way to learn about a business than by speaking to a person operating a successful one? Textbook authorities can explain what you should do; profitable entrepreneurs tell you how they did it.

The people who work, live, and supervise their businesses every day explain exactly what you will endure and encounter should you decide to go into one of the 50 ventures covered in this book. You are given tips, suggestions, facts, and information about costs and profits that can only come from people doing it rather than just observing.

You will get the answer to the first question that must be asked before you consider pursuing any commercial enterprise: "Is it right for my purse and will it suit my personality?" Being able to afford a business only means you are halfway there. Enduring its stresses and strains, seasonal fluctuations, customer-client pressures, and hours needed to service the venture are also major points of consideration.

For many, profit alone is not worth the commitment. To enjoy what you are doing while earning enough to support yourself is a critical need for many sensitive people. This book gives you the answers to help you make the right business choice.

The proprietors interviewed have provided varying estimates of start-up and operating costs for their businesses. This will give you an awareness of the approximate amount of investment money needed.

However, there are so many variables such as the rent for your location, number of employees, amount of inventory you will maintain, and expenditures for advertising and promotion that it is advisable to make a precise breakdown of your cost expectancy.

By getting the dollar amounts for the following list of items, you will have an accurate understanding of how much you will need to invest in the business of your choice.

GENERAL START-UP COSTS

Start-up investment	$ _____
Inventory	_____
Fixtures and equipment	_____
Installation of fixtures and equipment	_____
Remodeling and decorating	_____
Licenses and permits	_____
Professional (legal and accounting)	_____
Cash cushion	_____
Total start-up investment	$ _____

Operating Expenses—
3 Months

Salaries and wages	$ _____ Mo × 3	$ _____
Rent	_____ Mo × 3	_____
Telephone	_____ Mo × 3	_____
Utilities (light, heat)	_____ Mo × 3	_____
Office supplies	_____ Mo × 3	_____
Shop supplies	_____ Mo × 3	_____
Debt interest	_____ Mo × 3	_____
Advertising	_____ Mo × 3	_____
Maintenance	_____ Mo × 3	_____
Taxes	_____ Mo × 3	_____
Legal and accounting	_____ Mo × 3	_____

Operating Expenses—
3 Months

Insurance (fire, casualty, workers' compensation, disability, liability, etc.)	_____ Mo × 3	_____
Miscellaneous	_____ Mo × 3	_____
Total estimated costs for start-up and 3-month operation		$ _____

DETAILED START-UP COSTS

Advertising and Promotional	Estimated Cost
Business cards	$ _____
Slingers, mailers, ads, posters	_____
Business logo design	_____
Signs, outdoor	_____

Business Organization Costs	Estimated Cost
Accounting fees	$ _____
Decorating and remodeling	_____
Deposits, utilities and rent	_____
Insurance	_____
Legal fees	_____
Licenses and permits	_____
Telephone installation	_____

Office Operating Expenses	
Stationery	$ _____
Invoice forms	_____
Purchase order forms	_____
Cash register	_____
Pens, pencils, and so on	_____

Furniture and Fixtures	
Desks and chairs	$ _____
Filing cabinets	_____
Wastebaskets	_____
Typewriter	_____
Lighting fixtures	_____
Counters, shelves	_____

Tools and Equipment	$ _____

Inventory	$ _____

Loan Money

Should you need to secure loan money from a bank, you will be required to present a Personal Financial Statement (PFS) listing what you own and what you owe. By providing the lending institution this list of your assets and liabilities, a determination can be made of your net worth. Most banks will supply you with a PFS form which requires the following information.

Personal Financial Statement

I Own

Cash	
Bank accounts	$ _____
Other	_____
Securities-quick-sale value	_____
Real estate-quick-sale value	_____
Furniture-quick-sale	_____
Car-value life insurance	_____
Cash-value life insurance	_____

Personal Financial Statement

Savings bonds	_____
Other assets	_____
Receivables	_____
Total	$ _____

I Owe

Current household bills	$ _____
Installment contracts	_____
Car	_____
Appliances	_____
Personal loan	_____
Other	_____
Real estate mortgage	_____

(describe _____

_____

_____)

Other loans	_____

(describe _____

_____

_____)

Total	$ _____
I own	$ _____
I owe	$ _____
My net worth is	$ _____

In addition, the bank will also expect you to bring in your start-up cost tabulations along with an estimate of projected income for the first fiscal year.

Insurance Needs

Once a routine addition to operating a business, liability insurance has become costly in many situations, and, at times, difficult to get. Lawsuits are so commonplace in the United States that this country is known as the litigious society.

Insurance protection to cover all contingencies is obviously an essential cost of operating a business. Review the insurance checklist with care to determine what you need to have your business completely protected. There are still ample companies that would like to get your premiums. Therefore, take the time to shop around for the best rates.

Checklist

Inventory

Building

Office equipment

Show equipment

Vehicles

Records

Currency or security

Employee personal property

Smoke and fire

Water

Floaters

Theft and burglary

Floods

Windstorm and hail

Explosion

Riots

Vandalism

Plate glass

Lightning

Business interruption

Life and health losses
Workers' compensation
Disability
Key executive insurance (partner)
Hospitalization and medical care
Life insurance
Workers' compensation claims (if caused by improper repair or negligence by service technicians)

Liability claims
Product
On-premises accident-employees
Nonemployees

Vehicle accidents
Collision
Bodily injury
Towing
Theft
Property
Liability

Trade Publications

One way to get an updated understanding of the trends, problems, and outlook for any business before you start it is to read the trade publications that cover this kind of commercial operation. Names and addresses of the major ones are listed at the end of each oral history.

Recommendation—Buy six back issues and you will get a comprehensive view of what is happening in any retail field or professional service.

2

Actor's Agent

For the past 25 years, Gloria Troy, owner of the Gloria Troy Talent Agency, has earned her living being the anonymous link to the successful careers of many actors and actresses. While many of her performers have achieved fame and fortune, Troy still operates her agency from a tiny office in New York City.

It's a business where the fortune comes to her clients. For her it is a way of survival that she loves. A former singer, she has never lost her need to be connected to show business where actor loyalty is as thin as sheer cloth.

Too often, she explains, the performers she escalates to fame by exposing them to just the right auditions, leave for other agents who have plushier surroundings and presumably better connections.

Troy had seen her son work in every area of show business and then leave it to put the uncertainty and the rejection behind him. A member of the Screen Actors Guild, American Federation of Radio & Television Artists, and Actor Equity, she finds the business today more crowded and difficult. However, there is nothing else she would consider doing.

Talent agent Troy tells you why.

Gloria Troy

It's a little tougher for a person who has never been in the business to become an agent. Anybody can become a manager, but if you want to become an agent you have to have some kind of background in the business, because you are handling people's careers. If you worked two years for an agent, or even with a manager, for that matter, you get the needed expertise. You know what to do and whom to contact. At one time you had to have a city license just to be sure you didn't have some sort of criminal record. It's no longer needed. I've been in this for 25 years, and things have changed. Today an agent has to be bonded in the event that you go under. Money from the bond is used to pay your clients.

Unions

Then you get your union franchises. When you go to Actors Equity, you move upward and it's a little frightening. About 10 to 12 people there ask you questions. Mainly, they are interested in things like, "will you go see showcases" and "are you willing to represent minorities." They are really looking out for their people. So you say yes to everything and do it. It seems like everyone in the world is becoming an agent. There are more agencies now than there ever were. Managers are increasing, too.

No Advertising

We are always looking for new people but I don't advertise. It's word of mouth. I didn't ever have to, because I had a following. They put out this book called the *Ross Report*; all of the agents are listed in there. That's all you really need. The pictures keep coming every day, and the phone calls. Actors talk to each other. They say, "Gee, how do I get up to see so-and-so?" Well, buy the *Ross Report* and send out your picture.

All of the franchised agents are listed in here. They have franchises for the Screen Actors Guild and Equity. You have to be franchised; that's what makes you an agent as opposed to a manager. Managers don't need anything, except a room and a phone. That's all.

Then people come to you and you read their resumes and hope that they are telling the truth. Sometimes resumes are falsified. This one actor walked in and had a resume that would choke a horse. I was very embarrassed but the agent in the other room asked him who the producer was on a certain show, and the actor didn't know. When asked how many of these things he did, it was only two projects. He got the job anyway. He was a good actor. He just thought he had to puff up his credits.

I like it when they come in and say they haven't done anything. If they belong to SAG (Screen Actors Guild) or Equity and they have off-Broadway credits, I am inclined to believe them. If they have Broadway credits, of course, I believe them. I like it better when they tell me about college, the productions that they have been in at school. They can't claim commercial credits unless they belong to SAG. What makes me decide to take on actors is their looks and how they speak. I have them read copy. If I see talent there I take a chance. But when they start moving up a little bit, they leave you for another agent.

Contracts

A lot of agents sign all of their people. We don't. We just sign the ones we know we can keep happy. Because we get a lot of client flack such as, "I'm the same type, how come I didn't go out on that call?" We do have signed clients, but they are people who work all the time. It's a nice relationship. You see, in California they have to sign with one agent. New York City is a freelance town. They can be listed with many agents. Sometimes it gets to be a rat race. It's a question of whether someone is perfect for a part and it depends on who gets there first.

In terms of creating visibility, it's a long process. You send out pictures and hope to place one of your clients. Call on the phone and introduce yourself, like any business. You have to be in touch. You are only as important to an advertising agency as the job you did with them yesterday, because there are so many agents banging on their doors. A lot of people put out head sheets, a picture montage of your clients. But that is only for modeling. Those also get sent out. It could produce placements.

Earnings

There is still a 10 percent commission in this field, as that is all the union will allow us to take. After a commercial runs for 21 months, we send a letter 120 days before and not less than 60 days before the commercial ends to renegotiate if it will be used after that time. You get 15 percent additional with the approval of the ad agency and that's included in the check for the performer. Of course, you also try to get more for your talent, but the ad agency might refuse. It will offer you only the minimum rate. You try to get more for the next 21 months. But if the agency says no, we take the union scale.

Payment

The checks come to the agents and are put in a wash account which has nothing but talent payments. Then I issue a check to my client, deducting 10 percent. If somebody made $1000 I deduct $100. Occasionally, you have to put in some of your own money to cover costs. Certain banks charge you costs; you have to put a couple of thousand dollars extra in there.

Expenses

The overhead situation—office, postage, phone—is getting more expensive every day. The rents are astronomical, as you know. You can't get a four room office for less than $3000 per month. It depends on how many employees you have. It's very hard for one person. You have to be in the business and successful before you see any return. If you are a crackerjack, within six months you should be seeing some kind of money, if you have booked somebody in a play, film, or commercials. Today salaries are very high.

I would say it's going to cost between $4000 and $5000 a month. To expect to break even, you would need about a year or more if you are good, lucky, and have great people. Years ago if there were 50 people on a call that was a lot. But now we have what they call casting consultants, and I don't know how many members of the union there are, but there are tons and tons of them. There's a lot of people for the one job—maybe 300 to 400. Ten years ago there would be half that many because there were half that many agents. But now they see so many people. Everything is so expensive that they are looking for the best talent they can get. Commercials cost a fortune, so they see a lot of people to justify the money that they spend. You might realize $30,000 to $40,000 profit within five years. The ones that do the best, of course, have five to seven agents. Each person multiplies the other's productivity, and usually they all have their own little departments to work in. The union encourages us to get sub-agents licenses for them. They send us a letter and ask us to list our sub-agents. I would call the union and say I want a person to be a sub-agent and then fill out the proper papers. You pay a fee.

Hours

There are a lot of agencies that open up at 10 A.M. and close at 6 P.M. That's not the nature of my business, because as you know, I work with a lot of children. I'll have someone call me at five minutes to 6:00 and tell me they want 30 kids for tomorrow. It's due to the fact that I work with children that there are long hours. The ad agencies close at 5:00 and 6:00. The casting consultants never seem to close. They are hired by ad agencies. They don't want talent coming to their offices. These consultants have their own facilities and audition equipment.

We have one girl on a show here that is doing very well. Not a week goes by without a call from California regarding her. They see the soap operas and inquire about her. A lot of calls come from California so we make submissions and send them in. We send a videotape, if requested, and if the client has one. The first thing we do is ask if there is a representative coming here if our client can't afford to fly to the coast and back for an audition. It's too much. Some of them pick up the costs if they want them badly enough. Most of the time, they have someone come here to see them.

This is such a weird business; one month the money is just flowing in, and the next month nothing. It depends on the commercials, how they are running, what cycle you are in, and how long ago they were paid for.

New People

This agency is pretty open. We try to see as many people as we can, but only by appointment. For the first five years I was in business, every Thursday, without fail, people came in. It was open house. It got pretty hairy. They were lined up in the hall. We had to stop that. Now it's appointments. You must see new people, though. If somebody calls me and they have a very thick accent, I know I am going to have a problem. It is going to be very difficult, unless someone is looking for that type, a person who speaks Russian fluently, for instance. Once I got a call for somebody who speaks Arabic. I just happened to have him. A man called me and said he spoke Arabic fluently, and I said fine. I had him on my list, and he got the job.

Client Control

The most aggravating part of the job is wanting clients to leave. They come in and talk with you, and you say thank you very much, we will let you know, or we will call you when we can, or I want to think about it, but they just hang around and hang around. So I have to tell them I am really very busy. Actors should be more sensitive to agents. Also, people send in pictures and call two days later asking if I got the pictures. How can I remember? We get about 150 pictures a week. It's annoying and time consuming.

Problems

We're only told who gets the job, not who fails. Or if somebody behaves really badly, I hear about that. The biggest offense is being late. The actors say I'll be there, but then I get a call from the casting person looking for them. Not telling the agent or casting person when you're not going to show up is unprofessional. They try to get there, but traffic in New York is horrendous. You can't go from here to there without having to waste an hour. So allow for that and allow for getting lost. When the production manager calls and asks, "Where is he?" my answer is always the same. "He knew he was supposed to be there, he's not at home, so he must be on his way." This is a very aggravating part of this business.

Actors sometimes contact the casting directors. Role call is something new. For a fee, your picture is put on special film suitable for telex monitors. Let's say someone from Grant Advertising wants to meet Bob Smith. He will call this outfit. From its main office a picture is piped through to the agency with a resume. A lot of actors have signed up for this, and it hurts the agents. This is really a threat but some agents don't worry because all their people are signed. Well, I say good for them, but not all my people are under contract. The actors love it, and I don't blame them. I suppose if I were still a performer, I would like it, too.

It's hectic but I still like my work.

Trade Publications

Variety
154 West 46 Street
New York, NY 10036
(212) 869-5700

Back Stage
330 West 42 Street
New York, NY 10036
(212) 947-0020

Showbusiness
1501 Broadway
New York, NY 10036
(212) 354-7600

3

Antiques Store

Regrettably, of all the associations contacted for information about starting a business in their fields, only the National Association of Dealers in Antiques, Inc. (NADA), responded.

The NADA provided excellent guidelines on what is needed to operate an antique business profitably. It is a business that people can start later in life after a process of self-education that will provide the basic awareness of what qualifies a piece as a genuine antique, how to acquire inventory, and how to determine pricing. A solid foundation of understanding can be achieved by reading the many books on the subject directed at dealers, studying the trends reported in trade journals that cover the field (get at least six back issues), and establishing a complete reference library that permits a dealer to determine the real market value of various items.

Can Start Small

The character of an antiques shop will be the same if it is a tiny roadside establishment with an inventory of $4000 or one dealing in period furniture with a variety of pieces in stock that amount to several hundred thousand dollars. Also, contrary to basic retailing that demands stores be shiny and slick, with products displayed in a neat, orderly manner, the primitive look is often an asset. Age is a major attraction as it is one of the fundamental assets of an antique.

Stores with a weathered look have enormous marketing appeal. Shoppers in search of bargains or discovering a special antique treasure are often more inclined to check out rustic shops on rural roads. Therefore, a small location is as appealing as a large facility.

The NADA points out that most of the people in this business have been collectors and became dealers by selling the items they had purchased over a period of years—instant inventory. However, with enough start-up money to invest, antique merchandise can be purchased at auctions, farm sales, and from other dealers. Of course, it is important to assemble enough items with considerable variety to attract customers.

An antiques business can be launched anywhere: in a home, barn, or small store. Since antique hunters do not look for slick surroundings to buy, the place for your retail establishment is less important than what you have to sell. Having a lower overhead, more money can be used to attract customers through advertising, sales promotion, and other traffic building methods.

There is still another operating option for a prospective antiques dealer—the no-shop selling approach. These dealers conduct business by mail order and by selling their wares at shows held throughout the country. Costs for show-sellers include booth rental, transporting merchandise, travel, hotel expenses, and dining. However, having access to a highly concentrated number of potential buyers generated by these shows can produce a substantial amount of sales in a short time.

Inventory and Growth

While inventory will vary from shop to shop according to size and volume of business, the ideal situation is to be able to turn over all your merchandise about two and one-half times each year.

The earnings potential? The NADA noted that for an inventory totaling $30,000, the expectation is that it should yield an annual gross of $70,000.

The growth expectancy, to a great extent, depends on store location and the economy of the country. Other factors impacting prospective sales are:

Skilled buying practices

Knowledge of national trends

Sensitive awareness of what sells best in your area

Satisfying local demands rather than national trends only

Careful specialization—never to the total exclusion of basic variety

Guarding against overstocking to meet a trend so as not to be left with unsold merchandise when some other type of antique becomes popular with shoppers

Mark-Ups and Profit

Mark-ups vary as some dealers operate on the "keystone" profit margin, adding at least 100 percent to establish the retail price, whenever possible. Others operate with an increase of 33 1/3 percent. For big ticket items a mark-up of 20 percent is generally used.

Of course, overhead expenses are often a major consideration in what a dealer must charge for merchandise. According to the NADA, the 100 percent mark-up is generally the rule for storefront operations. The anticipated net profit yield is for about seven percent. This is earnings in addition to the owner's base salary.

Help from the NADA

The NADA serves all of the states, Puerto Rico, and Canada. Members share information and experiences that can offer insights on increasing sales.

The monthly magazine published by the NADA covers new legislation, alerts readers to the most recent reproductions, lists upcoming forums and seminars, and has one in-depth feature article about antiques. The publication is only available to members.

As a highly professional organization, the NADA is open only to dealers who have an established survival rate: two years experience as a shop owner and three years for "shows only dealers." The NADA membership is also open to show promoters, purveyors to the trade, and antique educators.

Inquiries about membership and annual dues should be sent to:

National Association of Dealers in Antiques, Inc.
7080 Old River Road
Rockford, IL 61103

The Real Thing

Of course, general guidelines on operating a business from a major association in the field are indeed helpful, but what is it like to live with the real thing, actually operating an antique store?

Candice Denslow, owner of Hathcliff and Company, a European antiques store located in Armonk, New York, provides insights and awareness that is rarely, if ever, revealed by any professional association.

Candice Denslow

Like so many other women, I am one of those people who found it hard just to sit home and take care of my children. I wanted very badly to do something in business that would give me a feeling of accomplishment and at the same time make enough money to feel independent.

Although I must admit money was an important goal, I really wanted to develop an income by doing something I would enjoy—not just anything.

Background

After I graduated from college with a degree in literature, I became a copywriter for an advertising agency in Boston. It was a creative position that gave me a great deal of satisfaction. Then I got married, had two kids, and moved to Armonk, New York, where I'm living now. But when the kids started to go to school I found myself caring for an empty house most of the day. This was absolutely boring for me.

However, before going into the antiques business which is what attracted me most, I decided to prepare for success. I know it just doesn't happen by renting a store. You need to know what you are doing. That's why I went to the New York School of Interior Design and learned how to distinguish antiques from old furniture.

Beginning

I started by opening a small shop in my town, stocking it with merchandise that I thought would sell in my area. This was my first lesson in product marketing. Something everyone interested in this business should consider doing before acquiring any kind of inventory is to determine if what you plan to sell is right for your location. The mistake I made was taking in merchandise that appealed to me but did not sell well in a town with an older, affluent population. I was selling furniture that had an informal country look, and it did not move.

My first store was opened in 1982 when the buying trend in the area was more to elegant pieces than casual ones. Eight months later I had to close my business. It was a very depressing setback that prompted me to wonder if I could ever become a successful retailer of antiques. In fact, you start questioning yourself about whether you will ever succeed in any business.

Marketing Research

Clearly I had failed by not knowing what should be sold where. I then consulted marketing experts—in advertising market surveys are made continually for clients—and got some critical guidelines from specialists. A quick analysis of my failure by the pros indicated that I had opened up my store in an area where most of the residents were older, well-to-do people who were interested in a formal look.

I was told that the pieces I was trying to sell, pine that had a country look, were better suited for customers in high power professions who like informality at home as a way of relaxing. People into formal antique pieces are the spit and polish type individuals who keep cleaning and polishing their antiques all of the time.

People who work day by day on jobs that are very stressful are less concerned about nicks and scratches. Becoming upset about the wear and tear of furniture would only add to their tension level. Therefore, they tend to be more at ease and don't have the white glove attitude.

Waitressing Interlude

I had decided that I would build a clientele for antiques before I opened my next shop. Also, by establishing a list of customers who gave me orders for specific items, I would be able to establish credit with suppliers.

Now how was I going to do this?

My plan, which seemed to be outrageous to many people, was to take a job as a waitress at a plush country inn near my home. The patrons at this place were very much into the antique buying world. Since people remain at this inn for days and often for a week or two, it gave me the opportunity to get to know them well enough to speak to them about my antique business interest. At the appropriate time I would explain to the guests that I would be opening a shop again in the future. I asked them if they would be interested in being informed when the store would be opened.

This is how I began putting together a valuable list of potential customers in advance of my new business venture. Now, what I discovered as well was that many of these people who would be customer prospects were immediately interested in acquiring special pieces that they wanted and had been looking for. In fact, just about all antique enthusiasts are always looking for some addition to their home collections.

After having a large list of orders from people who I decided were honestly interested in buying, I decided to try to fill their demands by making a trip to Europe to see if I could find what they wanted. In this way, I would have the chance to see how well I could do as a retail shopper for waiting customers.

My only concern was over what would happen if the pieces I found were not bought by my customers since they might not be exactly what they ordered. I settled this problem with myself by deciding that by that time I would have my new store and sell the unbought merchandise from there.

Getting Suppliers

Having compiled a really substantial list of buyers, I then started contacting suppliers with whom I had remained in touch even after my first store folded. I kept them alerted to the client list I was putting together and that certainly helped maintain their interest in me as an imaginative retailer. Having the names of ready buyers has an impact in this business.

By the time I opened my second store in Armonk, I was an antique merchant not only a lot more experienced than I was before, but one who had established a large number of customer prospects. In this way I could manage to have the suppliers give me a credit line for 30 days before I had to pay for the merchandise I would order.

Now I had a month to sell my consignment furniture to get the money to pay for the merchandise and enough profit to subsidize my first trip to Europe to locate the pieces for the orders I had. Obviously, my best bet was to move as much of my inventory as possible as quickly as I could. Very simply, I had to offer my merchandise at a very reasonable competitive price.

A basic mark-up in this business is 100 percent. But like all things, that will vary from dealer to dealer. The difference is not on the down side. Not at all. Most of my competitors mark their pieces up from 200 to 300 percent.

Antique buyers have a high intensity drive to find what they like. If they spot something that they have been looking for a long time—in fact, just an item they want very badly—they might bargain a bit, but they will buy it. Price is not a deterrent to these shoppers.

Suppliers know that such driven buyers will often yield a bit in making purchases. If they find items that are fairly close to what they want, they just might compromise and buy them. For the suppliers, having their merchandise seen by antique consumers provides them with the opportunity to expand their sales and earnings.

First Buying Trip

Now to get into the more highly profitable part of this business, I had to make trips to Europe to fill the orders I had from my customers. During my first trip I met a woman on the plane who was an antiques dealer from Virginia. She gave me the names of people to contact while I was on the Continent. I think the reason she was so gracious in sharing such information with me, much of which it probably took several years for her to accumulate, was that basic good natured, Southern hospitality, and the fact that I was not a competitor of hers since my store was located in the North.

When I arrived in England, I was still very nervous about being a novice antique buyer on her first search-and-find mission. What the pleasant woman from Virginia told me was helpful but also made me realize that I really still needed to know a lot more about finding the items I was looking for. Especially when I was about to commit so much of my meager earnings into this speculative investment. In the back of my mind was the nagging understanding that my customers could always say that they were not interested in buying the pieces I had found for them. I certainly did not yet have the confidence of being a sophisticated buyer. That would take much more time.

While I was in the antiques market area of London, I saw a beautifully dressed lady walking around, obviously knowing exactly what she was doing. I had to make a quick decision—speak to her and get some guidance as to how I could make proper purchases, or just look and envy her apparent experience.

I waited for her when she entered a shop. When she came out, I, with my heart thumping out of my chest, introduced myself to her. She was so pleasant, she made me relax immediately. Also, she was eager to be helpful. That's why I encourage people interested in this business to meet and talk to the pros who make a living selling antiques. Like most people who have certain skills, they are willing to be informative and helpful.

After talking briefly to my new antiques friend, I invited her to lunch with me. In this kind of relaxed atmosphere, she gave me an enormous amount of information—truly, tips and guidance it would have taken years for me to discover on my own. One tip was just terrific. She advised me to go to a certain place where truckers gather with loads of antiques they bring in from the country. The truckers are entrepreneurs of a sort themselves. They own their loads of antiques and old pieces which they intend to sell to suppliers or anyone offering the best price. I was told to go there and compete for the pieces I wanted to buy.

In this way, the lady explained, I cut out the dealers, people like me who own their shops and mark-up the merchandise for retail sale. This worked out to be a regular practice for me from then on.

U.S. Truck Sales

I was so impressed with the selling of merchandise from a truck I did the same thing when my orders were delivered to the United States. Actually, I learned that it is done by other antiques dealers as well.

It works out fairly simply. All my purchases—the special orders and inventory I wanted for my shop—are packed into a trailer van and loaded onto the ships that transport the entire trailer or container to the United States. Since these huge trailers remain at dockside for up to four weeks, it provides antiques dealers with an opportunity to sell merchandise right from the van.

I contacted all the people I had made special purchases for first to have them come down and see the pieces I bought for them. Leftover merchandise was then sold to my customers who were general antique shoppers. On one occasion I chauffeured two women working at NBC to the dockside van and they both bought a considerable amount of merchandise. I then happily gave them a free ride back to their Rockefeller Center office. I did this routinely for any customer I thought was a real buyer prospect. After I sold what I could from the truck, I transported the remainder to my store.

New Store Business

Today 60 percent of my business comes from direct orders from customers. Continuing my no obligation policy to buy or not to buy, I now make a buying trip to Europe nearly every six weeks to two months to fill special orders. On the Continent I go to England, Belgium, Denmark, and twice a year I go to France. It can take me as many as four trips to locate the precise item a customer is looking for.

Today, I know that these trips are nearly fully productive, as I am a much more experienced buyer now. Whatever merchandise is not bought by my special order customers, which is not too much, I know I will eventually sell at my store.

To maintain a repeat business, it is advisable to give your customers certain conveniences. If a shopper wants a piece but is not sure about buying it, I encourage that person to take it home and live with it for several days. I do not charge for the delivery or the pick-up should this consumer decide not to keep the piece. This is just a customer service that I know will pay off later in other sales to this individual.

Since the key to a successful retail business of any kind is repeat business, I offer my customers my take-back policy. Should one of my patrons tire of some furniture after several years, I will take it back and try to sell it for them, or give them a credit toward the purchase of anything else they would want to buy at the store that is in stock, or what I will have in the future.

General Tips

Today it would cost from $40,000 to $60,000 to open a modest antique shop in a small town. A shop in the city would be a much more expensive initial investment as urban rents are extremely high.

Location is very critical. My store in Armonk is about a 30 mile drive from Manhattan and I do get many customers from the city.

A one-person operation should keep a shop open seven days a week, if possible. If not, it is certainly advisable to be open over the weekends when people make their shopping excursions to locate antique pieces they want.

A seven day operation should earn the proprietor about $50,000 a year. While this figure will, of course, vary considerably, it does show what a savvy antiques dealer can make depending on how much effort and time is put into the business.

The best season is the warm weather months. I'd like to point out an important source of customer recommendations—the real estate salespeople in your town.

Also, I feel that it is wise to provide free delivery service. Most dealers do not do this today. I offer free service for pieces delivered to my customers' summer homes no matter how far away. It's a good investment since a customer having to bother locating a trucker and arranging the details of transportation could very easily decide not to make the purchase. Sure, this service cuts the profit margin, but I have made a sale that is making money for me against losing one entirely.

This is a fun business. The caliber of customer is high and they are, therefore, pleasant to deal with. Mostly the customers are affluent people ready to spend money when they find what they want.

If you like traveling, this business will be very delightful. Getting around is part of the antiques dealer's world.

Trade Publications

Antiques Magazine
980 Madison Avenue
New York, NY 10021
(212) 724-9797

Antiques Dealer
PO Box 2147
Clifton, NJ 07015
(201) 779-1600

Collectors Mart
West Kellog
Wichita, KS 67235
(316) 722-9750

4

Automotive Repairs

There is money to be made by an honest auto repairperson who has as much pride in diagnosing and correcting an ailing car as a doctor has in curing a sick patient.

For all the grime and dirt, skill prevails in this business. Seeing a smiling motorist leave with the pleasure and confidence of knowing his or her car is fixed and safe to drive still exhilarates Tim Dinan who owns an automotive repair shop in Norwalk, Connecticut.

Learning the business requires an on the job apprenticeship of several years. Also, there are private vocational schools where a person can learn the skills of how to fix a car and how to analyze symptoms indicating the trouble in an auto.

Also, it is a business that has a future as the trend now is to separate gas stations from repair shops. Already well established in the country are the places where drivers can buy gasoline only with no repair service. On the other hand, today there are more and more repair shops that fix cars only. In fact, major auto service chains have a policy of first come, first served.

From neophyte repairman to boss of his own shop, Dinan's blueprint for success is one that can be followed by any person interested in starting this business.

Tim Dinan

Before I bought the business, I was an accountant, stock broker, postal worker, and I was in the Marines for four years. It became obvious that I wanted to be my own boss when I found out I couldn't work for anyone else. I was unhappy being employed by someone else.

Start-Up Costs

I opened up my shop on August 1, 1985. Most of the capital expense was gotten on signature from a bank. For example, I got a $20,000 rotating letter of credit that I needed just to get the lease to this place. Without that guarantee, the guy wouldn't sign a 10-year lease. He wanted the guarantee that he would be paid $20,000 if I broke the lease.

As far as the start-up capital goes, it was another $10,000 borrowed on a straight line of credit through MasterCard, local hardware stores, and all the local parts houses that I would be dealing with. Then, there was about $12,000 that went into building improvement and buying lifts, tire machines, things like that.

Today, it would definitely be more because everybody that sells parts and equipment needed for an automotive shop always gives me a new "price sheet" showing an increase. On top of that, the rents and everything else in this particular area have gone up rapidly, to say the least. Take my lease. It goes up six percent each year, so eventually I'll be paying over $4000 a month.

My first profit took about three months. But then two months after that I broke even and soon after came the disastrous months. This was due to an employee I hired that just didn't work out, a costly mistake. He charged a lot of parts against the company for his own personal use that he never paid for. He worked out all sorts of deals with buddies of his that were charged against the shop. Plus, I injured myself personally and was out two weeks. It had a negative effect on the balance sheet for that month and almost put me out of business.

It is up to the accountants who audit all of our tickets and payables on a week to week basis to let me know if I'm making money or not. They tell me if I had a good month or a bad month. As far as the loans go, right now I'm just paying interest. For instance, every month it's about $300 in interest. The banks like to clear out a loan after a year or two and then have you take out a new one again just to show that you can come up with the money if you have to. With current interest rates so low, I'm negotiating turning my lines of credit into relatively long term loans.

Business Dangers

I don't consider my take-home pay as part of the profit for the company. There are two kinds of profits to consider: gross, which is before I pay all our expenses; and the net profit, which comes after salaries and insurance. We have an extremely generous insurance policy here, and taxes and social security taxes are paid. The investment that I have is potentially in danger. If the business folds, I'm going to be hit for about $30,000 the way things stand right now. It could happen, if the Arabs pull another embargo, or if I hire somebody like the kid I had who was ripping me off. Even a strike at the local plant could hurt me. I know because I worked for a shop during a strike. Day after day would go by and people just didn't drive their cars. And they certainly didn't drive them to repair shops. Two-car families would use one car. This went on for a month. Afterwards, guys got laid off. It doesn't seem likely to happen now, but it didn't seem likely then either.

Long Hours

The hours required to run this business are ridiculous—about 16 to 18 hours a day. I'm here from 7 A.M. to 7 P.M. officially, but the way things work out I generally leave about 8 or 9 P.M. at night. When everyone else is gone, I'm finishing up jobs or the paperwork.

Business Worries

The worries that I mainly have is the responsibility I feel toward my workers. As the employer, I have to run the business in a sufficiently efficient manner to maintain at least a modest profit on a daily basis so I can meet my payroll. That's the biggest worry. Also, I don't want to let my family down; I don't want to give my enemies a reason to crow; and I don't want to make my friends and supporters unhappy either.

My biggest concern is for my employees. Even when I was just working modestly and I had one or two kids working for me out of my house, I felt the same way. It's the hardest worry in this business. One week you have work, and then you don't know. This week I'm all billed up and I see some things for next week, but beyond that, maybe no one will come in. I saw it happen. I lived through it during the Arab crisis and I lived through an economic recession which made things very hard for another shop. I've been in the situation of being laid off due to lack of work, and I don't want it to happen to somebody else.

Slow Periods

Supposedly there are high and low seasons, but I haven't had anything but a high season in terms of the work available for me to do. People ask me how things are going, am I busy. I've always been busy, but I'm always concerned that maybe next week I will be slow. There undoubtedly are seasons, and I will undoubtedly find out about them, but I haven't noticed them yet. When I was working on my own without a shop, I was just so busy I couldn't keep customers happy because I just didn't have the time.

Attracting Business

Incentives to encourage business? The only thing that I've done was to offer a discount to some New Canaan teachers. That was frowned on by the governing body on the Board of Education in New Canaan. But I did get a positive response from several teachers thanking me for recognizing their contribution to the community. In this area it is tough on a teacher's salary since nearly all have to commute because they can't afford to live in this area. Even if business fell off, I can't offer discounts or specials. No, I really can't because I'm operating on a very competitively priced budget. To go under that it would hardly pay for me to open my shop.

Getting Loan Money

You've got to have a really good prospect to get loan money together. You have to prove that if you really had to you could get your own financing. You have to show them a balance sheet of your personal assets and liabilities. Great if you have a house, for instance, with only a first mortgage that is worth more now than when you purchased it. Otherwise, it's hard to get the bread. I understand the government has small business loans. I didn't go to them. I was discouraged from doing that because I was told you had to be practically poverty stricken, black, or Puerto Rican. So, I didn't bother.

Business Practices

There seems to be a lot of hostile, competitive feeling until you get to know the guy that's working the other shop. Everybody is afraid that repairs are being criticized by competitors. I try not to rap the other mechanic. It's been my experience that no matter how poor he is, no mechanic deliberately messes up a job. There is a lot of distrust from customers.

But there is this big greed factor, especially in rents, and it gets to the point where, basically, some guys out of desperation, just to stay in business, do jobs not needed by their customers. I don't really believe that customers are charged for work that is not done, but I do think there are some questionable jobs done and marginal jobs where, for instance, brakes are not really needed for another six months, but the shop needs money now. That sort of thing.

Personal Pleasures

What I enjoy about it is the fact that when I get a car that's basically a basket case, and I bring this car up to snuff so that the people can drive it with confidence, it just makes me feel good. I have taken something that was their worry and turned it into a happy asset.

When I had a job the boss was very quick to point out that I might have done work that did not please the customer. However, I take a lot of pride in doing the job right, and that is why the vast majority of my work was good. I knew I did a good job, but

I was never told. But I do that now with my mechanics. If they do a good job, I tell them. I let them know that I appreciate their efforts.

Business Tips

For people who might consider starting a similar business, the hardest thing is getting the right employees. You need the right chemistry inside the shop, also. What you basically have is people climbing all over each other all day long, going from bay to bay, requiring each other's help, and if you have people that don't like each other doing this, it's bad. They don't want to ask the person whose guts they hate for help, or ask to borrow his tool, or ask his advice. That really is the most critical thing—getting people who work together well. It's done basically by trial and error. If you hire people who you like personally, it usually works. At my shop, I've never had the experience, though, of having people who didn't get along.

Two of the guys I've got right now I knew personally before, and those are the guys I get along with best. In my opinion they are contributing most to the shop. And the other guy was hired on someone else's recommendation, and he is really the weakest link—not so much in work, but in attitude. There's nothing much I can do about it but control it. As time went on and the guy had built up some respect for me, things have gotten better. But it's not the same as being with someone who you have an immediate rapport with.

Training

When I decided to become a mechanic I took a course on motorcycle repairs. It was a course out of Venice, California. Then I was told by my godfather that there really wasn't much of a future in motorcycle mechanics, so I decided on becoming an auto mechanic. I worked at one place and got fired. I went to another place and got fired because I didn't know what I was doing. Then I went to another place, and got fired a third time. But I had learned a little bit. At the next job I started getting it right and lasted for three years.

The guy that hired me was a big fat guy named Charlie, a real gruff, bigoted son of a bitch, but he was bright and, in a lot of ways, big-hearted. Also working in that shop was a Polish fellow who was my mentor. He took me under his wing and showed me the right way to address a car with a problem. Because of him, I eventually became a pretty good diagnostician with cars. It takes a lot of patience and the ability to analyze a problem with the confidence that you are smarter than the car.

Of course, with the way they're making cars nowadays, which seems to be with all graduates from MIT, it's getting tougher and tougher to get smarter than the car. Still, that's the way you have to consider these seemingly impossible problems. You have to approach them with the attitude that the car or the system is not going to beat you no matter how exotic the engineering is.

Unfortunately, I haven't been able to keep up with all the literature. It's very hard when you're running your own business (the way I'm running it, anyway) to get a chance to read anything. I'm so tired when I get through working, I can't even read the comics.

A lot of my present success in this business comes from what I had done before—the fact that I had a corps of people whose cars I had worked on when labor costs were $15 an hour though now I'm charging almost double that, who came with me. And I'm lucky that my customers stayed with me. Why? I really think it's because they know the kind of work I put into a car—always the best that I can do. And just like anything else, when you see someone is doing his best and getting the work right, you keep coming back.

Trade Publications

Automotive News
1400 Woodbridge Avenue
Detroit, MI 48207
(313) 446-6000

Motor Age
Chilton Way
Radnor, PA 19089
(215) 964-4231

Service Station Management
950 Lee Street
Des Plaines, IL 60016
(312) 296-0770

5

Beauty Salon

Joe Magnotti, owner of Joe's Beauty Salon, Yorktown Heights, New York, drifted into the business after he came out of the Army. He earned his license in six months of training at a beauty school, the approximate amount of time required in most states, and then went to work for his uncle in 1954.

After buying the business years later, he was forced to move when the building he was in was sold and the rent skyrocketed. Trying to keep his customer following, he opened a new store in an inconvenient location, not far from the first one. It just didn't work out, and he was faced with the decision to begin again elsewhere or work for someone.

An established entrepreneur, he never gave any consideration to taking a job. But moving to a rural location situated on a busy street, he decided that the only way to develop business was to become a very modest priced salon catering to both women and men.

Price pulled in traffic. I saw his sign for a four dollar haircut and at this price got the courage to walk into the beauty salon to try one. I was comfortable immediately when another man was already there sitting in Joe's barber chair getting his hair cut.

Joe has made it in Yorktown, and here's how.

Joe Magnotti

I started as a salesman selling a line of major home appliances, and then I went into the Army. When I came out of the service and didn't find a job for a while, my uncle, who owned a beauty salon, said, "Why don't you go to hairdressing school, and you'll have a trade?" I went to beauty school for about six months, got my license, and have been in this business ever since. I then went to work for my uncle to get job experience in 1954.

I ran the shop for 10 years, and in 1963, I bought it. It was a five operator salon on Main Street in White Plains, New York, right in the *Reporter Dispatch* newspaper building. In those days it was a good sized shop—not today.

Loses Shop

I kept the shop from 1963, and the *Reporter Dispatch* sold the paper to the Gannett chain. Gannett then sold the building and moved to Corporate Park in White Plains, and this was the beginning of the end for me. The new landlord wanted me out. So this place that was in the same location since 1934 had to move. I had owned it for about seven years, but had to move in 1970. It cost me $15,000 to buy and in those days that was a lot of money. But the shop was a profitable establishment.

Just when I had the shop paid off and I was on my own and was able to save money—out. It was a profitable shop right from the time I took it over since my uncle had developed a big following. The business was there and I was able to keep it after my uncle retired and sold me the shop. I made a good deal. I didn't pay any interest. I had the loan interest free.

Starting Again

A shop like that, with what it was taking in, would go today for at least $50,000 or $60,000, maybe more. I had four people working, plus myself. Putting a shop in new would cost you a bit of money, easily $60,000 for equipment and carpenter work. If you buy a profitable shop, you should keep the same operators to hold onto the business that's already there. Say you buy a business from somebody and the owner and operators leave—so do the customers. Unless you keep the same help, you'll never do the business the previous owner did. That's important.

Of course, if you've got a shop that's going down you can pick it up for a song, like I did with my present one. The owner was in debt up to her ears. She had enough business, but it was badly managed. She was a silent partner, not a hairdresser. You cannot run a beauty salon if you're not a hairdresser. She was never there. You've got to be there. Employees can steal; this is a cash business. I'm not selling a product. Instead of putting it in the cash register, they put it in their pockets. They can steal you blind in a beauty salon.

This one cost me $4500. I could've picked it up for less than that if I wanted to fight her. She owed the landlord; she owed suppliers. I didn't pay her debts; I just gave the landlord the money.

Promotion

You've got to have the help and you've got to struggle for the first year in order to get a following. But if you're not in this area, like me (I came up from White Plains), what could I bring from White Plains to here? Nothing. In addition to advertising in the *Pennysaver*, I made a big change here. I turned this into a budget shop. I have 1968 prices here and it works. I would have never made it with the prices I had before. I charge $5 for a lady's haircut and $4 for men, and from $9 up for other work done for women. So with a low overhead and a volume business, I do very well. Remember, I had to start up again from scratch.

In the four years since I took over this one, I've found that today the shops that are making money are the very, very expensive ones, and the very, very cheap ones. The middle guy is hurting, because there are too many of them.

Unisex Customers

At one time, a man was never allowed to get his hair cut in a women's salon. This, I would say, has changed over the last 10 years. New York State has allowed men to go to beauty salons. It used to be that men had to go to barber shops and only women went to beauty shops. Today, this is what you call unisex. Some days we do have more men customers than women. My sign outside pulls in a lot of customers. They see it when driving by.

I didn't get a dime back from the $15,000 I paid for the White Plains shop. I just sold the equipment. That's $15,000 down the drain. In the early days after I got this shop, we used to sit around for days doing nothing. Small $25 ads in the *Pennysaver* did a lot and the sign outside worked, too. Price attracts customers, and workmanship keeps them. If you do poor work, you could charge a buck, but no one's going to come in. My hours are 9 A.M. to 5 P.M., Monday to Saturday.

The biggest profit makers are haircuts, and wash and sets; those are the repeats. Permanent waves you can't depend on because these are done every four or five months.

Outlook

Lately, I don't like the business. For the last 10 years, it has become cutthroat. There are no scruples anymore. Stealing employees from each other is commonplace. I always kept my help because I'm not a hard boss. There are a lot of people you can't work for, I don't care how much they're paying you.

I'm making a good living but expenses always go up. Like when I first got here the rent was $200 less than what it is now, so as the increases go up you take home less. The rent is more, the products cost more. I have two more girls working for me. I go home with a modest income, and that's all I need. I don't need what I did before since my kids are not home anymore. Also, my wife is working, my mortgage is paid off, and I have a few investments that I make some money from.

Each chair has to bring in at least $300 a week; if it doesn't, you're losing money. Remember, in addition to the salaries there are the extras for social security, and disability compensation cuts into a business with a small profit margin.

Customers

The customer is independent today; they're not like they used to be. There are more shops than there ever were. They have the choice of going out of here and going to another shop and pricing, doing this and doing that. Years ago there was more loyalty. Customer turnover is too much. The same for the help. The biggest problem is the help. You can not run a profitable shop if you haven't got the right people working for you. So what's the use of having nine shops? If you have a five-operator shop, you need 45 people and you can't even get 20 good ones.

Employees work on a salary and commission when they start bringing in customers. The usual percentage is 25 percent. But salaries can double before they are eligible to receive a commission.

Business Stress

You get a lot of complaints in this business, because most of the people don't know what they want. They'll come in and tell you they want one thing when they really want something else. It's annoying, but only happy customers come back. Today, we can please anybody—color-wise, permanent wave-wise, and haircut-wise. I figure about one percent of the customers complain no matter how hard you try. Some I've thrown out and told to take their money some place else.

The basic price for a wash and set usually starts at about $9. A styling haircut could run from $10 and up. And we do give women a basic haircut for $5 for a dry haircut—no wash, no blow dry, just a plain dry haircut. That's what they did years ago, when I was first in this business. There was no such thing as blow drying.

Anyone can run a beauty shop. All you need is a $10 license to open. You do not have to be a licensed operator. Years ago you did not need a license to be a hairdresser. It was on the job training. Today, you must have a license.

Location

When I lost my first shop, I bought another shop close to the old location. Although a lot of customers followed me there, I never built it up as it was a dead area. There was no traffic moving back and forth, so eventually the business started falling off. So the location is critical. When I was on Main Street I didn't have to worry.

Incidentally, I've been in this business 30 years and I haven't stolen an operator yet. I call the schools and place ads for help. I get students who I train to do things my way.

Weather

Weather affects the business. If it's a bad day, rain or snow, you're going to get a lot of cancellations. People are not going to come out and get their hair done. Holidays affect the business, too. That's when you're going to be busy. Your busiest months are May and June. Your slowest time is January and February because everybody's broke from Christmas and there's a lot of bad weather.

Special Tip

If you have good help, hang on to them. I know beauty shops that let people go in January and don't rehire until April. I keep my help. I don't care if I lose money. I give vacations with pay after they are here a year. That's the only benefit I give them. But they stay and people come back and find familiar faces, not strangers.

Trade Magazines

American Salon
100 Park Avenue
New York, NY 10017
(212) 532-5588

Modern Salon
PO Box 414
Prairie View, IL 60069
(312) 634-2600

Salon Talk
100 Park Avenue
New York, NY 10017
(212) 532-5588

6

Bookstore

Working in a bookstore is much like being in the serene and soothing atmosphere of a library. If you love books, you will never tire of being close to the written word bound in assorted sizes to be read for information or entertainment.

Being so close every day to the products of creativity can be a continually fulfilling experience for people happy just to guide customers to works of imagination and research.

Certainly there is an immediate and lasting personal pleasure to be involved with earning a living doing something you like. However, the demands of operating a bookstore profitably are somewhat more difficult today with the emergence of competition from chain store retail outlets.

Can it be done?

Indeed it can, perhaps taking more energy and commitment to succeed than needed for many other types of merchant businesses. But if you like it, certainly it is worth the effort, especially if you feel that the benefits of personal satisfaction have nearly as much value for you as money.

But to enjoy those subtle satisfactions of running a bookstore, you must prevail financially. The bottom line is still profit and survival. Ron Corcillo, who has been operating a bookstore in the small town of Norwalk, Connecticut, tells you exactly how it can be done.

Ron Corcillo

Beginning

Before opening a bookstore, I was in advertising in New York City approximately 20 years ago. I wanted to go into business for myself, and at first I thought of opening my own agency, but after researching that locally, I found that that was not a good idea. Basically, what advertising agencies in this area were doing was retail advertising. I was used to corporate and consumer advertising and not in the retail end.

I also found that it was a very tight kind of community as far as that went in those days—very few agencies, and most of the potentially good accounts were already taken. I talked to many agency owners, and they were not too keen on hiring someone unless you could bring business in yourself. I chose books as I always enjoyed reading. I couldn't believe that there wasn't a bookstore in this town. Having been a New Yorker, living and working there for a long time, I really wasn't familiar with this area. I decided that there was a need for a bookstore and I was going to fill it.

Financing

I did not need to take out a loan because 20 years ago you could start this business with less than $10,000, believe it or not. That was a bit of money then. It was in 1967 when I started. The approximate cost of start-up was about $8000. That was with a small stock which kept increasing. I lost sales right at the beginning because we didn't have the books people were looking for, but that was what the wholesaler gave us.

I did research. I talked to other bookstore owners. I talked to the Association of American Publishers. I talked to the American Booksellers Association; I had been a member of that, but I am not now. I talked to wholesalers. I read some books on how to start a business. And from that, I had some idea what to do. The $8,000–$10,000 covered start-up-stock, leasing of the shop. At the beginning, my wife and I worked alone. She does not work with me now; she has her own business. If I were to start this business today, in order to compete with the number of bookstores that have come on the scene, particularly the chain stores, in order to give myself a chance of success, I would need between $75,000 and $100,000. There's a big difference today. There were very few bookstores in this area 20 years ago, or, in fact, in the country. It's amazing.

Profit Outlook

It took about two years before I showed a profit, which is supposedly the rule of thumb for most businesses. You really need enough money to live on for two years without depending on the business. Most of the money I made during those first two years went back into the business for inventory and supplies such as displays. In the early years I expected to be able to take out of this business $35,000 a year. That did not happen for some time. I had come into the business making a good income, and I guess my expectations were a little high. But in terms of dollars in those days, profits were not high. I would think that would be the minimum you must make in this business, or you would be crazy to invest $100,000. It's hard to talk about 20 years ago versus today because the dollars change so much.

Advertising

As for advertising and promotion, we do very little because in this business the markup is not as high as it is in other retail businesses. I would say 10 percent is what most businesses figure as a minimum in advertising, but they start out with a 50 percent markup and we start out with 40 percent or less. So, right off the bat, you start out with 10 percent less.

The advantage that the book business has is that you are able to return merchandise, and the publishers do the advertising for you by promoting major books. The cost of returning books is assumed by us. It doesn't allow for too much advertising. I have found that advertising locally, which is all that I would want or am able to do, is really not effective unless you are advertising a sale or are giving the customer something special. The big "Sale" sign in the front of the store would not have been there 20 years ago—not even two years ago—but you need to do that today. In general, people have become used to discount shopping no matter what they buy. That's the tendency today. Nobody wants to pay full retail prices.

Work Hours

Hours are similar today to what they were when I started. We have not changed our hours that much. We are open six days a week, eight hours a day with one late night. We basically use from three to four part-time employees. On a full-time basis, we are down to one and a half to two over the year. Christmas is our busiest season. The early fall, due to school, is also busy. Summertime is slow.

Problems

Our biggest problem, I would say, is paying our bills. I frankly don't worry that much. I mainly worry about cash flow. Of course, we get some slow times when I worry that maybe we're doing something wrong, or maybe we should be doing something else, so we try to see what needs to be changed. There are so many variables, you wonder if it's just you, or if it's the town, or the economy. It's very difficult to figure out what really is going on when things are slower than they should be.

Our "A Buck a Book" sale just struck me as a good idea. It wasn't an original one. I read about somebody who built a very successful book business—a young man from Harvard who started this when he was in college. He ran a store with just a buck a book, and he has done very well, at a very young age, under 25. They are not used books. They are new books that we buy at a very low price. They are basically all types—books that were published over the last 10 years that are no longer in print, some of them bestsellers. Some of them were just books that you would more likely find in libraries. They are just sitting on publishers' shelves, so the publishers sell them at auctions to wholesalers for a nickel or dime a book. This is a way of recycling books that would otherwise just be stored in a warehouse.

They are very good buys, especially compared to what paperbacks cost today. And they are selling really well. Mainly it brings people into the store to buy other books. Even if they buy just those, we are still making a profit. But we do generate additional sales.

Outlook Gloomy

Today, almost everybody would need loan money to start unless you have a lot of money and you don't know what to do with it. Then why go into the book business? It's crazy today. That's why you see very few new independent bookstores opening up. It just doesn't make sense anymore. Compared to what it costs to open and with what other businesses people could invest in, I do not recommend opening a bookstore. Eventually this business will be entirely in the hands of the big chain operation.

Customer Relations

I think the customers buying at a small store are more demanding. They expect more personal service, and most of the people who come in here are willing to pay a little more for that. Even chain stores cannot give away books at cost, or less than cost, and stay in business. What they do is get you in and deceive you into thinking you're getting the books at a discount. And you're not. That's where they are really making the money. The main idea is that once you get the person into the store, they are going to buy something else—impulse buying. You really don't have to sell them. Most of the chain stores do not have salespeople to actually do the selling. Once you ask somebody something, they leave you alone. It's then up to you. The customers are not getting any great buys.

Responsibilities

I like selling books. I like books. I like people who are interested in books. I like being my own boss. I think I would find it very difficult to go to work for somebody else again. Especially after being in business for myself for so long. You're always busy in this business. That's another reason why anybody who doesn't want to work and work hard should never go get a bookstore. It's not a business where you sit around and read books all day, which a lot of people used to do.

Twenty years ago you could sit around all day and read a book while waiting for a customer to come in. Today it's a very work-intensive business. You are dealing with hundreds of publishers, wholesalers, and I don't know how many thousands of books that are being published each year. You have to pick salable books and decide what to keep, what to send back, when to send it back, how to send it back. You have to meet with salespeople. It's a learning experience. Today, I see only a few salespeople. It takes too much time, and I already know what my customers buy. That's what is needed to make the right choices. Each store is different. It can be in the same town, the same side of the street, and each store will have different customers. Anybody who has been in this business will tell you that. They'll go into one store and sell "X" and in the other store "Y," right in the same town. It's just a matter of who goes into those stores and for what reason.

The Store Personality

I would say we try to be a general bookstore. We don't emphasize bestsellers as much, because that's where you have to discount today. We have built a reputation for having hard-to-find books; books that are older; books that other stores don't have; books that are needed for college courses and for students in general. That's how we compete. If they want a certain book, they have to come to us. And they come, not just from Norwalk, but from all over New York State and Connecticut.

If you try to compete with the chains on what they're promoting and selling heavily and selling at a deep discount, you're out of business. Many stores found that out when they tried to compete with them on that basis, and they just didn't make it.

We do a lot of institutional business, which is another way of competing with the chain stores. That includes the local schools: elementary, middle, and high schools. I would say that accounts for one-third of our business. We sell directly to the institutions, in this case. We also supply libraries, including business libraries.

This should be a bigger part of our business; I just don't have enough time to go after it. We do do a lot of business with schools, but the public library is our biggest account. The public library and the Board of Education also order directly from the publishers. That's why our business with them is probably a minute part of their budget, but it is a very welcome addition. Schools come to us for class requirements, special orders for individual books that would be a hassle for them to order directly. The libraries call us mainly for bestsellers when they realize that they haven't ordered enough copies to meet the demand for certain titles. They might need them today or tomorrow, and they're not going to get them that fast from wholesalers. It takes weeks. So they'll call us, and we'll have them up to them in five minutes or the next day.

In the case of one library, we basically supply them with all of their books. It's a small public library and we act as its supplier.

Special Tips

If someone really loved the business and wanted to get into it, I would say buy an existing store. It's already making it and obviously has ways of competing with the competition. It would probably be cheaper than starting out and probably would be more likely to succeed for someone who doesn't know the business. To open a new store, I would say the main thing would be to try to sell items that the other stores are not offering. There is a lot of room for a bookstore to compete with a chain store. There are things that chain stores cannot sell profitably, and therefore, are not going to handle. To start up with that kind of investment today, there are probably a lot of other businesses that would be more likely to succeed and are less work-intensive, and I would really suggest that they try something else. If you really love books, you can do it, but it takes a lot of money to get started.

Getting Help

We have been pretty lucky finding employees. I have some excellent help. One or two were customers that became employees. Others were friends of my own children. I've had one family of four girls.

Book Association

I did belong to the American Book Association (ABA), but I left two years ago when I didn't feel the ABA was really working for the independent bookstore. It became a voice more for the chain stores, who obviously were paying them more money in dues. Also, the real problem was that there were two lawsuits against publishers for offering better prices to chain stores. The ABA did not back and would not get involved in supporting this litigation. As a result, a lot of stores left the ABA, and a lot of local and regional type organizations were formed to replace it.

What happened was some invoices were sent to the wrong bookstores, and that's how we found out. They were giving bigger discounts to the chain stores. Having hard evidence, it was not denied. They tried to deny it at first but then realized that they couldn't. The fact was that the ABA did not see fit to back all the booksellers, when it was supposed to represent us. There are benefits to being a member, but I didn't feel that they are enough to outweigh the disadvantages.

Trade Publications

American Bookseller
122 East 42 Street
New York, NY 10168
(212) 867-9060

Book Dealers World
Box 2525
La Mesa, CA 92041
(619) 462-3297

Publishers Weekly
205 East 42 Street
New York, NY 10017
(212) 916-1876

7

Boutique

During the 18 years that Phyllis Berman has owned and operated a ladies boutique, Simply Sweaters, in Pound Ridge, New York, she expanded to become a three store chain. When she reduced her operation to just her store in Pound Ridge, it was not because of poor earnings in her other retail outlets. She closed those when she could not get the dependable help needed for her absentee management.

A former buyer of women's wearing apparel, Berman opened her store and stocked it with manufacturers' distress merchandise which comes from overruns and store returns. Basically, she opened a quality ladies sportswear discount shop.

For people considering a ladies boutique but who do not have the kind of factory contacts and experience Berman had when she began, consider opening a branch of an already successful store. If you see one you like, inquire about making arrangements for starting another outlet with the same name to get the benefits of professional guidance.

Berman provides enormous insight into how to start and succeed.

Phyllis Berman

I opened my shop 18 years ago. I was still married to a dentist who owned the building where he had his office. I took one of the two spaces available for stores. One was empty at the time. I had worked for a ladies sportswear buying office. Then I married and had the children and stopped working for about six years. I got the idea to open a store from a friend who had a knitting business serving Jantzen and other name houses. She suggested that I consider selling her overruns on consignment. I scrounged up some tables and display cases. I painted all the shelves and then drove to New Jersey to get some sweaters.

Underway

My husband was to be paid rent from the money I made. I started making money right away. I was never in the red. Business grew very slowly. Every time I would get a little money ahead, I would expand my inventory. I knew some manufacturers who made sportswear and sweaters. I went to them and picked up their distress merchandise, overruns, and store returns. I got good buys, and gradually extended into other kinds of clothing. I met somebody who was with a skiwear manufacturer, and he suggested I carry skiwear at a discount. I did. That did very well for a long time, but then for some reason a few years ago it died.

I think part of the reason I did so well in the beginning was that I was offering something unusual for this high priced area. I was ahead of the times with discounted quality sportswear in Pound Ridge. People came from all over. But eventually lots of factory outlets and discount stores opened in nearby towns, so business slowed down. Then the gas crunch came in 1973 and people stopped driving distances to shop. I really felt it.

I tried to keep up with the trends in the area, nothing radical or way out. For a long time, kids' clothes sold well around here. Now I am going into exercise clothing—sweatsuits, warm-ups, aerobic outfits—because that seems to be what's moving.

Expansion

I did well enough in the beginning, so I expanded into the empty space next to me. Then I opened a store in Ridgefield, Connecticut and I put a woman who had been working with me from the beginning in charge of it. A few years later I opened a store in Nantucket, Massachusetts, where I have a summer place, and my daughters, teenagers by then, worked there. I also had a partner up there I trusted. Eventually it got to be too much. I moved into a different building about five years ago. I was paying more rent and not getting the kind of extra traffic I expected. Ridgefield was doing all right, nothing terrific, but it was helping pay salaries for all the stores, and I could move the inventory around to the best advantage.

I discovered that a man I put in charge of the Ridgefield store was cheating me. I fired him, but I never recouped my losses. When I was going through my divorce, I closed the Ridgefield store. My daughters got tired of working in the Nantucket store summers and I didn't have time to keep running up there, so I closed that one, too. Now I am back to one store and I find that I might have to move from here. There are not enough people in this area. I may have to move the store to a busier location.

When I need help I get it through recommendations or off the street. When employees quit, they usually recommend good replacements. I have never done too well advertising for help. The kind of people who respond aren't of the same caliber as those who stop in to inquire. When I first started the store, I only worked on Thursday, Friday, and Saturday. It wasn't a serious business for me. Eventually it became a full-time job.

Promotion

From the beginning I advertised in publications in this town and other areas near here. I need more than just Pound Ridge people. I have been fairly promotion minded, participating in things like Christmas Walk Night, when all the stores stay open and serve refreshments, and the sidewalk sale in the late summer that has always been good.

I like dealing with people, and buying, and getting ideas, and working on displays, but not keeping books. If I had to do it, I could learn, I suppose. I went to retailing school before I ever worked in the field and it was very helpful. But you really learn more by doing. I don't suppose anyone could start a retail business without some experience in what they were selling. I am in business now to make a living. Since the divorce, it does really support me and give me freedom from dependence on my ex-husband.

I never did a real study of the local market. I don't even know how you would go about it. I just observe people and see what sells. If something doesn't, I mark it down and don't repeat the mistake. People in Pound Ridge are wealthy but frugal. They are very careful with their money. They aren't big spenders, the kind that are trying to prove something. Some of my buying success is instinct, and some comes from my experience working for the buying office. You also learn by making mistakes.

Advertising doesn't work well enough for me anymore because I can't afford to put in very large ads. If you look in the newspapers, the very big stores place full page ads or even half page ads, which are very easy to see, more than mine. Mine are small and I don't know how to make them stand out.

Earnings

When it comes to potential profit for a store like mine, I know there are many formulas. You should be making so much per square foot, but I don't know those formulas. The National Retailers Association gives you all kinds of figures. I belong to it. It offers a tremendous amount of information. Also, the Association has meetings and seminars, but it's hard for me to attend them and it's very costly. But if you go, they do work for you.

Yes, shoplifting puts a dent in your profits. The professionals you never catch, you only get the ones that aren't too good at it. Once we caught a couple of pros and I eventually got the merchandise back through the police. But most of my customers here are very nice. I do have MasterCard and Visa, so I don't have to send out bills.

Problems

Occasionally women bring things back, and you know they ripped them. My policy is to deal with it myself. My sales help is instructed to call me. I have to make some sort of a judgment. Most of the time I give them credit or replace it. When I know that person has been in a number of times for that, I might not.

I accept checks. At times someone will come in and pile a whole bunch of stuff on the counter and whip out a checkbook. Most of the time the check is good. I usually ask for a credit card. You do have a funny feeling sometimes. Go with it. If you think that somebody is not trustworthy, go with that. One of the kids who worked in my store for only six months had a sixth sense about two people. She took down as much information as she could and it turned out they had stolen a Visa card. It's a good policy not to turn down checks because 9 times out of 10 it's going to be good.

Seasons and Sales

The best season is fall through Christmas. It used to be 40 percent of the business for the entire year. It isn't anymore. Business is good from August through December. January is a sale month, so the volume is good. February is pretty bad. But then business is about the same until August. In the slow periods, you can offer more bargains. I can make it with lower costs and bigger turnover here because I get the same customers. If something stays in the store too long, they've seen it too much. So I work with either fast turnover or smaller inventory. You don't make much money when you have chopped your prices for a sale.

There are stores that mark up merchandise so when they put it on sale they are still making money. I don't. The sale is just to improve cash flow. Like now, we are at the end of our winter season, so I had to mark what was left below cost, either that or carry the items over to next year. A lot of people don't want to do that. You want to get rid of everything.

Trends

I don't get into the high fashion trends such as clothes for the oversized. It doesn't last. You are already seeing the nipped-in waistlines. There is still a broad-shouldered look but now instead of big and baggy they have a small waist. I used to be able to get away with not having the very latest thing, but not now. This area is not terribly high fashion, but you do have to know what the newest thing is going to be. You do it by having an eye for what people are wearing. A trend starts slowly. It comes in a little bit to a store. You see something and you think that looks new, that looks right.

I like the business, as I said, and I don't get burned out because there are so many different things to do. I love to help somebody put together an outfit. I hate the advertising.

Outlook

I have no plans to expand again. When my partner and kids in Nantucket left, I didn't want the aggravation of trying to find someone, even though the store had done well. I kind of regret it because it was a wonderful area. Help was the problem in Ridgefield after my partner left. Catching the guy who stole from me and then firing him was probably the worst experience of my life. I fired him the week after Thanksgiving, just before the Christmas season, and thank God because I would have had big losses. I got somebody else, but she just wasn't capable, so I decided the hell with it. Shuffling the stock around, especially with Ridgefield because it was close, worked great for a few years. Actually the Ridgefield store didn't do that well, but it still did okay. But we were paying too many salaries.

It is very time consuming. We need to be open as many hours as we can, and, yet, I can't be there all the time. I like to be open on Sundays if I can get somebody I trust, someone I feel good about. I don't want to work on Sundays because I would end up always being in the store. But then if someone else was there I would be wondering, how is it going? What's going on? I can't relax. Maybe someone smarter would not be so concerned. I'm a worrier.

Trade Publications

Apparel Merchandising
425 Park Avenue South
New York, NY 10022
(212) 371-9400

Daily News Record
7 East 12 Street
New York, NY 10033
(212) 741-4000

Apparel World
386 Park Avenue South
New York, NY 10016
(212) 683-7520

8

Car Wash

For most of his adult working life, Joe D'Martino had the entrepreneurial thrust. Being his own boss was his lifestyle. For 18 years he owned a body shop where he painted cars back to their factory fresh look. Joe was a craftsperson who restored expensive autos for celebrities and executives to a showroom finish. Many were hand painted. For $2500 per car, Joe had the patience and the skill to achieve near perfection.

It was grueling work and D'Martino decided to find a business that did not deplete his energy as much as auto restoration. When he found a car wash on a quiet street in Yorktown Heights, New York, which was for sale, along with the property it was on, he bought it.

Having a naturally friendly and agreeable manner, D'Martino increased the business 25 percent the first year. With his skill in handling customers, he established a substantial repeat business that continues to grow. Most important, points out D'Martino, it is earnings with little labor. Just what he wanted.

The car wash business can be surprisingly profitable for little effort. Here's how.

Joe D'Martino

I bought the car wash in March 1985. Before that I owned a body shop. I purchased this car wash that has been here since 1970, and I also bought the property.

After I took it over, I found it more advisable to build a well for my water than to pay the high cost of getting it from the town. This addition cost nearly $15,000. It's worth it. In fact, one car wash in New York City run by a friend of mine did the same thing right in Manhattan. In the end you save money.

Costs

The acquisition of this place, which included the property so that I do not have to worry about a lease running out, cost $300,000.

This car wash could accommodate up to 1000 cars a day. It takes about 70 seconds to get a car through. Since we charge $4 a car we have a potential for grossing $4000 a day. Of course, that is ideal peak business, and in winter we hit it often.

Another cost is the disposal of the water into the town sewer. The town has a gauge on the well and it charges us a certain amount per gallon for the waste water. We get a monthly bill.

Building Business

I started the business when there was a water shortage and that was a help to me. It brought a lot of customers in who might not normally go to a car wash. That helped me turn the business around since the previous owner did not provide any feeling of personal service. I, having been on my own all my life, know how important it is to develop a pleasant relationship with customers. Make them feel good about coming and pleased when they leave that their cars have been thoroughly cleaned. Maybe it means an extra 10 seconds but it pays off. You have to be friendly and provide service.

By the end of my first year I had 25 percent more customers and grossed about $165,000. My guys take pride in their work. Many car washes are casual about the way they let cars out, often with water spots and streaks. Not here. I found people notice and come back.

Operation

We are open seven days a week. Of course, so many people who work during the week will bring their cars in on weekends. The seven day week is a must.

Snow really brings in the customers. This town salts the roads very heavily and people want to get that off their cars as soon as possible. Also, snow lasts longer around here. It melts slowly and causes lots of puddles that mess up the cars for a long time after the snowfall.

Our busiest period is from October until the end of March. When the weather gets warm people start washing their cars at home. During the slow season, we basically break even, so we do have to make it during the cold weather months.

Other Services

We do wax cars for a basic price of $50. If a car has to be compounded it costs more. Actually, I earn very little from waxing. It's a way of keeping my employees occupied during our slow times. Also, it is a service for customers whom we expect to see coming back again and again for car washes.

Employees

I have two full-time employees and usually about three working part-time, usually students. We are always able to get part-time help. Some young people come in to earn some money while they are looking for full-time jobs.

Equipment

There are equipment breakdowns mainly due to drivers who forget to put their cars into neutral. They will forget, step on the accelerator, and when the car lurches forward it strains the tension on the conveyor belt. Most of the repairs required are not too difficult for the average person who is somewhat handy. Fortunately, things that have broken and we have fixed, so far, haven't failed again. It's always something new.

Also, people who keep their feet on the brakes when in neutral break the pins on the conveyor belt. I tell them upfront to keep the car in neutral, let it run, and foot off the brake. But many do not listen. This equipment is worth about $120,000.

Incentives

I give customers a steady incentive: buy five car washes and get one free. Also, for my very steady customers I throw in an extra free wash from time to time. Good customer relations counts and brings them back. These are people who come in two and three times a week.

Also, I place coupons in certain publications offering a discount for coming in. It does bring new customers from a considerable distance. Many keep coming back.

Our $4 price any day of the week is a good incentive. Other places increase their prices on weekends.

Tips

I recommend a car wash to anyone interested. I love it. I worked 18 years in a tough business such as body painting and repairs. Here the machine does the work for you. Press a button and watch it go.

You put in a lot of hours, but it's not always busy. You get time to relax.

Loan Money

I was able to borrow to start the business. One bank turned me down even though I was getting the property. I wasted a lot of time with a local bank. I then went to a large commercial bank and got a loan for $125,000. My advice—go to the big banks first.

Trade Publications

Auto Laundry News
370 Lexington Avenue
New York, NY 10017
(212) 532-9290

American Clean Car
500 North Dearborn Street
Chicago, IL 60610
(312) 337-7700

9

Carpentry (Boat Repairs)

Frank Casey has rarely used his skills as a carpenter to build homes, remodel kitchens, finish attics, or construct offices.

As a young man without any direction and looking for a trade to learn, he became an apprentice carpenter at a marina. Casey applied for the job at the boatyard for two reasons: he needed a place to live, and he wanted the chance to acquire the skills of a carpenter.

He slept in the boats, read about carpentry, and watched the pros, who taught the youngster a craft that eventually would become a big business for him. Repairing boats became his specialty. It just happened that way.

Before taking the plunge as an entrepreneur, Casey had realistic visions of how he would compete for business and stretch it out over the slow months when the owners of the vessels in the marinas left their boats to slumber for the winter.

However, with the real estate boom expected to continue well into the twenty-first century, independent carpenter contractors will be in high demand. The unending need for repairs and special work by owners of homes and condominiums provides skilled carpenters with a bounty of opportunities to be their own bosses.

But for those who would like to use this craft to do something different, Casey, owner of Wood Boats, Inc., Norwalk, Connecticut, tells you how.

Frank Casey

I started doing this about 15 years ago. We officially turned it into a business and incorporated 10 years ago. We started in Stamford, Connecticut at one of the old boatyards there. I had worked for the boatyard for several years. My brother joined me two years later. We operated out of the Stamford Marina until we saw condominiums take over. Then, we packed up and relocated in Norwalk since all the marinas were still intact here. Our old marina had a tree right out in the middle of it. The tree is still there, but everything else is history.

The Beginning

I was a carpenter in the boatyard doing miscellaneous carpentry work. I never had anything to do with boats before. When I applied for the job, they asked me if I had ever worked on boats. Since I needed the job I told them yes. I actually lived on the boats that I was working on. The owners did not know. They just thought I was a hard worker. I would be there before anyone else in the morning and after everybody left at night. After I was all through, I would just climb into the boat. Every boat has bunks and its own bathroom and everything else.

I knew what quality work was, but I didn't know how to do it. So, I just watched and watched and read and read and asked a lot of questions. Then I would go to my foreman and I would say, how long do you think this will take? He told me and I said okay, and then I would do the job and then charge for that many hours. I received no expenses. I had a running tab that I would pay monthly at the local diner. My intention was to work full time learning the trade. As I kept working at it, I realized that as I completed one job, there was another job, and then spring time came, and there were too many jobs. When the winter came, the jobs fell off. I couldn't understand that. To me the winter was the time to get boats ready for the spring and summer. What I concluded was that there could be work year round. The better work you did, the more work you would get. I worked at the marina for approximately five years, and then we got our own place.

Start-Up

We rented a building on the property, set up our shop, and became boat contractors paid by the job. Of course, going into business for yourself, you have control over how many hours you work, how busy you are, and you can start to set your own destiny. We were working an average of 15 to 16 hour days. But that's what we wanted to do because we were still learning. We would set a price that was fair and competitive, and then do the job.

Money

We never borrowed money. We weren't brought up to do that. At the end of the week, we would look in the checkbook and find only $10 left. We would ask, who gets it? Or maybe we'll take five out. Who gets it, you or I, or do we split it? Brian would say, well, I still have some peanut butter, why don't you take it this week.

We both agreed that all the bills had to be paid promptly. From the day we opened our business, we had excellent credit in respect to paying bills, but we had no real credit established with banks for borrowing. And that was a problem in later years. But, once again, our concern was that we were good for the money, and our immediate creditors were more our concern than ourselves. It wasn't until much later that we borrowed money for gearing up the business.

The only money that we owe are mortgages, because all of our investments are on property. Our intention was always to invest back into the shop. When we had fully equipped the shop, we then moved from Stamford to Norwalk. Our expansion was limited as there were areas in the marina we could not get. We decided that eventually we would get into a position to work for all the marinas and not just commit ourselves to one. We wanted to give all the marinas an equal opportunity to get our services. This afforded us the option to pick the jobs we wanted.

Motivation

We grew up in a rich neighborhood, but we weren't rich. There were eight kids in my family and all of us worked. We used to sneak into the local yacht club every day until they thought we were members. So, the exposure was there. Our father brought us up to do jobs right—they weren't done until they were done right. That was his profession. He was a designer. We would do something for him and he would simply come in and say, do it again. No anger, just do it again.

Since everybody around here could afford the finer things in life, there was no point in doing a job at half price. We would not do work that was half good. That would certainly not satisfy our customers or us. But the policy at boat yards was that they would estimate the jobs, set the prices, and tell us how the job was to be done. This was not for us.

We set up our own terms that customers had to take or leave. We moved from the water to the building we're in now in 1979. We bought an old slum house that was about to be condemned as an investment. Another thing we learned from dad was to look for the nicest neighborhood we could find, but to make something valuable from junk. We rebuilt it during our free time. From the money we made selling our house, we got property one block from the water. This is not a problem for our business as boats are now transported by trailers. We could get to and from the marina easily.

Approach

We wanted to be busy all the time and to establish a reputation for good work. That was our special combination. Here, there is a demand for quality, and people are willing to pay for it. Other companies have left over the last 10 years since a certain amount of artistic talent is needed for this work in this area. Also, there is a lot of pressure here. However, when you are running a business, this pressure is really a benefit. There has never been a time that we were out of work. The great thing about this area is that there is so much work to be done. The only complaint you ever hear from anybody is for help.

Employees

I use four to five in-house subcontractors. These guys work for themselves. In reality, they almost work exclusively for me. They're good, and I pay them top dollar. I want them to take responsibility for their jobs. What I offer them is the facility to have control over a project, a spot on the bench, and a tremendous amount of good quality work that they like. They are all carpenters. Based on the nature of my business and reputation, I attract them, and I have never run an ad. At one time I had 15 employees here, and we had work for all 15. We still have work for 15, but I have only eight people here. I eliminated office help, and taught myself how to run a computer and set up a program, and I control all of my office work myself now. I did it just because if I ever cut off a hand or got injured, I would have a second trade.

I had not really enjoyed this business for several years. But this year I've come back to liking it again. It was the 15 employees. Too many. There's times in your life that you hit crises and you don't understand what the hell is going on, but it's going on. We were busier than ever, our reputation was going through a lot of changes—all for the better.

We had started owning property that we rented, and finally had the shop that we always wanted and improved the quality of our work, and yet I was depressed. I even told my wife that I wanted to become a housedad and give up the whole business, but she wouldn't go for it. My kids are wonderful. They are easier to deal with than the grownups. My relationship with all these people is now at its best. Success is not a guarantee that you'll be emotionally sound.

Payment

Our policy is to be paid as we go, not 50 percent down and 50 percent on completion. We put our clients in a position where they have to trust us. Once a week, they are given a detailed accounting of costs. They keep coming to look at their boats and ask questions. If they don't show up at all we keep them posted by mail and they send us checks for work done. With respect to customers, everybody is tracked daily. That's cash flow. Cash flow is needed to stay in business and to pay my bills.

Pricing

I do not have an average price for jobs. If people come in and ask what we charge per hour, I almost get offended because the cost is based on who is doing the work. We keep competitive with all the yards. We have been told that we should be $5 to $10 an hour higher because of the nature of the trade. What I did was to figure out our efficiency level. When I concluded that it wasn't what I hoped it might have been, I worked like hell to improve it. This resulted in increased profits as I could justify making my rate higher to make more money.

Everybody who works here, I can honestly say, is capable of doing other things, but there aren't many people capable of doing this in terms of what it takes. Some people have knowledge of boats and no knowledge of carpentry. Some people have knowledge of boats and knowledge of carpentry, but have not combined the two. And some just ended up doing this work as I did.

Promotion

I attend the boat show every year. To me, it's more of a convention where I can meet people and discuss what's going on with the business. I set up my booth with pictures of boats we did. I always get good comments and jobs. I don't just sit in a booth. I mingle at the convention, and get work that way too. I'm a member of the Maritime Museum, Newport News, Virginia; and the town Chamber of Commerce.

Tips

Would I do this over again? I don't know. I only did it to stop getting into trouble. Brian started it basically because it was the quality of work that he wanted to do. He always controlled the quality, and I always controlled the business. This is what we do best. John Gardner, from Mystic, who teaches small boat building and repair, says if you're planning to do this for a living, don't. Do it because you like it, and if it becomes a business after that, wonderful. I didn't start it with the intention of making a living or a career out of rebuilding boats. That's just the way it went.

Entrepreneurs must take risks. I think nothing about taking risks, but I don't necessarily think of myself as a risk taker. I would never involve anybody in anything I do unless I am confident it will come out right. I'll make sure that they come out better than I do.

The Plus Side

My customers are the greatest pleasure that I get from my work. They have all become friends. They depend on me. I always joke that this is kind of like their Boys' Club. I get along with their wives, and I get along with their children. I like to kid around and I like to be kidded and then, at the same time, I can turn around and tell them to leave me money. Because we are also doing business.

My wife is my bookkeeper. She does accounts receivable and payable. She is about as blunt as I am, and it is her job to pay bills. She can't pay bills unless there's money there. My brother Brian has no interest in the money whatsoever. He has no interest in the business whatsoever. He has no interest if he's even paid for his time. He would just like to be left alone to do it the way he wants to do it. He never wants to be rushed. He's a creative spirit.

Outlook

Wood boats have always been around. People, at one time, switched to fiberglass boats because they thought they were better. It's taken 15 years for people to conclude that they're not really better. They thought that they didn't require much care. But they look like hell if you don't touch them, just like your car if you never wash it. If you haven't got the time to get to it, you pay somebody to do it. All the guys around here are making around $40 an hour, but all the customers are making between $100,000 and $500,000 a year. The majority of my customers are millionaires. But millionaires are not what they used to be. My average customer owns three or four cars; he owns probably a little house up in a ski area or up on a lake; he owns a summer house and a regular home. Some of them own apartments in New York as well. And they usually have three or four kids who will go to the best colleges.

So, what does he get out of all of this? He has his boat. We just finished with one fellow who bought a boat for $200,000. Then he put $60,000 worth of electronics on it. Now there's $60,000 worth of customizing on it. People say he's got to be crazy, but this fellow is loaded. The hardest thing in my early years with this business was that I was meeting daily with these people and being awed by all this wealth. I stopped being so concerned with how much they were spending, only to make sure that they were being charged fairly for the amount of hours that they asked us to work. I established the relationship that they don't have to plead with me to do the job, and I don't have to plead with them to get paid to do it. It's refreshing to me to do business with them. One thing I do have is more time than they do. They take all their time in one big vacation. When the economy got bad, we were at our busiest. The last thing my customers were going to do was let it affect their lifestyle. But to give up? No. Giving up doesn't go with the entrepreneur. Most of my customers are entrepreneurs.

Trade Publications

Boating Product News
850 Third Avenue
New York, NY 10022
(212) 593-2100

Marine Engineering/Log
345 Hudson Street
New York, NY 10014
(212) 620-7263

Professional Builder
PO Box 5080
Des Plaines, IL 60018
(312) 635-8800

10

Catering

Bill Kaliff, a partner with his sister and brother-in-law in Festivities, a catering service, observes that this business can be much more challenging than just providing food, utensils, and decorations for special occasions.

Kaliff notes that catering offers many opportunities for creative cooking. In fact, at their store front facility in Norwalk, Connecticut, Festivities offers unique take-out specialties that are family inspired creations. Acclaim for imaginative dishes is one of the personal satisfactions of the business. He calls this recipe development.

While creative cooking is a plus, the love of cooking is a must in this business. Good administrative skills and off-premise supervisory abilities are also needed. And remaining calm and controlled when disaster threatens at the banquet hall is critical. Clients who retain a catering service almost always for pleasant occasions should never see the caterer worried about anything.

This is the way Bill Kaliff does it.

Bill Kaliff

I worked for Texaco for four years. I was in an executive training program for the first 18 months and then moved upward. When I left, I was a senior analyst. We started Festivities in 1984.

Collegiate Entrepreneur

When I was in college, I worked in a restaurant to earn tuition money. I got into the catering service while I was at school. A friend of mine, who was the general manager of the student-run cafe knew that I was into food and hired me on as manager of her catering operation. She catered for student functions and faculty receptions. It wasn't large, but it was fun. I worked about 60 hours a week while having a full-time school schedule.

Present Operation

We now work seven days a week, and on the average 16 hours a day. I never have time for recipe development here. I do that at home. Recipe development is experimenting with new ways to improve our dishes and setting new food trends. Our objective is to always be one step ahead of the food industry, whether it be our catering operation or in our retail section. We do this by research, reading, and tasting. We are really lucky because everyone of us has expertise in different areas. Marie, our chef, is the director of our kitchen. My sister Antoine is really logical, straightforward, and practical. She fits in between us. It makes for a good balance. I'm very impulsive.

We have developed a lot of off-the-wall recipes. We're now famous for our raspberry honey vinaigrette dressing. That's raspberry vinegar and really good Connecticut grown honey. People love it, it's really tasty. Our catering uses original recipes, either mine or Marie's. That's why we are doing as well as we are, because our customers can't say they've seen our specialties in a book.

Start-Up

We started off with a significant amount of money. We did not have to borrow. You can't really say that Festivities is a traditional catering business. It's not. A catering business can be started in a kitchen at home. That's really how my sister and I did start. We catered out of our kitchen while we all had other jobs. There was no overhead. We needed to buy the food, cook it, and then sell it. That is how most caterers begin. They see a market and they're good at what they do. When you get too big the law requires that you get a commercial kitchen. We wanted to do this full-time and we decided to go all the way. Getting a store, we felt, was a marketing tool for this business. Also, it does bring in extra revenue. With the store we do retail catering. People come in and pick up food for dinner parties, hors d'oeuvres, or desserts just for dinner.

We have a case with cheese and sausages, a choice of take-out cuisine, beverages, a frozen food section which features special entrees. We carry a full line of retail products for those who want to cook. We also carry exclusive table-top accessories for people looking for a little splash for their tables, as well as fancy food. We have four tables here set up for people to come in and have lunch, afternoon tea, a snack, or just coffee and cake in the morning.

In the course of two years, we have made productive additions to our service. Now we offer catered, delivered lunches for offices, corporation conferences, and other places.

High Failure Business

It's very difficult for food people to get loans without a significant amount of collateral. Banks hate food people because the failure rate is extremely high. You're dealing in perishables. You really have to be willing to take a great amount of risk to open up a food business. You have to love the business. We used our own money to invest in the business. We were fortunate enough to have it to invest.

It's Profitable

We made a profit after our second year. This was before paying ourselves. However, we put nearly all the profits back into the business.

We do have a steady clientele here. Small as we are, our catering business is fantastic. If we were just doing catering we would have an extremely profitable business. We have a combination of delicatessen, catering service, and little restaurant. But we provide all the services needed for a party, from food to waiters. We handle every aspect of a party. We're party specialists. Hence the name.

And that's really a major source of our clients. We provide hostess napkins, ribbons for packages, wonderful soup bowls and crocks to make a party a special event. We make artistic baskets to hold food or gifts. We offer a catering service with imagination.

Promotion

We have never used any incentives to promote our business. We have used some advertising. Word of mouth was a much better way. Some parties we did for a modest price just to get our name known. That's what we will continue to do. Satisfied customers send other people to us. The food business is primarily word of mouth. You tell a friend, who tells a friend, who tells a friend. And, henceforth, you get customers.

Work Schedule and Problems

Our shop is not open on Sundays. Sundays we do paperwork or visit New York to see what's new in the marketplace. We usually go down to Greenwich Village.

We have been really fortunate as far as customers are concerned. No one has ever complained about a party. We have had a really wonderful two years. We haven't had any bad experiences. People have received us very well. There are many horrors in this business as the reaction to even the finest cooking is unpredictable. In this area, we have not had any problems. There are growth problems as in any business. But we've had no employee problems. In the food business, workers are very transient. People have come for a short time but we expect that. Hiring our summer crew of college kids, we know that they will be leaving to return to school. We now have six employees.

Christmas is always good. But our retail operation has low points in January and February. There are some months which are better than others. December was fantastic. Last August was amazing. This summer is going to be super. We are optimistic about the future.

Association

We belong to the National Association of Specialty Foods. That is a group of gourmet retailers who have stores like ours. The Association is basically geared to promotion and marketing of retail gourmet food. It is extremely helpful. It has a couple of publications that are excellent and we study them. We get good information from this association. However, it's not a governing body or anything like that.

Learning

I was tutored for about one year in cooking. I had studied with certain chefs. I was taught how to bake by a wonderful woman. That's about it. Jane worked here, and I learned under her. I studied with a couple of French chefs who are famous in this area. Now I teach some classes. The year that we were developing this business I conducted classes at my home three nights a week.

Observations

I like doing parties the best. I like the planning, the creativity involved in putting the package together. I enjoy seeing the guests' reactions to everything, from napkins to ribbons to lighting on the table, flowers, food design—all those are intricate parts of a party.

I go to the customers' homes all the time. The first meeting is always at the store. The second appointment I go to their homes. That's where I finalize things. We talk about what is going to be served and in what room; how many waiters; how many kitchen people; how many tables; and how many chairs—things like that. We have organized parties in rental halls and many mansions throughout Connecticut. We did a 350th birthday celebration for Pepperidge Farms.

Tips

Make sure you have enough food. The worst embarrassment is to run out of food. Other things can go wrong. For instance, the band may not show up. We do full service catering, meaning we do every aspect of a party. If you know how to cook, you never have a problem with burning food. If you burn food you shouldn't be in the business. Have enough food and booze. Never run out of ice. Maintain control over the obvious which is a matter of basic common sense.

Trade Publications

Food World
5537 Twin Knolls Road
Columbia, MD 21045
(301) 730-5013

Foodpeople
Box 1208
Woodstock, GA 30188
(404) 928-8994

11

Computer Service

Part-time ventures can often end up as full-time businesses.

Ann Longenecker's Information Processing Company, Yorktown Heights, New York, began as an effort to earn extra income. Basically, it was an extended typing service using high tech computer equipment.

The capacity for expanding into a full-time business was all within the capability of Longenecker and her equipment. However, continuing to hold down a full-time job, she started to build her business working after hours and weekends.

Serving a suburban community where prospective clients had little access to her kind of technical versatility, she began to attract some large company clients. Many of these firms had taken low cost refuge in the new office buildings that proliferated in Westchester County about 40 miles from New York City, when rents in Manhattan skyrocketed.

The decision to devote all her energy to what has become a highly profitable computer business was forced upon Longenecker. Afflicted with multiple sclerosis, she had to leave her full-time job. Fortunately, by this time her side business was well under way.

Longenecker did it not only as a matter of need, but with skill and commitment. Here is her success story which can be duplicated.

Ann Longenecker

Information Processing Company

I process information for small companies that do not have a house computer and need only special services. These include payroll; data base management, which means keeping track of an organization's membership or the personnel of a company; and technical reports such as the one I did for the government on health-related terms for the elderly. I have also done a manual for a machine manufactured by Mitsubishi and a medical paper on heart bypass surgery.

As you can see, I handle a wide variety of projects, large and small, such as a personalized form letter or resume.

Background

For four years after getting my MA, I taught psychology at the college level while holding down a full-time job in personnel placement. Before earning my graduate degree, I worked at a travel agency and then in the electronics field for about five years. At one company, I actually headed the parts department, covering nine pieces of equipment it manufactured. However, I never had any computer training until I started my own business.

I started when a friend asked me to help her on a computer project. This is how I learned about computers. First I learned that you just don't go out and buy a computer. You must first understand what you need from a computer and what software is available for it. I read just about every computer magazine out on the market at that time. My friend had little knowledge of computers as well. In fact, we bought an IBM PC and had the man who installed it showed us how to turn the thing on and off. We were absolute novices. We learned the operation of the computer basically by reading the operations manual, and learning through trial and error. While it was very frustrating, I am a person determined to prevail, but my friend became very discouraged. The computer system was then put into my home as I had more time and drive to continue the learning process. When I realized that by pressing the buttons I was not going to break the darn thing, I just accelerated my mastery of the machine.

Illness Ends Part-Time Employment

The last time I worked full-time was the end of 1981. After much medical testing, I was diagnosed in late 1982 as having multiple sclerosis. I was at that time working part-time but had to stop and depend entirely on the computer business to supplement my husband's income.

Only after resting for five months was I able to start building my computer business again. My first job was computerizing all information for the rabbit club, and I was delighted. Since my friend had lost all interest in a computer venture, I bought the computer from her at a reduced price. The cost of the computer, software, and diskettes was about $3600.

At first I was operating off a used TV stand and needed somewhere to put the computer. So my next investment was a computer desk to hold the machine, manuals, and printer. That meant an additional investment of $400. Soon I realized that there were other needs for a home office where clients would come. I decorated the room with new carpet for $900, fixed up the bathroom for visitors, added a new couch. This amounted to about $600. To accommodate clients who wanted "letter-quality" print I bought a printer for $2600. Then came stationery, business cards, envelopes, postage, promotional pieces, ribbons, and so on. By the end of the first year I spent approximately $12,000. As a legal, full-time business, for tax purposes I can deduct a portion of my mortgage and utilities.

Getting Clients

Since I was with a personnel agency when I worked full time, I began by writing to 60 personnel agencies, enclosing business cards asking that they recommend me to their clients. Then, I picked about 100 companies out of the yellow pages and wrote to them. That took care of my first sales promotion campaign. I then began to advertise in the *Pennysaver*, starting with a quarter page ad announcing my new business. I got a few replies. I then had to take smaller ads due to finances. I use different types of approaches. I advertise either under my own name or the company name, depending on what seems to be attracting the most response.

At the beginning of 1986, I advertised for six weeks in conjunction with an accountant friend, hoping to attract business during the tax season. What a flop! I received not one reply to those ads, more disappointment. I ran another ad under my name and received three replies.

I do have a promotional brochure that I distribute at networking meetings for business people and to friends.

All this might sound discouraging. Developing a business takes time. In the two years I have been in business, taking a tax depreciation on my equipment, I am in the black. You've got to keep prospecting for clients. Mitsubishi came about through a local man doing a manual for the company who needed word processing work. The medical journal job came from a competitor who did not have the compatible equipment that the company needed to do the job. And how about this? I landed the government job through my ads in the *Pennysaver*.

Loan Money

My initial investment money came through a loan I took for a trust fund left to me by my father. I personally could not qualify for a loan from a bank based on my business, and I did not want to use my house as collateral. Now there would be no problem in getting expansion money as my small business is profitable.

Getting Help

For big jobs I use a network of other people in the same line of work to help out. They in turn give me work when they have big projects. The network was formed through personal contact—knowing people doing this type of work who also need help from time to time.

Outlook

Depending on the size of the business, someone working full-time with three employees can make $20,000 to $30,000 per year.

Someone else—who works alone, just using the backup network system—can earn up to $10,000 a year. I have found another way to increase my earnings when I am slow. I set up programs on other people's computers. Lots of computer owners need help putting special programs together. I set them up and explain how they can be used. For this type of service, I charge by the hour. Depending on the size of the job and the deadline, the time required to complete a programming varies.

Problems

Problems include bounced checks, nonpayment, waiting for payment.

Business Tips

Learning takes a lot of trial and error. You need to sit down and play with the machine to understand it. It's best to learn from another person. I found that manuals were not much help. I feel that one important piece of advice to someone getting involved in this business is to find a good office supplier. I use companies advertising in computer magazines, which I feel is the best source. I belonged to a group of personal computer users for awhile, but the members were too advanced for me. I eventually dropped out. There are personal computer user clubs throughout the country. Membership, however, could be helpful.

Think carefully about going into this business. The competition is substantial. But what business does not have plenty of competitors? There is usually room for another dependable service, especially in suburban areas.

Computer Components

Hardware

Component	Function
Central processing unit (CPU)	The CPU performs logic calculations, manages the flow of data within the

	computer, and executes the program instructions.
Main memory	Memory is measured in the "K" you'll often hear mentioned—for example 32K (32,000 positions). It is simply a storage area readily accessible to the CPU.
Mass storage	This storage is simply "nonmain." There are a number of devices available, such as disk, diskette, and magnetic tape.
Input device(s)	These units are used to enter data into the system for processing. An input device commonly used with computers is a combination keyboard and television-like display screen called a CRT (cathode ray tube).
Output device(s)	These display the data. The most common output device is a printer.

Software

Component	Function
Operating system	Software that tells the hardware how to run.
Applications programs	Software written to perform a particular function, such as word processing, accounts receivable, payroll, or inventory control "applications."
Compilers and Interpreters	Special software that translates programs into machine language that the CPU can execute.

Special Booklet

Available free from the U.S. Small Business Administration is the management aid booklet, *How to Get Started with a Small Business Computer*.

Write to: SBA
PO Box 15434
Fort Worth, TX 76119.

Trade Publications

Computer Decisions
10 Mullholland Drive
Hasbrouch Heights, NJ 07604
(201) 393-6000

Computer Products
PO Box 1952
Dover, NJ 07801
(201) 361-9060

Data Management
505 Busse Highway
Park Ridge, IL 60068
(312) 825-8124

12

Consignment Shop

Changing attitudes of the public regarding used merchandise has made the consignment shop a simple business to start and a profitable one to operate. At one time shopping at an establishment that sold used items of any kind was left almost entirely to consumers who were impoverished. Today, the second time around stores are places where shoppers can get stylish, expensive clothing and furniture in excellent condition at better than bargain prices.

Carol Gibbons and her partner, Rosemary Peppet, bought Double Exposure in 1985, stocking it only with choice clothes for women. Located in the affluent town of Darien, Connecticut, they get such a bounty of clothes to sell on consignment that they pick and stock only the very best offered to them.

Developing a reputation for offering fine tailored garments in almost new condition at extremely reasonable prices, the store has attracted a large and loyal following. With overhead amounting to little more than the store rent and a telephone, plus some advertising, the two women were a success from the day they started.

Gibbons explains how they did it.

Carol Gibbons

I did some part-time secretarial work for writers before starting Double Exposure. I've been in Darien for eight years. I met my partner at a Newcomers Club about seven years ago. We got to know each other well. Rosemary and I had talked about going into business for ourselves for about a year. We had tossed around a lot of ideas, but none of them seemed to gel. Then one day, the owners of this shop called us. I had never been in the shop before. Rosemary had been in the shop once or twice. They called us on a Wednesday morning in the middle of winter and told us that they were going to sell the shop and that they heard we might be interested.

I called Rosemary, and we went to the shop on Friday afternoon. Rosemary and I concluded, nothing ventured, nothing gained. One month later, we became the owners of Double Exposure. We had our husbands' support. They thought it was wonderful. And, sometimes, ignorance is bliss. This was March 1, 1985.

Start-Up

To start a business like this, it would come to $2000, not counting the rent. You would need money to invest in racks, hangers, accessories, light fixtures, telephone, and utilities. That probably wouldn't be included in the space you rent. There is no inventory cost as what we sell is on consignment. Considering what it costs to start up other retail stores, it is not too expensive.

We made a profit right from the beginning. We were able to pay our husbands back in less than a year, and take some money out for ourselves. But I think the interesting thing about this business is that we don't own anything. We earn half of what we sell. If we sell $1000 worth of clothes, our profit is $500. We pay our bills first, and anything left over is profit. We use one, sometimes two part-time employees. We spend a lot of time working here. This type of business is really a personality business. This is not just selling. You really have to sell yourself. This is a service. You really are selling a service. You are doing a service to the people whose clothes you are showing as well as to the secretary who wants to dress nicely on a limited budget.

The more accommodating you can be to both parties, the more clothes you are going to take in and the more clothes you are going to sell. We have worked very hard on that and that's one of the reasons for our profit. We get to know the people who consign for us and we get to know the people who shop here.

In the beginning we were here all the time. We were here Tuesday, Wednesday, Thursday, Friday, from 10 A.M. to 4 P.M. We had some help on Saturdays. Of course, we don't pay ourselves a salary. We had lots of enthusiasm, and we still do. We constantly get different things in for our customers.

We do not have to solicit consignments. They come into us regularly. There is one day a week when we both are here that we take our consignments. We printed up a little sheet of paper that explains all of the rules and regulations and answers most questions. Usually we work together on Thursdays. But we get wishy-washy about it. Today I am here by myself and I took three consignments. However, we will never turn down a good consignment brought to us on any day. If somebody came in with something fabulous off the street, we are not going to turn it down because it's not Thursday. But it's hard to run the shop when it's full of shoppers and marking consignments at the same time.

Operation

We received a little advice from the former owners at first. There were some things that we decided we wanted to change almost immediately. For example, the previous owners had people come in to pick up their checks for merchandise sold. We felt it took too much time to go through the files to find the checks.

From the beginning, Rosemary and I decided that we would mail the checks. It might take us a little more time to pay everyone, but in the long run, it would be a lot better than being disturbed at the shop. Since there were other things we wanted to change, we didn't ask for a lot of advice. We just went in and did our own thing. We learned the basic procedures from them, and gave them credit for setting up the contract process, most of which was pretty good and we kept. But then we just sort of adapted and changed things.

We streamlined things a little each time. Trial and error. The process is still basically the same; we just changed a few things. The mailing of checks is a little more professional. It keeps the money coming in and going out instead of sitting in the file. We charge one dollar for postage and handling, and people are happy to pay that. They get their checks quickly.

Promotion

Special signs, deals, flyers, and two-for-one are some of the incentives we use. We found that through word of mouth, more and more people were coming in. We do advertise occasionally. The former owners had advertised a few times, minimally. They ran the shop on a shoestring. One of the partners in particular was very, very careful about the money that went out. And there was no extravagance whatsoever, which is fine. We do take ads in programs and in the yellow pages, where there is a consignment section. One other thing we have to give credit to the former owners for is the name. We asked them why they chose Double Exposure. And one of the reasons was that the word "double" is listed near the beginning in the Yellow Pages. Alphabetical advantage. Since people see the name Double Exposure sooner we might be the first one called.

We have talked at great length about advertising and we do from time to time, especially if we have a lot of things that we think are fabulous and we want to sell them. We do a good business without much advertising. We certainly never have to advertise for consigners. We haven't actually kept any statistics, but we have written down all of the consigners who are new, and there have been a lot of them. It would be interesting to go back at the end of the year and count them. We now have our 421st consignment. We started with 100. This refers to the people who bring us merchandise. I would say at least half of those are new. The average number of articles a person brings in is about 20.

Earnings

There was a woman who was interested in opening up a consignment shop who discussed it with us. She asked if I live on the salary I was making. I told her that I could not live in my present house or maintain my lifestyle on the amount of money I make having a partner. However, one person willing to work six days a week, 9 A.M. to 5 P.M., could certainly make out well, could make around $30,000. It is possible to make a living. It depends on how much you want to put into it.

We were here pretty much all the time in the beginning. At this point we put in between 15 to 18 hours a week. We both work all day on Thursday. That's six hours. We each work one of the other two days, that's 12 hours. We have someone who works for us on Friday. We alternate Saturdays.

Stealing a Problem

Shoplifters are a real problem. We have learned to deal with them and the police. Rosemary has had one or two instances here where she has called the police. We follow through on it. We have spoken to some other shopkeepers here in town, and they have not followed through by prosecuting because they are worried about retaliation by the thieves. You get angry about it. That's just our attitude. That's our biggest problem.

Aside from that, the majority of people we deal with are very nice. We find that the people who have the best clothes, the most salable, the most desirable things, are the nicest consigners. They don't care what they get for their things. They are very easy to deal with. It's the people who have the less than wonderful things that are the most insistent that the prices be higher, that we must accept this. What I often say to people is, is this something you would wear yourself? And they would say, no, I wouldn't be caught dead in that. And I would say, then what makes you think that someone else would buy it? We've learned to deal with that. I think I myself have learned to say no because of this shop. Being in your own business is a growing experience as well as a financial one. You get to feel more professional, more secure, more capable.

We had to apply for federal tax numbers. We order things. We do so many things that we never thought we would ever be doing.

Seasons

January is kind of a low month, at least this past year. Right after Christmas people don't have that much money to spend, I think, and they're not much in the mood for shopping. Our sales have gone up steadily every month compared to the year before. My husband does this on a computer and compares everything on a day-to-day basis once a month. It's a very steadily growing business. We close the whole month of August.

After work, we go home, wash our windows, and see what our children look like. All of our consigners know that. We just have to because after you've looked at these clothes for three and four months, you're tired of looking at them. Your enthusiasm wanes. We need to recharge our batteries. We come back in September ready to go again.

Consignment Procedure

Something that we have learned is that when we make a contract with a consigner, we establish a price for the article. We can reduce it according to a certain plan. After three months we have the right to donate that article. That's written in the contract. Even if we discover something is flawed later, we can donate it. We won't sell anything that's spotted or dirty. Some people come back for the clothing they left on consignment that we could donate. It can be touchy, so we have learned over the months to be very, very careful.

Legally we have the right to give away items after three months. We have a signed contract. But you can get yourself into some really nasty situations with some people who come back and say they didn't know. You have to try to maintain good relations. We try to ask and be very careful. With very good items, we will double check many times and sometimes call the consigner and remind them that the article has been here over the three-month period and hasn't sold. We ask if they want it back. We don't keep things.

At the end of July everything will be gone. The store will be empty. We take in the fall line at the beginning of September. When July's checks get mailed, we insert a little mimeographed reminder that we will be open the first two weeks of September for consigning only. And we will be here for about five days. That will pretty well stock our shop. Then, we open in the second week of September. In the meantime, we have gotten enough clothes to start the fall line. People are usually waiting to bring in their clothes.

Associations

We do belong to the Darien Chamber of Commerce, which the prior owners did not belong to. We both are Darien residents. At the moment we just keep getting mailings from the Chamber that they would like people to work for them. They do things for small businesses by way of advertising, and they sponsor sidewalk days. We just felt it would be good public relations for us to belong to the Chamber. We haven't profited from them or have needed them as yet, but there may come a time that we will. They do a lot of seminars on shoplifting. They provide a lot of services for businesses, none of which we take advantage of.

Customer Reaction

We get compliments from people who like our shop because of the quality of things that we have. Also, it smells good, and it doesn't look like a used clothing store due to the improvements made. There is a consignment shop in another town that has a corner with a bi-fold screen in front of it. It's a little hard if you want to buy a nice dress to get behind a bi-fold screen to try it on. We have regular dressing rooms. We are carpeted. We are not in the basement of a shop on the main street. This was a house originally. It has a nice porch on it. It has a bay window that we use for display.

In the spring and summer we have a mannequin that we put outside to entice people to come in and see that we are a clothing shop. It's bright and feminine looking. People feel good about coming in here and that's important and would be my biggest piece of advice. Also, we never take shabby or shoddy items, only the best things we can get. In a town like this you have the advantage of getting a lot of wonderful things. We have become very selective. We have made mistakes. We take things sometimes that both of us know we shouldn't. Then we both look at each other and say why did we take that. We should just learn to say no. We have gotten much, much better at that, and people have said that the quality has gone up. And I really do believe it has.

The biggest danger is that things can look overcrowded because we have too many things. That is a big disadvantage. Nothing is more distressing to a customer than to come in and find things all crammed and jammed together. In a store like this, there is only one of everything. It's not like a department store where you have 15 of these, 10 of these, and 20 of these. Here you have to go piece by piece and pull out what you like and leave what you don't. If it's crowded, it's a struggle. We have had a problem with that. We could use another room. We get a little frustrated because we don't have the space to display merchandise well.

Pleasure

Other than making a living, we enjoy meeting with the people. It's a lot of fun to see a dress tried on by three people and all of a sudden, the third or fourth person looks fabulous in it. It finds the right owner. We tell people candidly how they look in the clothes they select. We are not like the boutique owners who buy in New York showrooms hoping they guessed right. It's not an insult to us if people don't buy. We are very honest with our customers. Meeting the public and being with people is what makes it fun and it's different every day. It's not like working in a retail store where things are predictable. Every article and every customer is different. Every consignment and every consigner is different. It's like a treasure hunt. You never know what is going to happen. At the end of the season, the store is empty. Being in the shop from 10:00 in the morning until 4:00 in the afternoon, the world's problems are outside of your realm. It's a little bit like therapy.

Once in a while a man will come into the shop, and we say we don't sell men's things. But that man might continue to look at the clothes, which makes us wonder about him. He could be buying for himself. But we can't let him try anything on because it's a ladies' dressing room. But you have to be polite.

Employees

My daughter works here on Saturday. We had a friend who worked a couple of days a week, and then she got ill and had to leave. Recently we decided that we needed one day a week off, to plan our own lives and do other things. Soon after a woman walked in who had consigned with us and shopped here. She asked about working one day a week. We didn't say yes right away, but went home and talked about it. Then we called her up and got her references. Now she works for us every Friday. I don't think we would have run an ad for someone for just one day a week. There have been two or three other people who have said they would be happy to fill in whenever we needed someone. It's nice to have someone who comes on a regular basis because there are lots of little things that only we know about. Now, our employee's learning and soon will be able to make some decisions on her own.

Expansion

We keep saying that we are going to open up another store. Maybe one day. We both really do enjoy it. I like having Monday off. I like having Friday off and not having to go into work on Saturday. But I love being here on Tuesday, Wednesday, and Thursday. I miss it when I'm not here. We get along very well, and we can always work out a schedule. We like being here together as we always have fun. We complement each other very well. We have a wonderful working relationship. We're both here to stay and we'll do it as long as it is fun.

It's really nice to have a partner. It's so pleasant to have someone to share the joys, the laughs, or the little problems with. I recommend going into a business with somebody else. It's easier to do that way, although not quite as profitable. In the future we might get more ambitious and open another branch. There's no stopping us now.

Trade Publications

Apparel Merchandising
425 Park Avenue
New York, NY 10022
(212) 371-9400

Discount Merchandiser
2 Park Avenue
New York, NY 10016
(212) 889-6030

Stores
100 West 31 Street
New York, NY 10001
(212) 244-8780

13

Custom Jewelry Designer

Sarah Kennedy, owner of The Cellar Workshop, Westport, Connecticut, where she sells her expensive custom jewelry creations, was inspired to go into the business after her home was robbed. All her jewelry, which she was extremely attached to, was taken. As a graduate of the Rhode Island School of Design, she decided to remake the custom pieces from memory.

Soon after, she opened up her combination art gallery and jewelry store in a cellar. Although she has long since moved from this below-street location, she has kept the name of her shop even when located in fancier areas.

Although there is considerable satisfaction in creating new design pieces that sell for thousands of dollars at times, it is a grueling, precise and often grimy work that is hard on the hands. Working with precious metals such as gold and silver is costly but the end products produce high profits.

After creation comes the selling. This requires a store in the right location and the time to be there waiting for customers. While Kennedy admits she is a workaholic, it is not an essential ingredient for success.

Kennedy tells you how to do it.

Sarah Kennedy

Before designing jewelry, I used to work for Lavern International in New York. It was a fabric and furniture design house, and I designed fabrics and did murals. I was right out of college. I went to the Rhode Island School of Design. I did not know then that I would be interested in designing jewelry. There was a whole chain of events that took place before I got into my business.

About six months after I graduated from college, I got married. My parents were opposed to the marriage and it became rocky. I had a child the third year but I was unhappy. It was this unhappiness and wanting to get out of this situation that made it impossible for me to stay home. I was always a person on the go anyway. To be sitting home taking care of kids, cooking, and washing wasn't for me. It wasn't my thing.

I was not quite 30, and I had been married for seven and a half years to a husband who would not let me work for anyone. When he wanted to go away on vacation, I told him to go by himself. I was going to start a business. The idea to design jewelry came to me after our house was robbed and all my jewelry was stolen. I was heartbroken. I decided that I was going to replace it, but I couldn't because mostly all of it was custom made. Somehow I realized that it was up to me to eventually redo the pieces.

Start-Up

I opened up a gallery mostly for painting and jewelry. It was a combination of the two. I had never done jewelry before. I had some crafts training but I really didn't have any interest in jewelry.

I opened up a gallery with another fellow who didn't put up any money, but we went in together. I put up the money. I went to the bank and I borrowed, on my own name, $3500. This was in 1971. The gallery was in Westport, Connecticut, underneath a men's clothing store in the cellar, hence the name, The Cellar Workshop.

I lost the fellow who I went into business with, who was gay, when he became involved in a heated and messy break-up with his lover. I took over the business after nine months and moved it to my present location. I borrowed another $5000 to incorporate and set up this expanded operation.

Costs

The first loan my first husband had to cosign for me. After I paid back the first one, the second one was no problem. The gallery was a success. It is limited just to painting and custom designed jewelry. I think my total overhead a month was $800 tops. That's how much it cost me to operate everything. My rent was $250 a month. It was incredible. It takes a couple of years to get established, especially with what I do. I custom design for people. I have walk-in customers, but my items are very expensive. I do exclusive kinds of work. And I have built up a clientele over the years. It took me about three years before I was making money I could take home. I was still married at the time and the business paid for itself. I was building up stock, building up inventory. You can't sell from an empty wagon.

I took my earnings and put them all back into the business. I had nobody working for me. This is a dirty business. The creative end of it is done in wax. Each casting has to be finished off, and it's extremely dirty work. It's hard work. I get a lot of kids that want to apprentice with me from surrounding schools, and they all come in bright-eyed and eager. But I can tell you that maybe there's one out of 10 in the last five years that continued doing jewelry after they'd finished apprenticing. It's dirty, hard work. You don't have fingernails. You have dirt ground in. You are using heavy braces to finish off the metal. You have to know what you're doing. And it's expensive.

Outlook

To start today, I don't see how you could do it without $100,000. You need good backing. You could start out of your home designing for people, but it would be a random thing. It would really be difficult. Around here they're getting $50 a square foot for rental space. It would be very tough. I feel sorry for young people starting out today. And for anyone starting this kind of a business, it would be difficult. I think you could start designing. You couldn't do it from a storefront in an upbeat town. I was lucky that I started when I did. A great deal had to do with my situation. And also, what I do, how I do, was an evolution. It evolved. I went into business to get away from home. I was into illustration and painting. I never had any background in creating jewelry.

What I learned over the years was self-taught and expensive. You make a mistake, and you wasted your labor. You have gold that doesn't sell. Obviously, it doesn't lose its value, but the workmanship is lost. There are lots of little hidden traps. You buy gold at your current market value by the piece, and the people who sell it tack on a 17 percent surcharge because of their profit margin. Also, when you go to sell it back to refine it to be able to make something new, you pay another 17 percent.

You are always in the position of losing, and the only time you make any money is when you sell a piece. Also, gold is lost due to spillage. That means you need about 20 percent more in weight to cast a designer piece before it is ready to be sold. You also lose an additional 15 percent of the gold when you're cleaning the piece out because you're cutting off screws with gold on them. Also, it can't be separated from the dirt. All lost money. And you're talking $338 an ounce right now.

Getting Underway

Painting did not pay my rent. Westport is a very funny town. You have to recognize what sells here. I could never make a living from just selling paintings from my gallery. And I produced everything that was in that gallery. That was part of the joy of doing it. That's what I wanted to do. I didn't want to be a salesperson. My thing is creating. And what produced revenue was my jewelry. In the beginning I did everything from painting mailboxes to painting murals on people's dining room walls. I did it all. Whatever I could do to make a living, I did. But it was the jewelry that paid off, and it's the jewelry I'm paid to do today.

When I finally got divorced, I was already supporting myself. That played a very major role in my going into business because I knew eventually I would have to earn my own living. I wasn't going to be another statistic; you know, the problems that divorced women have with no visible means of income. And, I wasn't going back to my parents. So it meant that I had to succeed. I had no out. It motivated me. I took me seven years to build that business to the point where it could support me and the children. I have two children, whom I have educated. We share expenses, my present husband and I. It's a joint effort. I was divorced in 1979 and separated from my first husband in 1975. It was almost six and a half years before I felt I was able to take care of myself.

Promotion

I go on a daily basis. When I'm slow, I'm the kind of person that doesn't sit back and let things happen. I'm out there. Today I advertise like crazy—in the *New York Times*, the local papers, the magazines. When I get slow, I call in the photographers to take pictures, and I name all my pieces. It's my trademark. If you open up the *Times* next Sunday in the Connecticut section, you'll see Icy Fingers, a wedding band. And, I call it Icy Fingers by Sarah Kennedy. Then I describe it. I can't just sit and let things happen.

For years I never advertised. Up until the last six years I did not advertise. Maybe around Christmas time I'd run some ads. It was an indication of how I was feeling about myself. I was hiding behind The Cellar Workshop. I didn't want to put my name in public. I didn't feel secure enough to push me, to sell me as a product. And that's what I'm doing. It's my design, and it's me that I'm selling. I was very uncomfortable with that.

When I got married the second time, and through lots of therapy, I really started feeling good. And then I started advertising. I had a pretty good following at that time too, though. I kept getting praise. I kept being reinforced because people kept telling me things were so great. In the beginning when people were telling me how great things were, I felt that they didn't know anything. I didn't believe what I was hearing. What do they know? Their credibility came to be in question. But as time went by, and it was reinforced over and over again, I began to think better of myself and I got confidence.

Word of mouth builds my business. I put my name out, because a lot of people know who Sarah Kennedy is, but don't know what The Cellar Workshop is. There is a conflict now. When I advertise, it's blank, by Sarah Kennedy. The store name is down on the bottom, so my husband will get the calls. People will ask him if his wife is the jewelry designer. I'm going to have to start double listing it in the telephone book and things like that. May is always notorious for being slow. When it's slow I create. I build things up. I am always busy.

Employees

I have two people working for me now, and I am looking for another right now. I need two people full-time to finish off jewelry. It's very hard. There are two jobs I don't let go of—creating, and dealing with people. If I don't talk to people, I lose my touch with what they want, and I can't do that. Most people, when they come in, want to talk with me anyway. It's hard to find employees. I go to universities; I advertise. Sometimes people will come in and I'll ask. I have to train somebody and I start at $5 an hour, but it's so hard to find the right people. You have to be the kind of person whose personality can handle a lot of different things.

Professional Association

I belong to the Jewelers Board of Trade. We all do. We're all listed. They provide nothing. I am not thrilled with them. The amount of financial information you have to give them I resent. They want your returns, how much money you make, everything. You are listed with them. There are certain places that you do business with that won't accept your credit unless you are a member of the Board. That's restriction of trade, and if I wanted to make a big mess out of it, I could. This really upsets me.

Outlook

The jewelry industry, I think, is one of the most trustworthy. The individuals that you meet are helpful. They were terrific to me when I started. One man in particular gave me more information about stones, showing me what to buy and what to look for. I learned on the job. A Mr. Weber told me about a Mr. Bauer, who in turn told me about this one or that one, and all of these things help you develop.

There are many different casting companies listed in the yellow pages. But after 15 years, I wouldn't trade the one I use now for the world. I used other ones on the side. It's just a question of opening up a book and setting up an account. Anyone can do it. You just have to have the guts to do it. Just do it, and have a little money. I went on the principle when I started, I had $3500 and I wasn't going to buy a two carat diamond. I started with lots of little silver pieces. I bought a lot of Volkswagens-I didn't buy Cadillacs. When I sold my Volkswagens, I bought Buicks. I kept building. I didn't waste money on pencils with my name on it. I only spent money where it made money.

Everything in the shop I have produced. I never stop working. I went to bed early one night last week, and my husband walked in and there I was talking to myself. When he asked me what I said, I repeated it, where I usually mumble. I was describing how to design something. It never stops. I can't. I'm not content to sit.

Hours

My shop is open from 10 A.M. to 5 P.M., Tuesday through Saturday. I always go in an hour early and stay another hour late, and always put in a couple of hours on the days that I'm off, which are Sunday and Monday. It took me about 10 years before I took Mondays off. I was only taking Sunday off. I need that space and I need to feel it's okay to do that. I come from an old Jewish family where you work. I now take some of that time off and do other things, except for Christmas, when I am there seven days a week. When I first started, it was all the time.

I really used it as an emotional crutch, which served me well. I couldn't afford child care the first year; my daughters were 4 and 18 months. My mother took care of them that first year completely. Then, I was able to hire an au pair, but my mother was still there. I had tremendous family support and I was able to do a lot that I wouldn't have been able to do without them. What would I have done with my children?

Business Pitfalls

I think one of the most important things is realizing a need. Segmenting your market. Location is everything. Don't spend money that doesn't make money, and try to keep your costs down as much as you can. Costs are everything, your material costs. You must always try to buy cheap and sell dear, but for true value. It takes knowledge of the market. You really have to know what you're buying and selling so that you don't commit a fraud unknowingly.

I will never forget, I bought a sapphire from a dealer that was supposed to be genuine. I had set it in a ring. Some years later a customer wanted me to put it into a different kind of setting. I took it apart and made a new setting for her. Of course, she wanted to get it appraised. I was very busy at the time so I sent her to another jeweler in town who would give her a fair appraisal. When he looked at it, he called me up and told me it was a doublet.

A doublet is a laminated stone. The top half of it was sapphire, the bottom half was glass. The dealer had sold me this as a genuine, 100 percent sapphire. I stood by it. I replaced it. It was a loss, but I learned. I do know what a doublet looks like. There are certain things that you learn, and there are certain things that require caution. You have to allow for those things to happen—and for breakage and for theft, as well.

Record Keeping

I hate book work. It's not me. I'm at the creative end of it. I like people. I do farm the book work out. I have a bookkeeper and an accountant. But, you must understand it. You can't let it go because you won't know what you can afford and what you can't. You must do some of it, especially in a small operation like this one.

Another difficulty is getting help. That's very upsetting. I've had a gal now for three years. We get along very well. It's a small shop and we work closely and she understands me. Don't forget, these people are following through. They have to know what my hand wants them to do. When help comes and goes, that's very frustrating. It interferes with the flow of your business and your ability to earn money.

Customers

The worst thing about this whole thing are the hours you must be here, because it's retail. You are tired, but you must be there. You are committed. People get very angry when they come to see you and you're not there. I am here. I do not take lunch. I am here all the time. That's the big drawback.

My dream is to someday wipe out the shop, not have a physical shop, have my own studio by appointment only, taking what I want to take. That's what I want to do someday. I don't think I would feel as compulsive about producing as I do now.

Robbery

I've been held up at gunpoint. I had a diamond on, and the safe was open, but the door was closed on it. They didn't realize it. It was a Monday, and I was closed, but I was working. It was about two weeks before Christmas, December 16. They walked in with a loaded gun. I didn't believe it. Nobody walks around with a loaded gun in the middle of Westport in the afternoon. The man threw me down on the floor, and I realized he was not fooling. He tried to cut my finger off with gardening shears. I really got hysterical at this point and I pushed my burglar alarm button, which goes directly to the police. It's like dropping a quarter into a candy machine and saying, where's the candy. I got so scared that I lost my vision and my hearing. The blood was pounding so hard in my head I just couldn't see or hear. He ran to the front door and I thought, he's going to lock the door and kill me. But he saw that I pushed the alarm and he ran out. He got nothing.

He was wearing white gardening gloves, so as not to leave fingerprints, and he got all dirty from pushing me around. He ran out the dor and kept running. I called the police and told them that this was not a false alarm. It was raining and water gets in the alarm system. The police were all over the place. They came in like a dragnet. They caught the guy. He was jailed for six months. When he did the job in my shop, he was out on bail. There was nothing you could do. I have insurance, but it doesn't cover half of what I have. It's so outrageous, I can't afford it.

When that robbery happened, within six months time I had a trained German Shepherd. I had him for eight years. He was a protection dog, trained for attack duty in Germany. He cost $2500. Today those dogs start at $6500. His death was a tremendous loss. The dog was my best friend. He went to work with me every day. He went everywhere with me. When I married Jack, he asked, where does the dog sleep? If I had to make a choice between Jack and the dog, Jack would have to leave. But, there was no problem. They got along fine, and the dog slept in the bedroom.

Enjoyable Work

The reason that I'm here is that I enjoy the creative end of the work. If I've had a bad financial day, it doesn't flatten me as much as when I've had a bad creative day. I can come home in the dumps, if I've been working on something that is not working out; I'm drained, I'm unhappy, I'm unfulfilled. That's the most important part. But it's also very important when someone buys it. That's the end result. You have given birth to it. That's one part of it— the creating of it, the conception of it. The execution of it is another part of it. It's a three part process. When they all blend together, it's exhilarating.

Trade Publications

Jeweler's Circular-Keystone
Chilton Way
Radnor, PA 19089
(215) 964-4468

Executive Jeweler
1050 Timber
Forest, IL 60045
(312) 295-2483

National Jeweler
1515 Broadway
New York, NY 10036
(212) 869-1300

14

Dance School

Most people have special personal ambitions that ultimately never become anything more than recreational pleasures. There are people who learn to play an instrument well enough to entertain at their friends' parties, and many young talented athletes who never develop their early promise into successful careers.

For Canadian Doris Driver, a youthful ambition became a later life business vital to her financial survival. Discouraged by her parents, having few places to learn dance in Canada in the late 1940s, Driver persisted, studied, came to the United States, overcame personal failures, and became a successful proprietor of a dance studio. She owns the New Canaan (Connecticut) Academy of Dance.

Having been a member of the Ballet Corps of Radio City Music Hall, performed in summer stock and in the road companies of Broadway musicals, today she is earning a living teaching a skill she always loved—dance.

Her story is an inspiration for anyone who has the capability and interest in opening a dance school. It is a business where there is always room for one more.

Doris Driver

Back in Canada, my family didn't want me to dance. However, I persuaded them to let me take ballet lessons when I was 12 years old. They were against it, so I got a job instead after the Second World War when I finished high school. I did architectural drawings for the Canadian Navy just to get money to study dance at the Royal Academy in Toronto. After completing my training and passing the two Academy exams, I decided to go to the United States. It was very difficult to get into the United States after the war unless you had a job. But, you couldn't get the job without being there.

I finally got into the United States with $400 my father begrudgingly gave me. I stayed with some friends and I got in the Ballet Corps at Radio City Music Hall in November 1947. I thought, this is going to be a snap. But it really wasn't. I went to live with a young couple with a small baby. It was a dreadful place.

Marriage and Divorce

Then I got married. I had a husband who did everything—he was an actor and dancer—much more talented than I was, that's for sure. I had two children and was very happy being a full-time housewife. One day he left me, just like that. He came home and said, "I'm leaving."

I was left with the house we owned in Lewisboro, New York. I hung onto it for a couple of years, and I fixed it up and managed to sell it five years later. There was not much of a real estate market at that time.

Opens Dance School

Then a friend offered me her school in New Canaan, Connecticut. It was a tiny thing. I had given up instructing 10 years before that, when I got married. In 1968, I bought the school for $350. My friend was a good dancer, but not a good teacher. What I got was mainly space, with a few mirrors on the walls and a record player and some of her students.

She was very helpful. She showed me how to do the banking. I'd never done anything like that before. She showed me how to set it up and introduced me to the students. I started off with about 35 students. Now, I have about 175. I guess the $350 actually bought me her students. I still use that space today. I started out paying about $10 for the afternoon in 1968, and now I'm only paying $25 for an afternoon.

Space Problems

The big problem here, and anywhere, is finding the space. You need a great deal of square footage and a fairly high ceiling. Taxes are so high, and it's so hard to find space today. I would have had a lot of competition here in New Canaan had there been any other available space. I think the Odd Fellows had a hall, and some of the churches have space that they rent. That would be the most expensive aspect. There is one other place in town. The rent is double what I'm paying and it's half the square footage.

Even in New York now, many dancing schools are having a terrible time, even though they've been in the same place for years. Many had to move out because the rents are too high. Most of the time you use your hall is when the children are out of school. You might have a class in the morning for some mothers but not too often. You really don't have that many hours during the day or the weekends when you can use it. Actually there really isn't much to setting up a dancing school.

Promotion

I am the worst advertiser in the whole world. I had to get people to do it for me because I just cannot sing my own praises. I feel that word of mouth is the best way to get students. I had sent out brochures that asked "where did you hear about us?" About 75 to 85 percent was word of mouth. Of course, I put ads in the newspapers and have performances at the end of the year, and other events. I guess people sort of hear your name, but they don't pay attention until somebody else says yes, that's a good school. Brochures are sent out every September.

Staff

I have wonderful teachers, and I think I choose them well as far as getting the right people for the right job. I have six teachers at the moment. It sounds like a lot, but they don't teach all that much. They specialize. I have one teacher that teaches modern ballet, and she's fabulous. She works about three days a week. I teach a class of my peers. It's tough because years ago I danced with them. Also, I have a bad foot now, and they still keep going. With adults, you have to get something going, and keep it going on the same day for years.

I taught alone for a very long time. I had very few assistants. The people I had been teaching in class decided I needed more help. I'm not an aggressive person. I had children I had trained to perform for some teachers when my foot was getting worse. The teachers loved the way my kids danced, and they told me they wanted to teach at my school. That's when it started growing.

Earnings

I realized a profit right away. I lived on very little for a few years. I really was below the poverty line. The first thing I did was to get rid of extra expenses and just get right down to basics. I even had tenants living with me to make money. I put most of the money I earned from the school into advertising and bigger shows to attract students.

There are no requirements for teachers in this country. Anyone can hang out a shingle and say "I'm a dance teacher." You could. There is nothing to say you can't do it. If you're really good at advertising and publicity and you're gung-ho, you can make it into an enormous business. One dancing teacher that I know is not a great dancer. But with publicity and learning a few new dance steps, she developed a business which she is now selling for $400,000. I don't want to sell this business. I know I could sell it. Since I'm in the Masonic Lodge and I don't know how long the Masons are going to keep the place, it really wouldn't be fair to sell the business to anyone.

Time Commitment

I didn't devote nearly as much time to the business in the beginning as I do now because I had kids. I wanted to be home when they got back from school, so I only taught a couple of times a week. I didn't build it into a big thing. Since I've moved to New Canaan I spend almost all my time either choreographing, making costumes, or cleaning the studio. They don't do anything at the Lodge. I've even sanded the floors. I take the vacuum over on Saturdays, scrub around and clean the place up. I try to keep it pretty.

I have a tape recorder right by my bed, and I'll play the music that I have to work on for dancing. I'm an insomniac, and I might wake up during the night and I'll get my book and go over all the bills. Right now, I have a recital coming up and I'm thinking about how I'm going to place the people. The logistics of getting all these people on and off the stage. Will I have a blackout or a full curtain. These things keep going on and on in my head.

Problems

The parents are the horrors of the business. Most of them are nice. But, every year you get one or two you just wouldn't believe. And then every so often, you get a very sad kid, and you'll know that something is going on at home. I've had things like mothers calling me and complaining that their child got a partner they didn't like or felt left out because the other kids were friends and hers doesn't make friends easily. I put kids in for exams the other day. You tell them time and time again that you have to have ribbons on your shoes, you have to have this and that for these tests-no nail polish, and so on. Then, with all the running around and preparation, I see one kid with ballet slippers with big pins on either side. Stuff like that just gets on your nerves. Things that they know they shouldn't do.

Payment

I collect the money in the fall for the entire year. It's worked well for me. Most schools have a session in September and then everybody comes back in January to sign up again and pay the other half. But I like to know who I have and who I'm going to have. A real commitment. I give them up to December to pay the last installment. They should know by then whether they like it or not and if they're going to go on for the year.

I had a mother the other day who paid her last installment in December and in January the child decided she didn't want to come back. The woman wanted her money back. You feel terrible. I'm inclined to give it back to her, but if I do that, I have to give all the other people's money back. It wasn't good for my income tax the first year because it all came on one side and then I had nothing from January through June. But once I got underway it was okay. Then, I get the books all cleared up early.

Tips

For people who want to start a dancing school, I certainly wouldn't let anybody pay as they came. They have to pay in advance and, like all colleges, YMCAs, any of those courses, you have to pay for at least the first 10 lessons. Before that's finished, get paid for the next 10. Especially something like a dancing lesson. If it's paid for, people are more apt to come.

I find that people will drop out toward the end. I find that February and March is a very low time in the school. Kids get restless, and you haven't started getting on to the big recitals yet. You've got to have something going almost every part of the year. I have something almost every month. At Christmas time we have a very big performance. Before that I have exams that older kids can take and I prepare them for exams in New York. In January it's getting back to business. In February I have photographs—a photographer comes to take the kids' pictures. He's not cheap, but if they want the photos, they can buy them. It's hard work and I don't get anything out of it. I work all day just posing these kids in different positions, making sure they aren't looking too terrible, that their feet are in correct ballet positions. We have something going on almost every month.

Passing the exam provides a kid a certificate from the great ballerina Margot Fontaine. I really have always maintained it's a teacher's exam, because it's your work. If you have a pretty high standard of teaching, most of the kids will do well on the exam. It's the Royal Academy tests from England. They're given in the British Empire, Australia, South Africa, and Canada. I, coming from Canada, passed these exams, and I think they're wonderful for the kids. They really have to be perfect. They know that they're going to go before someone who is a real professional who is going to judge them. I always have anywhere from 8 to 10 students per year able to do this. I spend a lot of extra time with them. They are the ones that really want to go on and dance professionally.

There are national associations, but I prefer the Royal Academy to any of the American ones, simply because that's where I was trained. It's very prestigious in England and everywhere else but here. You can pay dues to belong to the Royal Academy.

Personal Rewards

I get the most pleasure from choreography. I work the hardest on that. I love to have an idea and see it work. It doesn't always. And the class that I teach for my peers, I have a lot of work to do on that. I really have to work out combinations of steps and I spend a lot of time on that. I take most pride in the choreography and in having good dancers with clean technique. I like having really good dancers. I can't stand sloppy stuff. I like turning out good people, and I think I do.

The students come and go. I don't take much enjoyment from the little three and four year olds. But, you have to take them because the parents are so keen to get them dancing at that age, for whatever reason. It doesn't make any difference to me. Eight or ten is a great age to start. But they want them in at three and a half; the minute they stop wetting the floor. And I've always contended that it must be the parents who really want to dance. I really feel that that's the way it is. I give those kids to a lady who is wonderful with them. I don't take them unless I have to.

Outlook

I can't afford to retire so I think that I'm going to have to continue with one leg tied up. It's not from dancing, it's hereditary. I have a weak foot that's been broken and it needs to be realigned with an operation. What can I say? I'm in a profession I have loved all my life. I'm lucky.

Trade Publications

Dance Magazine
33 West 60 Street
New York, NY 10023
(212) 245-9050

Ballet News
1865 Broadway
New York, NY 10023
(212) 582-3285

Theatre Crafts
135 Fifth Avenue
New York, NY 10010
(212) 677-5997

15

Delicatessen

Baloney—don't just say it, sell it along with ham, liverwurst, potato salad, and all the other goodies you find in a delicatessen store, and you would be surprised at how much money you can make.

Air Force vet Mike Magee took only one year to gross over $127,000 in a small store located in Norwalk, Connecticut.

Too limited a retail operation, you might think.

Hardly. Magee, a young married man with a child when he bought his first delicatessen, eventually owned three stores and almost expanded into a chain operation. But Magee likes pleasing people with sandwiches, small talk, and genial advice. He likes people contact and not administrative routine.

He is still serving sandwiches at Mike's Deli, Norwalk, Connecticut, raising his family, working with his wife, and loving it.

Mike Magee

Before going into the deli business, I was in the Air Force, married, and had a child. When I got out, I couldn't go back to school because of my family. I finally got a job with Grand Central Market, a local chain. I worked there for about a year and a half and then bought my first store.

My uncle, who is a priest, came down one Sunday when I was working in the market. He said that as long as I worked on Sunday,

I might as well work for myself on Sunday. He lent me the money. I bought a deli; that was 13 years ago. It was a steal. My second child, another girl, was born in March and I went into business April 1. I jumped in with both feet. It was frightening, but what the heck. You have to take a chance.

I had myself, and my wife used to come in with the kids to help. We were a couple of immigrants with the kids in the store and my wife feeding them there. The first couple of years were tough. Real tough. But, knock on wood, business went uphill immediately.

Costs and Profit

My first store cost $6000 but I showed a profit right away. When I bought the business it was doing an annual gross of $36,000 a year. It was not enough to pay the lights. My first year I grossed $127,000. That was a lot of money back then. My accountant said that the place was too small. We had one parking space. The dimensions of the store were 13 x 24 feet. There was no room. It was a hole in the wall. When I was a lifeguard in Stamford (Connecticut), I used to go to a deli there that made great sandwiches. So I did the same, and people used to line up outside the door. It was incredible. From day one I made a profit.

Steady Business

There are no low seasons. Business drops a little in the winter, but that is due to the end of the boating crowd and the hiatus for landscapers. But it did not affect my sales too much. These big sandwiches really draw people. I have a picture at home when I first started of a sign that said "Coffee, 15 cents a cup." There were no other incentives other than the sandwiches and the nice family atmosphere. Also, we developed a good rapport with the neighbors. I was a young guy trying to make a living in the deli business, and they became my regular customers.

Long Days

When I first started out, the store hours were 6:00 in the morning until 8:00 at night. I lived in Stamford then, so I would get up at

5:00, and I wouldn't get home until 9:00 at night. It was tough. But it was well worth it. A lot of people who are in business don't see their children grow up. My wife and kids were here. It got to a point that my wife would open the store one day, and I would open the next. So, my off days I would be home with the kids, get them ready for school, feed them. It was great.

Start-Up and Expansion

It would take about $50,000 today to open up a deli, which would include all the inventory, cases, and fixtures. That's the right way. You can do it cheaper, but not if you would want to have a nice operation. Today, the rents are brutal. I used to have three stores altogether. Now I'm back to one.

This is how I got three stores. I went out to Ohio to visit some friends and stopped in a place called Mr. Hero, a small sandwich shop. I thought that something like that would work really well in Norwalk (Connecticut). When I came back from vacation, I found a vacant store in Norwalk. It was just right. I put a binder on it, and a couple of months later I had it opened. After I had the Norwalk store for a couple of years, my accountant had a client who was selling his deli located on the beach in Westport (Connecticut). My accountant and I bought it and became partners. We were there for six years, when the man who owned the property died. It was put up for bid, but we did not get it. The new landlords, having heavy financial obligations, raised our rent $3000 a month. This Westport store was mostly a seasonal business. Rent can kill you.

I had sold the Norwalk store for $30,000 when I got the one on the beach. The people who bought it sold it for $35,000 and the new owner has since turned down $65,000. This was all in about five years. And I'm finished with the one at the Westport beach.

Employees

I have about six employees here. When I first started out, it was just my wife and I, and a couple of part-timers. One girl has been working for me for 11 years. She came into the original store one day, and I asked her if she was interested in working part-time. Employees are tough. They are hard to figure. You get someone in and you explain the job to them, but before long you find out that they are useless. It's not what they don't know, it's just that a lot of the young kids think you just stand by the counter and wait for a customer to walk in. But behind the scenes, there is the preparation of the salads and general maintenance of the store. It's hard to make young kids understand.

There is a lot to learn on the job. When I managed Grand Central Market, there was a lot of responsibility. But I didn't own it. It wasn't mine. When it's your business, you want to be at the register all day. You want to see the dollars come in. They're your dollars. There is a pride in ownership. I remember when I first started, people would come in and ask for Mike Magee. I would tell them that I'm Mike Magee. Being young, they'd ask for my father. When they realized that I was the owner, their attitudes would change.

It was a problem too with vendors. They were basing the business on what it was before I bought it. I told them not to judge how I'm going to make out. It's a whole other ballgame. A prime example was when I called an ice cream company. When the guy came in he wouldn't give me a case because the store was too small. So I bought one. When I moved my present location, the guy wanted to give me two cases. I told him that since he refused to give me a case down the street, we were not about to do any business with his company.

Plusses and Problems

Something is always cropping up. When you're in business, it's not like a nine-to-five job. For example, 3:00 in the morning the alarm goes off, you get a call from the police department and find that someone threw a rock through the window. The rest of the night is spent trying to board up the window.

The good definitely outweighs the bad. I make a living, and since I'm at it so long, I enjoy a feeling of independence. You have to realize that the store can live without you. Many people own a business and feel that they must be there all the time. They think the store can't survive without them. My wife works here every other day, and she is fantastic. She's quick, organized, she's the epitome of efficiency. My wife also does the books. When she has her day here, I can go off and do whatever. I work Tuesdays, Wednesdays, Thursdays, and Saturdays. There's still banking involved, so I still have work to do on my days off.

My summer is the high period. It's the area. It's the boaters, the landscapers, the kids out of school, the softball players. It all blends together. It starts with the early commuters, to the kids going to the beach, to the lunch crowd, to the people coming home from work. We have a Lotto machine, so it's also the Lotto players. It's a very busy day.

Licenses

In this business, you have to be licensed for everything. To sell cigarettes, you need a sales tax license, which they charge you for. Imagine, you pay to collect sales tax to send to the state every month. Wow. You need a license to sell milk, beer, lottery tickets for the state. They get you coming and going. This is an annual expense amounting to about $300. You can't operate without the licenses and permits.

I have had the lottery for about five years. It's a big drawing card. A lot of people come in to play and 8 out of 10 will buy a pack of cigarettes or something else. You don't make a big buck off the lottery. You work on five percent. If you sell $100 worth of lottery tickets, you make $5. But it brings people in.

In this business, the mark-ups are all different. For example, in milk there's no mark-up. Coffee has a tremendous mark-up. There's no mean percentage. There are no associations that I belong to.

Customers

After working in the retail business as I did as a kid, I can tell from looking at people how you have to treat them. You can tell if you can kibitz with them a little or not. I'm a pretty good judge of character.

We make a very good sandwich, and the food is very fresh. It's quantity and quality. My 10-ounce cup of coffee sells for 50 cents, where other places in town are charging 70 to 80 cents. Coffee has gone up, but it hasn't gone up that drastically to jump the price like a lot of stores have. On the sandwiches, we give a fair amount of meat at a fair price. That's what is needed for success.

The personal touch helps. We get a lot of customers that we see every day. You learn how they like their coffee. You learn a little about them; they learn a little about you. Over the years, I've made a lot of friends with my customers.

Tips

I would say to anybody who wants to start a business that it's a little tougher now than when I started. It's like buying a house. It's a lot more expensive now. You just need the right combination: finding a good location in a populated area, and not going in over your head. You go into an area to see if there is industry, if the area is densely populated, if the location is on a busily traveled street. And your merchandise—what you sell shapes the character of the store. I'm basically a deli, so I don't sell a lot of groceries. Here it's the sandwiches and the rolls that people come for. You have to have a certain percentage of groceries to have a beer license. I don't have a deli beer license, I have a grocery beer license. You have to be willing to pay your dues. You have to work at it. It doesn't come easily. I had a woman come in one day who wanted me to give her a lottery ticket because she thought I was lucky. I asked her why she thought I was lucky. She said, look what you have here. I told her I didn't win it, I worked for it.

Trade Publications

Deli News
12028 Venice Boulevard
Los Angeles, CA 90066
(213) 391-4180

Grocer's Spotlight
25689 Kelly Road
Roseville, MI 48066
(313) 779-4940

Progressive Grocer
1351 Washington Boulevard
Stamford, CT 06902
(203) 325-3500

16

Delivery Service

Anita and Patrick McAllister operate a successful delivery service that they established in 1975 in the swank suburban town of Greenwich, Connecticut. You might wonder just how much business can be generated from a largely residential area where nearly everyone has a car.

More than might be expected. The bulk of the McAllister business comes from commercial sources such as corporations that prefer to have their mail picked up privately at the post office and then taken from the companies and delivered directly to the post office in the afternoon.

Unlike cities where most facilities are usually within walking distance, suburban areas require driving to almost everything. With mail such a critical part of any operation, having a dependable, private delivery service pick up and deliver is well worth the cost. Also, merchants such as drug stores and food establishments that deliver, as well as retailers in need of items to be shipped or picked up that require a van or truck, use the McAllister service.

A reasonable amount of business for the McAllisters even comes from residents of this affluent town who call the delivery service to pick up bulky purchases rather than stuff them in their cars. Often the autos are small imports that have very little room for sizable merchandise.

Theirs is a profitable business and easy to run.

Anita and Patrick McAllister

PATRICK: Well, before we became McAllister Delivery, I worked for an express delivery service. It was run by a husband and wife team who split up. The business was left to me. But it was mainly a moving business at that time. There were some deliveries. My wife came in to help me run it. We eventually let the moving end of it go because we couldn't find people who really wanted to work. With the moving end of it, all you could do was to go up the street to the local tavern and pick up all the bums that hung out there and give them $10 a day. Finding employees to do moving work is very difficult so we dropped it. The hardest part about the delivery business is learning the town. After you've mastered that, it's a piece of cake. It's not easy work but it's not hard.

Start-Up

ANITA: We had clients from the moving business but no small trucks for a delivery service. We just went out and bought what we needed in 1975. Barclays gave us the loan. We bought two trucks and a car. The car was used for small deliveries. Soon after that we purchased two vans.

PAT: I bought two vans for under $7000, and today I can't even buy one. The total outlay at the start was about $11,000. If we were to start today, it would cost at least $30,000. We have one part-time employee.

I go down to the post office at 6:00 A.M. and pick up the corporate mail and delivery it to all the corporations in Greenwich. In the afternoon we pick up all of their outgoing mail and take it back to the post office. A big part of our business is mail, I'd say about 60 percent. We only have one account outside Greenwich, and the only reason we have that one is that they used to be in Greenwich.

ANITA: As long as you stay in your own area, you're okay. The beepers were my idea. Since we're always out on the road, I thought they would be helpful. Pat has a phone in his truck so that if he gets a page he can contact me. We bought a house because we needed it. We would be very well off if we saved money, but we love spending it.

PAT: We never took salaries. If we needed something, we got it. The money was there—very little in the beginning, but it was there. A year before we bought the house I said we couldn't afford it. In a year she saved $25,000.

Work Routine

ANITA: You get tired, you get disgusted. At Christmas time it's the worst. Now the hours Pat has to work are cut down because I'm working.

PAT: I put in between 10 to 13 hours a day. Sunday we are off. Our ads say we're open 7 days a week, 24 hours a day. January through April is very slow. Holidays are a high time. The corporate income is 60 percent and for deliveries it's 40 percent. Our regular clients consist of a hardware store, liquor stores, a wedding and gift shop, a clothing store, and Western Union.

ANITA: Greenwich is a delivery type of town. The people don't mind paying for the service. We dropped the drug stores we serviced years ago because we would be out till 10 P.M. every night. Today, not too many drug stores deliver. We specialize in personal service.

Recommendations

PAT: If people go out to get customers, they could make $25,000 after a few years. But pick a town that is in a free zone, one that doesn't require licenses. The licenses are very easy to get but very expensive.

ANITA: You need a lawyer to get through all the red tape. A free zone is where you're really not stepping on anybody's toes. Greenwich is the only free zone in this area that I know of. You wouldn't want to start in a town any bigger than Greenwich, which is 48 square miles.

PAT: We only started advertising on the side of the trucks last year, and we just made it into the yellow pages this year. All of our referrals were from word of mouth.

Employees

ANITA: If we could depend on our employees, I'd love to sit back and take some extra time for ourselves. The youngest we hire is 16 years old as a driver, but to deliver the liquor you have to be 21. We look to the high schools for finding employees. It amounts to about two hours, five days a week, no holidays. And for a high school kid that's great because we pay $85 a week. We pay way above minimum wage, but none of these kids want to work. They feel they can pick and choose their after school jobs.

PAT: Customers move and new customers come in. Sometimes it feels like we're losing with every new one we get. Snow is a problem in the winter time. Dogs are sometimes a problem but not so often because we carry dog biscuits.

Banks are very receptive to loan requests. We're trying to refinance our house right now, but if you're an independent businessperson they don't want to know you.

ANITA: We knew a banker whom we met through one of our clients. Within six months we borrowed almost $30,000.

PAT: Reputation has a lot to do with it, as well as the outlook of the bank and its size. You have to get the right banker.

Location

ANITA: You need an affluent section where there are a lot of people with nice homes. Location is a big part of the success of a business. Fairfield County is one of the richest counties in Connecticut. We're in the right location for doing what we do.

PAT: I'd love to talk to somebody who could give me ideas about how I could improve the business, but I don't see how you can improve it unless you're really working hard. Even when things get tight, we know that we're not depending on anyone else for our income. Also, we don't feel threatened by anyone like many people do on their jobs.

ANITA: Every time we get a new customer, we raise the price. We may lose a customer but we will gain another within a month. We have established a lot of good will and that brings in clients.

Trade Publications

Automotive Messenger
American Trade Building
Hazelwood, MO 63042
(314) 332-0210

Motor Transportation Hi-Lights
2425 Devine Street
Columbia, SC 29205
(803) 799-4306

Steering Wheel
PO Box 1669
Austin, TX 78767
(512) 748-2521

17

Dry Cleaning

What happens when you are approaching 50, have spent all of your working life as a dry cleaner, and then lose your job because the store where you are employed is sold?

You get another job, no problem at all for a man of such extensive experience.

How about getting your own business!

That is exactly what Dominick Luce, owner of Mr. Fabricare, Croton-on-Hudson, New York did. The mental transition from earning income instead of a paycheck is not easy. It makes most people very hesitant. But the drive to own a business of your own is one that is at a peak in the United States. Be a boss and not be bossed. A very special kind of freedom.

The friendly, easygoing but highly professional dry cleaner, Luce went on his own. He found a store in a shopping mall, bought the equipment, and got the customers. Many followed him from his old job to his new place. With his wife and student son helping, his business has grown from the day he opened the door.

Soon there will be no more 12-hour days as Luce is making enough at the end of his first year to think about hiring part-time help. He's on his way and here's how he got it all together.

Dominick Luce

I was fortunate, more or less, because somebody bought the place where I used to work. I was there for 8 years, but I have 30 years experience. I started when I was about 13 years old.

I decided to start my own business two years ago. It took me about three weeks to find this store, which is nicely situated in this shopping mall. The rent is $1500 per month. I started basically from scratch, buying all my machinery: a spotting board to remove stains and grease spots, a 45 pound cleaning machine, and a 50 pound dryer that takes 45 pounds of clothes. I separate the loads into dark, light, soft, hard, and silks. If the load consists of coats, there are fewer garments; if it consists of silks, it's more. It depends on what I put into the machine.

Cleaning Materials

I use chloric ethylene. That's a synthetic solvent. I buy it by the drum and I have it pumped right into the cleaning machine. The chemicals are delivered to me the same way as gasoline would be. They pump it right into my tank. It's like they're pumping gas. Then there is soap that is added to the dry cleaning solvent. The average cost of chemicals per month is about $500.

The hours are long. We put in about 12 hours a day, 5 days a week, Tuesday through Saturday. My wife helps out.

Advertising

I advertise in the *Pennysaver*, a whole page ad. I also have circulars made up and put them in the parking lots and the train stations. I advertise with a local weekly that gives me a 10 percent discount. Also, I advertise in special Croton and Ossining advertising type books sent to families in this area.

I'm at a breaking point in the operation but I haven't matched the amount made on my last job. At this location, I'll expect to make as much as I earned before by October 1986.

Outlook

When I'm going at full capacity, I will have a presser working for me and at least two part-time girls. When I'm grossing about $2500 a week, then I can afford that. Now I'm still paying off machinery. Once I'm over the hill with payments on the machinery and everything, then it should be clear profit. My salary is now $350 per week. When fully operational, I should double that. It takes five years to pay off the machinery. The cost was $51,000. That's not all my expenses. We had to cut a hole in the roof for the chimney I needed. When I get everything done, my investment will come to at least $75,000.

Operation

I do clothing repairs, tucks, shortening, and letting out. I bill this on an hourly basis. I send the shirts out, so, actually, it's not profitable. It's just an accommodation, but I do make five cents a shirt, ten cents on some. We don't do sheets either; the turnaround is too long. It takes two to three weeks. There's no profit in it. There's a small markup on shirts.

Customers

The customers are not hard to deal with. You may get three or four who always complain and are never happy. The majority are very nice, understanding, and if there is a problem, I help them with it. A lot of places won't give them that time. They try to rush them in and out. A lot of places are not qualified to answer their questions. You have a lot of foreigners in the business now, and most of them can't speak English. I don't think they really know what they are doing. They can't communicate unless they have a counter girl or somebody that can talk for them.

The most unpleasant part of this lifestyle is the long hours. I'm still trying to get it off the ground. Once that happens, I can work four or five hours, take a break in the afternoon, and then come back later, if necessary. I like it. It gets into your blood and becomes a part of you.

Training

The National Cleaning Association (NCA) is the place to go for training for a person thinking about opening a business like this. It has a training school for beginners and one for manager training. The office is in New York City. I did on-the-job training. Personality at the counter is important.

Major Daily Expenses

Hangers are one of your biggest expenses. You use them for everything. They're about $23 a box; that comes to about six cents a hanger (500 in a box). The plastic bags are about 6 cents also.

Seasons

The prime part of your season is October to January. February and March start slowing down. April is also high because of box storage and coat storage. We provide those services. All that lasts right through July. Last year I gave free box storage in order to bring customers in. April through July business ir okay. August dies down. September—three weeks into the month—is also pretty quiet. As soon as it gets cold, again they start pulling out the storage. You stay pretty busy right through December.

Trade Publications

American Drycleaner
500 North Dearborn Street
Chicago, IL 60610
(312) 337-7700

Drycleaners News
PO Box 2180
Waterbury, CT 06722
(203) 755-0158

National Clothesline
717 East Chelton Avenue
Philadelphia, PA 19144
(215) 843-9795

18

Exterminating

Aaron Mitchell, the former president of Ozane Exterminating Company, New York, is an example of making it on your own in a business for which he had no skill.

A management person for many years at an exterminating firm that was once among the biggest in the country, he became weary of unfulfilled advancement promises and decided he would like to be his own boss.

Never actually a bug killer, but an administrator who knew the business side of exterminating, he purchased a failing one-man operation, got in-field, on-the-job training from an employee, took a course on extermination to be licensed, and made it.

Seven years after acquiring it, he sold it for a considerable profit and, being at retirement age, made enough to enjoy full-time leisure.

This is a success story that can be duplicated by people with a commitment to run a business rather than be employed by one. Here's how Mitchell did it.

Aaron Mitchell

I had been working at various types of jobs, mostly secretarial, office work, that sort of thing. Then I finally arrived at a low point in my life. I got a job in the office of an exterminating company that was the largest one in New York City and probably about the second largest in the country. I worked there for about 12 years, starting when I was about 34 years old. It was a good job. About that time I got married and thought about my future. When an executive of the firm left to start his own company, he asked me to come along with him. Since I felt I was in a dead-end situation, I agreed. Although he promised to give me an interest in the business, I soon realized it was not going to happen.

At the age of 50 when most people said I was out of my mind, I decided to go into business for myself. It turned out to be the smartest move I ever made. I could always get a job, that was no problem. Fortunately, my wife supported my decision. Since she was working, we could get along financially. The important thing was that I wanted to be my own boss. I felt that what I did for others, I could do for myself.

Start-Up

The president of the exterminating union, whom I had spoken to from time to time, knew I wanted to buy a small company. He told me he knew a man who wanted to sell his business. We met and I bought it for $7500. What intrigued me was that this business, started in 1923, had deteriorated to just a one-man operation. The business grossed then $10,000 a year. Of course, that's very, very little. He operated out of a hole in the wall, an office with 10 cubicles. He paid about $35 a month rent for one. He even stored his chemicals there. If you wanted to mix them, you went into the public bathroom. I hired a man immediately and then I went to New York City Community College two nights a week to learn about pest control and to be licensed by the Board of Health. Even though I basically knew the terminology of the pest control business, I really didn't know the mechanics of what to do.

Growth

Although I knew the management end of the exterminating business, I had never worked in the field. I would go out as an assistant to my exterminator, see what he did, sort of on-the-job training.

It may sound demeaning, but I didn't mind. I was doing it for myself. On a $10,000 gross, I paid my assistant about $5,000; chemicals and rent cost me an average of about $3,000. It was really a no-profit operation for the first six to eight months. That's when I found out that I did have sales ability.

I went out to get accounts. One shipping yard was serviced by a big company. It couldn't understand how I could compete. I said to any big company, you're just another account. To me, you'll be my big account. And, I'll tell you this, if you want service and I don't have a man available (he didn't know how many I had) I will be there myself to do it. He gave me the account on a month-to-month basis. He gave me a three-month trial. If he liked it, fine. If not, no hard feelings.

One day after I had the account, when I called the answering service I was told the shipping yard in Brooklyn had an emergency in the office, a roach or some trivial thing. I was there within 35 minutes. I deliberately took my old Cadillac. It looked impressive. I was wearing a suit jacket. I pulled up in front of the office where the purchasing agent could see me, took off my suit jacket, and put on work clothes. I told him that since I did not have a man available, and since I had promised him, I would do it. He was very impressed.

Exterminating is something everybody needs: private homes, businesses, food institutions, and buildings. There is a 100 percent market out there. Also, when people cut back on service, they will drop the luxurious items. The ones they don't want to get rid of are the garbage collectors and pest control service.

Promotion

I never advertised or made up brochures. In my particular line, advertising doesn't matter. If someone needs an exterminator, they will look one up in the yellow pages. I found that I had to do it by picking an area and seeing prospective accounts. I made personal calls. I would say, all I would like to do is leave my card should you need an exterminating service. I'm inexpensive and provide good service. I represent a company that's in existence, established in 1923.

Chemicals

In my 13-week course, I was taught about all the chemicals used in the business. Chemicals change every few years. It's amazing. Roaches, for example, the hardiest of any species, will eventually be able to resist whatever pesticides are used for a while. Roaches are fossilized in rocks millions of years old exactly as they are today. There has been no change. Chemicals come in quart size, bottle size, and can size, and the pest control companies around sell them in any quantity. Rodent control is more difficult.

Within six to eight months I started to get new business through references and word of mouth. Give people decent treatment for their money and personalized service. I tried to sell myself. It may be wrong, but I sell myself, and then I sell my product. I found that in most cases it worked. I was selling personal dependability.

This is a 12-month-a-year business. There is a seasonal emphasis. Of course you have a termite season that occurs in early spring. And you would be busy mostly with that type of work. In the summer you have heavy breeding of roaches, and you will be busy around that time. Ants, too, in the country. You schedule service to accounts on a weekly, bi-monthly, or monthly basis, depending on what is actually required.

Of course, you try to get your big accounts. I succeeded and just in the same fashion. I got Aqueduct, Belmont Race Track, Pan Am World Airways. It was mostly sales effort. Someone who worked at my shipyard account told me that he knew they were having trouble at Pan Am at a particular department and hangar. I called to make an appointment with the purchasing agent and told him that I was well aware of a problem that they were having in hangar 14, and I would like to go in and take care of it without charging them anything. Let me go in and clean that place up. If I do the job for you, I would like to get the work. I was making an investment. In out-of-pocket, it would come to about $40 worth of chemicals and my time. Unfortunately, I had plenty of time then.

Again, it was one of those simple things. I was able to clean up the problem and got the account.

Emergency

The airline account had an incident. The union and the workmen were going to walk out. They were working down at the new terminal at Kennedy Airport. There were mice all around since there was a lot of marsh and wet areas there. The men refused to work unless the mice problem was taken care of. I was called. I went there with two men. I stopped everything I was doing. I put on dirty clothes. As soon as the men saw us, they cheered. We went around and sprayed and they went back to work. What we did was saturate breeding areas. By putting this film of oil on the areas, it killed off any possibility of breeding.

I was on my own for six years, and then I sold the business for $75,000. My gross during that sixth year was about $100,000. The new owner has done even better. He increased the business to $300,000. He is doing this with about six full-time employees. I stayed in the background as an advisor.

Problems

The chemicals are only dangerous if you have very young children. When mixed in water most have a milky appearance. An exterminator would have to be very careless to put it near children. It looks like milk. Basically, you lock it all up.

Most exterminators today wear an inhalation mask. There is a big danger if you don't learn how to use chemicals properly. You have to be careful about flushing it down drains. Today, the environmental people are very strict.

Tips

You might think it is better to have a large account that pays $1000 a month than a homeowner who pays $35. Big clients are important, but those small ones are your bread and butter. It's easier to lose a big account. A lot of people are shooting for your business. But nobody is going to go after your little Mom and Pop store or private homes. A company has to have a good balance.

Trade Publications

Pest Control
7500 Old Oak Boulevard
Cleveland, OH 44130
(216) 243-8100

Pest Control Technology
4012 Bridge Avenue
Cleveland, OH 44113
(216) 961-4130

19

Financial Planning Service

Ed Neugroschl, a former school teacher, is an entrepreneur who has always been willing to take daring risks. His ambition to build a commercial enterprise of gargantuan proportions had motivated him to experiment with a massive expansion before he was ready. He failed.

But for Neugroschl, founder of Finesco Associates, Inc., a personal financial planning service located in Lincolndale, New York, this substantial setback did not prompt him to terminate his business but only to postpone his plans for expansion.

Neugroschl, who spent several years acquiring skills as a financial planner when selling insurance, started the now highly successful business in 1978 operating from his home. Being a former teacher was an extremely important asset in the early growth of the business.

His wife, Jill, also a teacher, was not only the woman behind him but next to him helping the operation succeed.

This story of his early success, near failure and his ultimately prevailing, offers guidelines that could be used in many other businesses. For anyone considering starting a business as a financial planner, the blueprint for making it is in the story of the Neugroschls.

Ed and Jill Neugroschl

ED: I taught math in high school. I had taught for three and a half years. The year before, Jill and I got married and moved to New Milford, Connecticut. Our location had a lot to do with getting out of teaching because the drive to the Bronx was a bit absurd. I could not get a job because anyone I went to assumed I was looking for summer work. Just by virtue of the fact that I was a teacher, I couldn't get a regular job. Finally Metropolitan Life Insurance Company hired me to sell life insurance which I did for six years. I studied and got a CLU degree, which is a Chartered Life Underwriter. It took me two and a half years.

In 1976, Metropolitan Life came out with a product called the Tax Shelter Annuity, mainly for school teachers. As a former teacher, it was natural for me to sell. Also, it was something I could believe in more than life insurance itself. I was never good at selling life insurance.

JILL: If I weren't teaching, we never would have made it.

ED: Basically Jill's income was supporting us. I think in my best year at Met I made $15,000 which is less than I made in my last year of teaching.

Beginning

By 1978, the annuity I was selling was no longer competitive. It had a front end load on it, while other companies had products with no charge. I decided to quit my job to start my own financial planning company. I was doing tax returns for myself and some friends in 1973. By 1976, I was doing it for pay and I had built up a small tax practice. The only training I had were the courses that I took to get the CLU, which included tax courses. I had no training in the forms; that was self-taught. Realistically, unless we're getting into very complicated returns, one can learn how to do them by reading the publications the IRS puts out. By 1978 my tax knowledge had expanded. I had taken advanced courses leading towards an MA in financial services.

I also became a chartered financial consultant which helped because that was geared towards actual financial planning and individual tax considerations. The concept of my company was to provide services to school teachers and to do it with the endorsement of the union.

JILL: Up until that point I was teaching in Yonkers and became very active in the union there. I was secretary of the Yonkers Federation of Teachers. Prior to that, and also during that time, I met many union officials. I attended American Federation of Teachers conventions and New York State United Teachers conventions. In 1978 I stopped teaching when our daughter was born. My contacts with all these union people was very important to developing Ed's company. It was his idea, his concept, his putting together, but I was able to provide the right ears to listen to what services he was offering.

ED: In December 1978, after the first month on my own, I earned $20,000—more than I made at Met in one year. I operated out of my home and did it mainly working with people I knew.

JILL: What I did was to contact my teacher friends in Yonkers. So while I was home with the baby, I was making phone calls and getting to a lot of client prospects.

ED: I was able to also work with life insurance. I've always thought life insurance is supposed to provide money in the event of death, but, unfortunately, at that time in the insurance industry, the emphasis was on something called whole life which included a savings feature in the policy. I knew that people could do better by buying something called term insurance, which is just pure protection, and earn more investing the money elsewhere. Along came these no-load annuities and I had the ideal vehicle to be able to work with it because of its tax benefits. I was able to replace whole life insurance with decreasing term and an annuity, and people did a lot better than if they stuck with the whole life. I was a bit ahead of the times as a couple of years later it became very popular to do that.

Expansion

Taking a second mortgage on our home, plus my aunt dying and leaving us a little money, I was able to buy my first computer in April 1979. Today it would be considered a toy, but at the time it cost $8000. But with that computer I got a jump on other people in the industry, because very few of them knew anything about computers. I was able to program, and to demonstrate that my concept worked as far as insurance and annuities were concerned. In May 1979 I formed a partnership with a person I had met at Metropolitan Life. After we formed the partnership we took a suite of offices in Pleasantville, New York. We hired two people, and remained as partners until December 1979. We took a bath due to the expenses of setting up the business, meeting the rent, and having a payroll.

Sustaining

The operation itself did not fold. But times were very rough. In fact, Jill had to sell some of her gold jewelry, gold coins. That definitely helped. The partnership ended up losing about $17,000 over a period of six months.

JILL: A big break came when our service was endorsed by the Dobbs Ferry United Teachers. The president of the union was a personal client. Today we have 36 unions that have endorsed our service. We call it the Financial Planning and Advisory Service. With the endorsement we get a billing line in their district which allows us to have the tax sheltered annuity money sent to us, a place to run our seminars, and an outlet for our material. In exchange, we provide two hours of free counseling for each union member per year on a variety of topics. We don't solicit the teachers, they come to us. We also send them newsletters which come out periodically. Each union gets two seminars per year which are free, and about 20 to 25 percent of the teachers come to the seminars.

ED: The partnership dissolved but I kept the space. The 1200 square feet was broken up into three different offices. I took over all the assets of the partnership and in essence absorbed the loss. I continued on my own. By that point, Jill had already joined the company on a part-time basis, and I had the endorsement of four unions. In February 1980 my former partner became my employee. Then Jill, because of her contacts, started bringing in endorsements that now amount to 36.

JILL: In February 1980 I started working full-time. I would come into the office once or twice a week with another endorsement. It was a full-time job meeting with the presidents of the locals. Some of the locals would not endorse a particular financial company because they did not want to deal with the repercussions, if there were any. Obviously, as our reputation grew, most of these problems did go away. We have picked up some locals who originally said no. There are some that we will never get because they simply don't endorse anybody.

Growing Too Soon

ED: Coming into 1981, we had 20 locals, and our reputation in Westchester County was excellent. In January 1982, we had a meeting with a committee about a state-wide organization. Three months later we had our chance to handle New York State. As a test, we had to set up operations in two regions picked by the state teachers union. If a year later these branches were successful, we would probably get state-wide endorsement. My dream.

JILL: You have to understand that the rest of us that were involved were not as confident as Ed. We felt that we were not ready for such a large scale operation.

ED: I did. But we needed about $500,000 to establish the offices in these regions, which were far from our headquarters. I expected a loss of $200,000 in the first year, and to take a smaller loss in the second. We didn't have enough money to get started on this.

In four months we blew $200,000. We closed the offices upstate immediately. We had already moved into our present, larger offices here. We were in debt for $200,000 and practically bankrupt.

It was my first experience with failure and I didn't like it. If I were to do it again I would be a lot more conservative. At this point we were down to seven people working, six in sales earning commissions only, and a secretary on salary. We had just laid off 16 people. That year, 1983, was a year of survival.

In 1984, we got a lot of breaks. Recognizing the fact that we were no longer going to expand geographically, we decided to start getting away from teacher's unions and start dealing with the general public. So our new business in 1984 was about 50 percent teachers and 50 percent from other sources. Since 1984 it's been uphill. We've been paying the bills and showed a profit last year.

Promotion and Awareness

We tried some advertising on the radio which got us nowhere. We probably picked the wrong radio station, or maybe we didn't stick with it long enough. Our main source of new clients was from people recommending us.

When Finesco was started, financial planning was something that most people knew little about. There were few degrees given out in it, and I believe no universities had programs to prepare planners for the sudden boom that followed in the 1980s. Major corporations set up financial planning departments and more people became aware of what we could do to help them.

JILL: Now the public wanted specific services from a financial planner. We began getting calls from people asking about our credentials. Since we have been in the business for so long we could provide total planning services, unlike the alleged "financial planners" who really sell insurance or stocks. And everyone at our company has a degree to back him or her up as a financial planner. The educating of the public has helped us.

ED: Having the credentials, and having the name and the exposure through the unions, was a tremendous help in getting those other clients. As those new clients came in, they would refer other clients. And, when you're dealing with people who have money, their friends also have money.

The only marketing I believe that has worked for us are the personal contacts we make at seminars, and sending out our newsletter to prospective clients after we are endorsed. Seminars we ran in places where we weren't endorsed didn't do any good. Endorsement is very important.

For example, as a speaker at a regional conference in 1979, something called "Teacher to Teacher," the room was set up for 40 people, and we ended up with over 65. Every year since then my workshop attracted more and more people.

Outlook

You have to be open with your clients and create an atmosphere where they are willing to confide in you. No matter how much you know, you must remember that people react emotionally, not logically. Also, now unions are seeking us out; we're not pursuing them.

People walking in off the street pay $100 per hour. If they come in through a union endorsement, they get the first two hours free and then they pay $40 an hour.

JILL: Our schedule is flexible. Often we don't get here until 10 or 11 A.M., but we're here seeing people until 9 or 10 P.M. You can be as productive as you want to be. We enjoy it.

Trade Publications

Financial Planning
5775 Peachtree/Dunwoody Road
Atlanta, GA 30342
(404) 257-0110

Financial Service Times
537 Newtonville Avenue
Newton, MA 02160
(617) 244-1240

Financial World
1450 Broadway
New York, NY 10018
(212) 869-1616

20

Fitness Center

A health oriented population in the United States today is as concerned about toning its muscles as it has already become about good nutrition.

The surge to achieve hard bodies, or just to physically look and feel fit, has soared in the 1980s. An imaginative assortment of equipment called Nautilus attracted both men and women to laborious weight training exercises. Looking good is in, and it is a profitable and growing business for the continually increasing number of health and physical fitness centers mushrooming around the country.

Fitness is not only a business for cities and big towns. While vacationing with my wife at the small beach resort town of Lewes, Delaware, we discovered a spanking new Nautilus center nearby. Both of us into fitness, we wondered how this facility could survive in an area where there is largely a flood of people only in the summertime.

Very simply. Throughout this coastal state there are massive developments of condominiums, and in many places large apartment buildings. Today, wherever there are people, there will be a market for fitness.

Bob Baff, owner of his own fitness club in Yorktown Heights, New York, extremely short of investment money, had to do it all wrong when he started. He had a poor location, opened before the fitness boom, and faced other drawbacks. Still he prevailed and has a very successful operation.

147

Bob Baff

Before I opened my fitness center, I was doing physical therapy. I had a practice which involved working six days a week divided between a nursing home, private patients, and hospitals.

After I graduated college in 1969 from Long Island University with a BS in physical education, I went to Columbia College of Physicians & Surgeons where I took a one-year intensive course in just physiotherapy. I completed that and I started work at a medical center as a physiotherapist. After about two years, I took further courses in physiotherapy and I supplemented my income in doing home care—going to see patients in their homes after they were discharged from hospitals. That I did after my regular job as a therapist.

About two years went by and I then went into private practice with two other fellows. Eventually this partnership dissolved. I then had my own practice for about 10 years.

My therapy practice was locked into a fixed fee that I could not increase. People paying were not getting reimbursed at a higher rate. I now had a ceiling on how much I could charge. I then decided to open this place.

Exploring

I had a family all this time. I got married at 19 and I'm now 42. It was nothing less than survival. I have two children.

When I started this business seven years ago in Yorktown, New York, people didn't know what Nautilus was; they didn't know what aerobic dance was. But I had to get into something other than the physical therapy. First, I shopped around. I looked at franchises. I made lots of friends. One friend owns Arrow Staple Company, and he told me to try Wendy's, which was to be an up and coming thing. I got in touch with the attorney that represented Wendy's, and I sat down and had a very enlightening meeting with him. I realized that I couldn't afford it. I didn't have any savings. All that was left for me was to start from nothing. Franchises were out.

Start-Up

I had no reason to be in business. I broke every single rule. I was totally undercapitalized at $7000. The equipment that I first signed up for cost $25,000. Then there's the lease for a place without showers or anything else. When I came to this building, the windows were boarded up. I was knee high in water. That's why no one wanted it. IBM used to be here; they moved out. BOCES used to be here; they moved to the place up on the hill. What prompted them to move was that whenever it rained, water would come in.

The ownership kept changing. Then there was a fire here. It became a ghost area. The bank owned it when I signed the lease. It was in receivership. The bank didn't want to be a landlord. It didn't want to put another nickel into this place.

I believed I could turn it around even though this was the pits. There was no exposure to anything, boards on the windows. My wife thought I was totally out of my mind. What they wanted for rental was a lot, but I convinced them that there was nobody waiting on line behind me. I got it then for what was a lot for me. Today it is a bargain. Right now it looks good but then people thought I was nuts. There was nothing here. The building next door which is now a professional building was totally vacant. There was nobody here, only the Chinese restaurant. All this space was empty.

Getting Underway

I got a 10-year lease. I figured it doesn't hurt me to have a longer lease. I originally rented 3000 square feet. I now have 10,000. When I opened up, Nautilus was an unknown and I couldn't pay the rent on just that. In fact, what is my men's locker room now was where I had all my Nautilus equipment. To buy Nautilus equipment you have to put 50 percent down, and in 80 days you get delivery, COD. Nautilus was just getting popular, and the company was not geared for fall production, so it was a long wait for delivery.

I tried to borrow money but I was rejected by every bank. Finally, I borrowed money from my family. I was lucky they believed in me. I also continued working—doing physical therapy—because

I had to keep putting money into my fitness center just to keep it going. It was a primitive place in the beginning. My kitchen table was my desk. I didn't have a water fountain. I had an ice chest with water. I didn't have enough money to get a contractor to estimate my construction. I did all the electrical work, all the plumbing, and everything else by myself.

From conception to the opening in 1978 took nine months. But I didn't pay rent until the place was ready. I started two businesses—one was a Nautilus fitness center and the other was for gymnastics. In short, I was very small, and I felt I was losing business because I was very small. Gymnastics began paying its way. When we created the business, Nautilus was supposed to be the big money maker. But Nautilus wasn't an in thing yet. What it was going to take for me to have Nautilus work was to put it in a bigger area. I started with 10 machines.

Expansion Needed

For a long time Nautilus wasn't producing a decent return on my investment. What I chose to do was to go more into debt and expand my operation. I took the successful business—gymnastics—and moved it out into a larger space all by itself, away from Nautilus. I then changed all the walls and put Nautilus into a much bigger room and added a new line of free weights. That started to work for me.

I had started with 3000 feet divided between Nautilus and gymnastics. Gymnastics was successful. Nautilus wasn't. I put the successful one out into its own building. However, seeing a future for Nautilus, I borrowed again to provide more space for it. I took a chance. Now I have 3000 feet for just Nautilus, as well as the separate facility for gymnastics. I started gymnastics training for kids from two to 13 years of age. Now I have them from 12 months to 30 years of age.

It was time to expand even further. I decided to lease more space in order to accommodate a larger cross section of the health-oriented market, which was growing all of the time. The added space was for exercise and aerobic dance for women. But the exercise section was not getting enough traffic and was not a profitable part of my operation.

More Changes

I analyzed what was working for me here and what was not, and changed the layout again. I kept the space for the women's and men's exercise classes but decided to eliminate the nursery area and turn it into a gymnastic school. Fortunately, the space was available for me to break down walls for expansion that included a physiotherapy room for me.

Why not add my own specialty—physiotherapy—to the business? This produced needed extra income. I'd do personal treatments for people with bad backs and diabetes. I don't use ultrasound equipment but do pain management. I have three tables in the physiotherapy room.

Free weights is a big part of fitness, even more than Nautilus. But these two are the major attractions of a fitness operation. Racquetball, which had become very popular, has leveled off and is not a major factor in a fitness center. In fact, the big places that have tennis courts and racquetball find they must now offer a swimming pool to help maintain membership that feels it has joined a club rather than a health center. My place is totally fitness. A gym where people can exercise. These big places cannot offer memberships for only one type of activity such as exercise classes. They require full family membership even if you end up using one facility.

Costs and Market

A basic place requires at least $150,000 investment today for the space and all the basic equipment needed to attract people. It is hard to predict when the break-even point can be reached since this kind of business involves heavy expenditures for equipment and overhead. I have been in business for seven years and was only able to manage to barely survive for the first five years.

Keep in mind that people have a different objective of earnings. I suffered from a relatively poor location and an area where there was not too much interest in fitness—certainly not much in 1978. Now it has become a big thing in this country. It started in the 1980s. Now there is even a substantial market in home exercise equipment. Fitness has become fashionable in a big way, perhaps in the last three years. Up to then the momentum was building.

Now people getting into this business have an established market. I got into it when the public still had to be conditioned and educated to the value of exercise.

I did so much myself, which meant I was just keeping the business together. With a budget for help, I could have expanded my operation by actively marketing the fitness center. You need adequate capitalization to open up on a large scale immediately. I am confident that I would have gotten a bigger return on my investment money than by having to take the slow expansion route.

Location

Location is critical and parking facilities in a suburban area vital. I am lucky since the mall I'm in is building up all around me. In fact, the new post office will be located near me and all the empty space in the back has been rented. But I was isolated for a long time since I did not start with enough capital to pick the best location when I started.

Employees

For this business, a person can get good employees since many people like to work in a fitness center, so they can guide individuals to better health and better looks. Trim, firm bodies do look better.

Hours

I'm here from 9 A.M. to 1 P.M. and I'm back at 3 P.M. and then leave at 8 P.M. I like to get back to my family. I have good instructors and trainers and finally can live a more normal life leaving my business with excellent employees. We are open seven days a week, Monday to Friday, from 9 A.M. to 9:30 P.M.; Saturdays 9 A.M. to 3:00 P.M., and Sunday 9 A.M. to 1 P.M.

Tips

If a proprietor gets off to a slow start, it is important to have his gym facility appear to be alive and not look like he is dying. I used to invite friends in to work out and keep a lively, spirited atmosphere that new customer prospects could see at my place.

I recommend the areas for women and men be separated. Body conscious ladies, especially, do not want to be too visible to the opposite sex. Each really wants their own space away from each other. Most fitness centers do have rooms for women only. It makes them more comfortable.

Don't forget this business requires continual advertising to attract new customers.

Trade Publications

Fitness Industry
1545 NE 123 Street
N. Miami, FL 32239
(305) 893-8771

Recreation, Sports & Leisure
50 South 9 Street
Minneapolis, MN 55402
(612) 333-0471

Sport Fitness
2100 Erwin Street
Woodland, CA 91367
(818) 884-6800

21

Fruit and Vegetable Store

Selling fruits and vegetables, once a perky business in the summer, is now a profitable venture year-round. This is certainly true of Mike Cotic's Country Market, a small, old, charming store located on a rural road about two miles north of Croton-on-Hudson, New York.

Drive by quickly, and you can miss it. But stop and browse between the tight aisles of the display bins, and you will find an endless flow of people paying for their fruits and vegetables at the tiny checkout counter.

The small parking lot at times barely accommodates the continual stream of autos bringing customers to the store. But regular shoppers at Mike's are there the entire year, with hardly any noticeable drop-off in the winter. In fact, business is so steady that the store is open seven days a week throughout the year.

Cotic decided to be his own boss after his job as a tractor operator ended when his company moved to another state. He bought the store and the property in 1981 for $68,000. He was offered $425,000 for it last year.

With luck and hard work here is how Cotic did it.

Mike Cotic

Most of my life I was a tractor operator. When the company I worked for moved to New Jersey, I decided to go into business for myself. However, it did take me about a year to find the thing I wanted to do. In between I worked for the county police as a dispatcher. One day when driving by this place I saw a sign up that it was for sale.

Within one month I got an agreement to rent the store on this country road for one year with an option to buy. It cost me $68,000 in 1981. By the end of my rental year, I bought it. I was able to get a loan from the bank that will be entirely paid off shortly.

During my rental year, I got some help from the former owner. Most important was going down to Hunts Point Market in the Bronx to buy the produce. I learned the whole procedure as he went with me once, and then I got into it on my own. I did get a list of people the former owner bought from. But basically I built up my own source of suppliers as I learned from doing it how to make the best purchases. In time, the people there would offer me deals on their produce. One thing, you have to bargain at the food market. It's part of the system.

Spoilage

Once we get the fruits and vegetables at the store, they move out fast. However, a certain amount goes into the refrigerator and then out into the warmth of the store, and that causes spoilage. We suffer a lot of loss, which is true of everyone in the retail produce business, with green vegetables. As soon as they are exposed to air, hot or cold, they begin to go bad. Then we have to trim off the rotted parts, and that means we lose weight and money at the cash register. We really do not make any money with greens. It is basically a customer accommodation.

However, we do make up for this loss with our fruits. They hold up very well.

Increased Business

From the day I opened the store, business increased steadily. Of course, people who come to a small store like mine expect quality products and are willing to pay for it. If they are looking for lower grade produce, they can get them cheaper at a supermarket.

Another thing that helps is being available to customers. I'm at the store, after I go into the city to buy my produce, every day of the week from 6 A.M. to closing, which is 7 P.M. I'm friendly with customers and advise them what to buy when I'm asked.

Extra Revenue

The grocery items I have here are mainly another accommodation for customers. Every produce store sells milk, eggs, cheese, and bread. The cake, jams, newspapers, and magazines are my way of providing more shopping convenience for my customers.

I do a big wholesale business here, as well. In fact, about half of my revenue comes from the wholesale side of my operation. It is especially good during the winter months. I supply hospitals, nursing homes, restaurants (from public ones to those operated for employees by big companies in this area), and delicatessen stores.

It started when a chef I knew started to order wholesale from me. He then increased his orders. When he took another job, I delivered to his new place. The person he replaced began to call me for produce when she took a job with a large company that has an employee dining facility. And that is the way it continued, by word of mouth. Today, my wholesale volume accounts for one half of my business.

Employees

My wife and son work here and my father helps out, also. I then have a part-time woman for the counter and a part-time driver.

Present Value

Not too long ago I had a quarrel with my son whom I am breaking in to the business. In fact, he does some of the buying for me. Well, I got so mad that I decided to put the business up for sale. I listed it with an agent who handles commercial properties. I had no idea what price to put on it and left that to the real estate person.

Well, she brought me a buyer from Manhattan who loved this small place in the country, and I was offered $425,000. I paid only

$68,000. I took it off the market when I straightened things out with my son. I love it too much to sell it at this time. Also, by next year I will have paid off my bank loan, and that will bring my profit margin up a bit.

I really am not ready to sell yet. I'm doing something I enjoy and I'm dealing with customers I like.

And what I like most is—this is my place.

Trade Publications

Food Merchants Advocate
303 South Broadway
Tarrytown, NY 10591
(914) 631-4100

Food Trade News
119 Sibley Avenue
Ardmore, PA 19003
(215) 642-7040

Modern Grocer
15 Emerald Street
Hackensack, NJ 07601
(201) 488-1800

22

Golf Club

When you read the story of Bill Warner, who owns one of the most successful golf clubs in Connecticut, the Silvermine in Norwalk, you will discover a person with a rare blend of business savvy and compassion. Bill concluded deals to construct his 27-hole golf course that many people would be reluctant to propose. They were a mix of rural integrity and sound judgment.

Warner is in a business where there will be room for expansion—possibly always. There are more golfers in this country than there are courses for them to play on. And the situation will not change in the foreseeable future. In fact, it is likely to worsen before it improves as more and more people take up the recreational sport, and acreage for golf courses is taken by real estate developers.

Establishing a golf course is a costly venture today, one of the businesses where success is almost guaranteed if a number of basic guidelines are followed. Warner explains how to work with developers.

The Warner success story, rooted in a disappearing do-it-yourself, pioneer work ethic, is indeed an inspirational one.

Bill Warner

At 14 I was an umbrella boy working at various clubs. I enjoyed putting up the umbrella and I liked working with people and not having to sell anything—just to provide a service. I especially enjoyed cooking hamburgers for a year. After four years in the military service, I went to St. Lawrence University, already knowing that I wanted to go into the golf business. I met my wife at school, and we got married after graduation. We came back and started a golf club business. I talked to my dad and my brother, Jack, who is my twin, suggesting that instead of going into the construction business, why not open a golf course? My dad had built homes for 40 years.

Start-Up

We started looking for property and my brother spotted this Lauden Farm in our area. This was in 1958. We decided that we wanted to turn the property into a garden and install a golf course. The old people who owned the farm were very warm to that idea. So we made a deal that involved no money down at all. We proposed buying the 64 acres in 10 years. Meanwhile we would pay them interest on the purchase price of the property until we were in a position to pay for the land. We then bought 15 more acres from a neighbor, as well as other land on the same basis.

The farmer was very elderly and in ill health. He just couldn't do the farming anymore. We happened to come along just at the right time. This man was born on the land and really didn't want to part with it. We mixed humanity with business. We told the man he could live on the property for the rest of his life. We would give him money to survive and make his last days contented ones. He would have his private garden without having houses all over the property. That started us off.

Eight of us designed, built, and created the golf course. We bought a bulldozer and worked from sunup to sundown every day, seven days a week. As people in the community became curious, they would come up and find out that we were putting in a golf course. They would then give us their initiation fees and dues. We took their money before it was done.

Costs

To get the short nine course open for play cost us $60,000. That was 1958. Today, it would cost about one million dollars. We did all the work ourselves. We hired a young guy to run the bulldozer and we paid the notes on the bulldozer. When the job was completed, we let him have the bulldozer instead of pay. He just had to continue making the last payments on the machine. He was a young man who used the bulldozer to start his business. Now he is a very successful developer in Norwalk (Connecticut). He has done very well. This is how we did it. We just had everybody pitch in knowing that if they helped with our dream, we would reward them down the line. This is how we built the golf course.

The $60,000 was a family investment from houses that had been built and sold plus what we could borrow from the bank. Many people said we couldn't do it and were very surprised when we did. We did it with a lot of luck and a lot of hard work. We worked every single day from the crack of dawn until dark for two years before we got it going. But, it was a labor of love. Improvements that we make now are expensive and must be maintained. You have to use your crew for maintenance plus construction, so it makes it a lot more difficult and a lot more costly to expand today.

Membership Fees

The initiation fee in the beginning was $100, and the dues were $100. So, you could play golf for $200 a year. Today a family membership is $1200 and initiation is very low at $300. Basically it's the most inexpensive club in the state, for a 27-hole golf course. Also, we are the only privately owned 27-hole golf course in the state of Connecticut. We have 65 acres now in Wilton that we have added on to it, me, my brother and Dad. But Dad is retired now so my sister, my brother, and I bought his share. Technically, the three of us own the golf club now.

Employees

We have a total of 37 employees during the peak season and nine in the off season. But during the high season, we vary between 37 and 40. We've been lucky since good workers are scarce. A lot of people have been with us for many, many years. But we get a lot of young people, too, high school kids that come looking for a summer job and then stay on with us and learn the business.

Of course, we have a lot of family. All of my children and my brother's kids and my sister's kids have worked for the club and then went off to do their own things. Only one has expressed an interest in club management, and that's my daughter, Kathy, who is graduating this year from college where she studied club management. She will carry on the family tradition.

Promotion

There were no incentives in the beginning to attract customers. We did no advertising. People would drive up the road and all of a sudden see a golf club that they didn't know about and were absolutely surprised. We are tucked up in a corner here. They would stop and say that they wanted to join the golf club. We never put an ad in the paper, used radio, or anything of that nature. It was just by people playing and then bringing their friends. It was just by word of mouth that we did it.

Earnings

It took about three years before we started going into the black. This has always been a tough cash flow business. Your properties increase, your land values increase thousands of times over. They are very valuable. But the cash flow to cover everyday expenses always has been a problem in the golf club business.

When we first started, the very first year, we opened a pro shop. The Weeburn Country Club was selling out its merchandise so we bought the pro shop inventory when the owner retired. He had beautiful, expensive bags and shirts and all top-line equipment. We made a package deal and bought everything. We looked like we were really fancy and ready to go. We were very impressive.

Many of our first members are still here today. It's 28 years and they remained with us. It's like a big family. We share their problems with real interest and much understanding. When the going got tough, they supported us. It's been a great relationship over the years. We just celebrated our 25th anniversary and had a big party for everybody and gave out medallions to the charter members with silver keychains, and they all were very appreciative. It's been a very successful enterprise.

From the profits, we got a fleet of golf carts, and that's a big source of revenue. The dues structure more or less just covers operational expenses such as overhead and things of that nature. You try to get the dues to wash out the expenses. It was a very big struggle those first three years. We had a tremendous battle. I had a family, and we just took enough salary to handle our emergency expenses that we had. Kind of subsistence for the first couple of years.

We had a real problem with Uncle Sam because the IRS ruled that the excise tax on dues was payable to the government since we were operating as an individual instead of a corporation in the beginning. So, we went to the membership, and the membership all got behind us and put up a $200 debenture bond and bailed us out. And over the years we paid those monies back. When we got in a jam with Uncle Sam, the members came through to help us out.

Problems

Taxes are still a problem for a golf club, especially real estate taxes. Towns always want to tax a property as building lots or commercial property, rather than as open land. So every few years we have to remind them that we went to open lands. It's a real battle with them. We fought with Wilton, because half the golf course is in Wilton and half the golf course is in Norwalk. We had told them that it was best to give us open lands. We promised not to sell it or develop it for 10 years. They finally agreed to open lands, but we had to hire lawyers and struggle for four years to accomplish that.

We made a subdivision of the upper nine holes, which we call Grey Hollow, because of the new concept in the area called cluster housing. Houses were built around the perimeter of the golf course. These houses are owned technically by the 24 homeowners who bought them. Also, they each own the land, amounting to 1/24 of 65 acres. Now, they're paying the real estate taxes on the Wilton properties. The Wilton property is now at a special tax rate. We still pay the open land taxes. We just went through a reassessment this year which required that our attorneys negotiate with the town to get it down. It's always a struggle. You always have to be on top of it. You can't let it slide, or you'd really be in a lot of hot water.

Town officials see land and they think taxes. And sometimes thy don't realize that it's better to leave it as open land rather than to have another housing development that would mean more firemen, police, schools, and all the things that go with it. We had our battles with the State of Connecticut because they were going to put a road near our property. We had to make sure it didn't affect the golf course. We convinced them, but at one time they wanted to cut right through the middle of the golf course. It turned out to be a little too expensive for the state. There are a lot of unpleasant things you have to overcome.

Sharing Responsibilities

We have to hire people to run the club: chefs, waiters, waitresses, golf pros, an office crew, pro shop people, clubhouse function people, an outside maintenance crew. We share management responsibilities. I'm in charge of the pro shop, office, and clubhouse areas. My brother, Jack, handles the outside crew. He buys the fertilizers, fungicides, and all the necessary materials for the outside. He also hires people for maintenance. We've been doing it this way for 25 years now, and it's worked out very well.

Professional Development

I have always been very active in the club manager's association. I was treasurer and president. I've attended many seminars, learning from the bottom up. Even when I was in college, I knew I was going to go into this field, so I took a lot of courses in club management. It did pay off. My daughter's decision to go into the business was a very big surprise. There was no pressure from me whatsoever. This was just something that she wanted to do. She's a good student, made the dean's list. I'm very proud of her.

Connecticut Club Managers Association has taught me a lot. Every month we have a local seminar and then we have national conventions and regional seminars. Most of the club managers in this area go to them religiously. They are very, very important, since we get updated on the newest labor laws, safety equipment, hiring, and firing. You've got to be on top of it because things keep changing. If you don't, you can get behind very quick.

Growing Larger

The pro shop area used to be a garage for milk trucks and that's one of the original farm buildings left, along with the maintenance facility which used to be the barn. When we built the golf club, we took down 22 buildings. We had to cut them down to make room for the golf course. We dug 11 ponds to put in the water hazards. Everything was manmade, not preexisting.

The clubhouse was started in 1960 and we put another addition on it in 1964. It was very small. It's still not big, as we thought we were going to be only a golf club and not a large social club with the tennis and swimming pools that we have now. That's why we went with 27 holes of golf and 60 golf carts. We have all the latest pieces of equipment. We have been continually putting a lot of money back into the club. We installed two paddle tennis courts a couple of years ago. But it kind of died. They don't use them very much. It just didn't catch on like we thought it would.

Pleasures

The greatest reward is seeing the young people who come to work for us succeed later in life. They come into the club at the age of 16 or 17 while in high school. We are proud that the kids have done such a great job. The ones that have worked for us, the majority, have gone on to become really successful. Several have gone into club management, to such places as Marriott and Disneyworld. They got their first taste of the business here and enjoyed it. Some of them have opened up their own recreational businesses. One fellow who got his training here opened up a marina, a restaurant-type thing, and has done very well. I also coach a local high school golf team, which is very satisfying. Once the kids learn golf, they continue forever.

Outlook

I think that there is still tremendous need for golf courses. I think the concept of building a golf club with the housing around the perimeter can be a successful business. The houses around the perimeter give you the nucleus of your membership. The houses would help pay for the construction and the operation of the golf club.

That still is my dream if I would ever do it again, to find a tract of land that is large enough to put houses around it. You don't have to commute to New York. I live right on the golf course. I just come over in a golf cart. My sister lives on the golf course. My brother lives in New Canaan. We always cover for each other and get some free time. We close in the winter time. The rewards are not having the pressure of punching a clock from nine to five and commuting to New York and checking train schedules. It's wonderful.

I look out over the green fairways and think that it's such a pretty oasis. We are at the highest point in Norwalk and have a great view. It's so tranquil looking out over the fairway, seeing the evening sunset. It's a great way to live.

Trade Publications

Golf
380 Madison Avenue
New York, NY 10017
(212) 877-0901

Golf Course Management
1617 Saint Andrews Drive
Lawrence, KS 66044

Golf Industry
1525 North East 123 Street
North Miami, FL 33161
(305) 894-8771

23

Hobby Shop

He succeeded in the hobby shop business selling old comic books to collectors, but Michael Raub, owner of The Dream Factory, Norwalk, Connecticut, said you can do it selling anything from toy trains to dolls.

The collectible craze extends into a huge list of items—so many that Time Books puts out the *Encyclopedia of Collectibles*.

While his store is his chief source of profit, Raub adds to his earnings selling items through direct mail. Also, he has a number of convenience publications, the current popular magazines that he stocks, to supplement his income.

Can you make a good living from selling collectibles or from some other kind of hobby shop?

Indeed yes. In fact, Raub's success with the comic books has been so substantial that he has been considering opening a second store.

It is interesting, how often you might wonder passing a series of stores located on the main street of Anytown U.S.A., if these merchants are doing well. They are, for the most part, and Raub tells you why.

Michael Raub

Inventory

The market has changed a lot over the past five years due to mail order selling of certain items. Comics and related items are now available strictly to specialty shops, which, of course, helps hobby shops. A few items are sold on a nonreturnable basis. Once you get them you have to sell them yourself in the future. This is for the new comics. Everything in the store pretty much are new items, current items, except for one area. We have a set of about 10,000 back issues that collectors can buy right here. However, we also do mail orders. We get merchandise from wholesalers and also from people who sell us their collections. For every five people who start to collect, there is always one person who gets out or decides to change what they buy. These people sell to us.

What kind of mark-up would a 20-year-old comic book have over a current issue? That really depends. It's a fallacy that old things are worth money. Old things are not worth money. Old *Life* magazines are worth 50 cents or a dime. A lot of people will drag that stuff in, and it's not worth anything. We don't sell used magazines. Comic books which are 50 years old may only be worth 50 cents. I have one in the window that's 40 years old, and it's worth $1.50. And it's in fine shape. Scarcity creates the value. There's a comic book that came out last month that sold retail for $3.95 new. It is now worth $20. It just isn't available. That's what makes it valuable. It's an item that everybody wants and is hard to get.

A small publisher in Connecticut put out a comic book in early 1984 and the first edition is worth over $100 now. It was written up in *The Wall Street Journal* at the end of 1985 as one of the items that was considered the best investment of 1985 for collectors. It is a $1.50 item which turned over a profit of $98.50. Imagine if someone had bought 100 copies.

Start-Up

My wife and I are both avid collectors. But nothing in the store came out of our collection at all. I continue to buy a bit of material every week for myself. I always have. We researched the market by going all over the country. The business my wife was in a year ago enabled us to travel a bit. She was a computer programmer for Dun & Bradstreet and she did a lot of traveling. We visited stores in California and even as far away as Hawaii.

We went to a lot of shops and there are a lot of these specialty shops around the country. We saw what they were doing, really studied the ones that were successful as well as the ones that were not. We decided that a specialty hobby shop could be profitable. We went mainly to comic book shops of which there are well over 25,000 in the country right now. In fact, a weekly newspaper comes out every Tuesday that covers news about mail order and things for sale. There is such a big market for these items that stores from small towns such as Lombard, Illinois; Clinton, Massachusetts; Milford, Massachusetts; and Oakland, New Jersey advertise in this publication. Notice I didn't mention the big cities, like New York City, which has over 20 comic shops alone.

Store Opening

You have to carry a large variety of products and not be very limited in what you offer. I opened in September 1985. We put up an initial capital investment of about $25,000 to cover fixtures. This was pretty much a turn-key building. The floor and everything was here, was new; we watched it being built. We had to get fixtures, stock, cash register, and shelves for displays. In the early months, we didn't realize that we needed a full line of reading material. I don't think that someone who just sells old comics or new ones can survive. You must sell a lot of other things that interest people.

For instance, say you would come in here with say, three children; you are going to be bored looking for just comic books. We want people to browse, so we now have a used and new paperback books section, and special trade paperbacks for senior citizens. We have just about every magazine that gets published. The more successful you are, the better you are in getting the most out of every dollar that comes into the store. If I get only 50 cents out of that dollar, the other 50 will be spent elsewhere. If a customer spends the entire dollar's worth here, I'm successful.

We use part-time people. We have some young boys that do stock work for us, boxing and that sort of thing. I have a girl that works on the cash register about 20 hours a week and a few others that fill in for her.

Investment Money

We borrowed money against our home. We got a very good deal on the house and we were able to get all the money needed to begin. Then my wife got laid off from work. That was two months after we opened. But we were lucky to open before the Christmas season. We earned money right from the start. This is a hot business. I'm amazed at how fast it grew.

We reinvested virtually everything we could to expand our product line. For a while I had to supplement our income by taking some work in my previous profession—radio announcing. But it certainly worked out for us. We are now looking for a second location for a store. Our plan is to have a chain of these, at least three in Fairfield County, and elsewhere. Our particular kind of inventory mix seems to work very well and is not duplicated anywhere.

Earnings

The best way to determine if you've made a profit in a small business is after you've paid your bills, is there any money left? It doesn't take a genius or a computer spreadsheet to see if your pockets are empty or your pockets have something in them. Sometimes we overcomplicate profit and loss, and I think that's fine for a large company who has to answer to stockholders, or even a business that has a huge tax problem. For a place of this size, it's simple. We see growth.

We have items that come out every month. Every Thursday we get in new comics, costing us about $3000 retail. Everything in this store has a 50 percent mark-up. That was our original plan and we kept it at that. We also reserve older books for customers who can't afford to buy them right away. We never require a deposit.

Competition Contrast

The best form of advertising there is is another store like ours in this town. It has been there for five years and was the only one around. But we opened and operated differently, and that's why people came to us. It's like the difference between being served gruel or having a smorgasbord. Naturally, they are going to come here. The other store is very dark, sells cigarettes, and has pinball machines. Fairfield County people frown on this. The fact is they don't like it at all. We have had parents come to thank us.

Promotions

We advertise in newspapers, never on radio. We have an immense amount of co-op advertising available to us. Co-op advertising means that if we mention certain publications in our advertising, the companies that produce them will pick up a large percentage of that advertising cost, up to 75 or 85 percent. The comic book companies pay for our racks. We pay the cost of having them shipped to the store. Take the huge electronic sign outside. If I attach one of their comic book characters on it, the company pays for it. We have not used a lot of our co-op yet. My feeling is that if you use co-op immediately, it could be wasted, and when you really need it—a year down the road—it is no longer available.

The best advertising we had cost $25. I used it for the paper signs we put into the window when the building was being finished. The signs said, "We Have Dream Factory Coming—new comics, new magazines, toys and games." We kept a countdown sign in the window on how soon we were opening. And it worked. We did a booming business the very first day.

We chose this location because there's a lot of traffic that goes by here. It's very expensive. I would never pay this for our second location, but this is about $18 a square foot, which is high in this area. It comes to about $2300 a month just to open the door.

Work Schedule

We are open seven days a week. We just recently expanded our Thursday night hours because we get the new comics that day and that increases store traffic. We're now open until nine. Monday through Wednesday, 11 A.M. to 7 P.M.; Thursday and Friday until 9 P.M.; Saturday 10 A.M. till 6 P.M.; and Sunday noon to 5 P.M.

I do a lot of work at home since we computerized. Everybody who is in our super-saver program is on our computer. We know what books are coming out any given week, and we just print out a list. I bring the list in when the books arrive.

Loan Money

Loan money depends on your personal situation. You really have to line that up. No matter how good your idea is, if you don't have the personal possessions to put up as security . . . . There are small business loans and also digging out second loans and loans against whatever you own, equity loans. There is a way to apply for small business loans. There is money available. A lot of effort and research has to go into it. You have to list what you expect to make and how much your overhead will be.

Trade Shows

We go to trade shows. We went to one meeting of retailers in Chicago, and, at times, I felt like I was talking to Stone Age people. They're talking about nickel and dime situations, and they've been in business for 10 years. It's hard for us to imagine this. We have showcase windows; we do advertising. Most of these people have never even done a newspaper ad. We haven't advertised since last Christmas. We have a market of people who collect comics and are not going to stop in January and pick up again in June. If they do, it's going to cost them a tremendous amount of money because the stuff that was out in January now costs twice as much. And, they are afraid they'll miss something.

To a collector, we are a necessity. We promote a newsletter within the store, which is why we invested in a copy machine. We found that flyers are very good for us. We put it together ourselves, and we circulate it right here from the counter. We have people who come in just to get these flyers. We have a weekly art contest where people submit artwork. We give prizes of $5 in back issues. From a cost basis, we have invested $2.50. But it pulls in traffic.

Shoplifting

We had to get used to shoplifting. This area is tremendous in it. It amazes me how much there is. I've worked in stores of all sorts in the midwest where I was born. Shoplifting was not anywhere near the problem that it is here. I call it "t-shirt crime" because they're not old enough to wear white collars. There is no way of preventing it. I would really lose sleep if I had to wonder just how much is taken out of the store this way.

Tips

Research before setting up a shop. A year ago, we were in San Francisco for a week, and I spent the entire day in stores shopping around. I tried to make little notes, and I still do that to this day. I was in New York last week and stopped in a few shops. You look for the setups, for what they have in stock, any special promotions that they have. Other shops put out newsletters.

What I enjoy most about my business are the last two words— "my business." It's ours. Nobody else can take it away from us. The fact that there is no one else to answer to.

Trade Publications

Craftrends
6405 Atlantic Boulevard
Norcross, GA 30071
(404) 441-9003

Creative Crafts & Miniatures
Box 700
Newton, NJ 07880
(201) 383-3355

Toy & Hobby World
11 West 19 Street
New York, NY 10011
(212) 741-7210

24

Home Contents Sales

It started with garage sales, and then a sudden awareness that there is a huge market for secondhand merchandise. Bargain oriented shoppers buy nearly everything at these backyard sell-a-thons.

Soon professional organizers offered their services to people wanting to convert closet clutter into cash. With pros who know how to price items properly and to arrange appealing displays of these household cast-offs, more money was earned by these residential merchants. The added revenue was more than the cost of the professional service.

A group of four housewives, Judy Sclier, Jane Feibusch, Hesta Forgang, and Annemarie Gordon, gaining invaluable experience organizing these sales, formed the Tag-Along Girls, Harrison, New York, to take on more gargantuan projects: selling the contents of an entire home. For senior citizens leaving their homes for the convenience of small condos, or divorced families deciding to sell their household belongings rather than divide them, Judy Sclier and her team of experts organize and run the entire sale.

It's an attractive arrangement for the customers. If the Tag-Along women accept a home for a contents sale, the owner sits back while the four women search every corner of the house for everything that can be sold. They clean, tag the merchandise, and use their staff to run the actual sale. Their sales commission is between 20 to 30 percent of the proceeds.

What does it take to get into this business? Judy Sclier explains.

Judy Sclier

Actually, as four housewives raising children, we wanted to do more than just being home all of the time. We got together and decided what would fit best into our lifestyle. We decided to become a home contents sales organization called Tag-Along Girls.

The reason for this sizable start-up group is that each of us had some basic information about different areas of household items, but not nearly enough. All of us took additional courses to learn how to determine if some old piece of furniture or lamp might qualify as an antique.

We entered the business really able to make sound judgments for our clients. If we had any doubts about an item, we would take it to our dependable appraisal sources and get an honest estimate of its value. In time this was less and less necessary as we became so well briefed about the market, always being updated with the latest literature and from our growing experience, that we were able to discover priceless items that people were just casting away or selling for less than their value.

Start-Up

In the beginning, we did garage sales as a way of becoming familiar with merchandise that were people's cast-offs, how they would sell, and developing a feeling about the public that comes to find bargains at these sales. This was a way of building our reputation so that eventually we could do only homes. But it takes a while before people get to trust you enough to turn over a whole home full of their possessions for you to sell. We did this while we were taking courses about antiques, lamps, china, silver, and just about everything that is sold from a home. This is the only way to get over the concern about picking up an item to evaluate and not being sure it has high price potential. Indeed, anyone going into this business must take a course also on collectibles.

As a result of our training and experience, we have almost never failed to find some item considered worthless by the owner that had a market value of over $1000. We have learned that in the shabbiest and dirtiest corners of a basement, we are most apt to locate precious items stored away and completely forgotten about.

We know that we always face the possibility of finding treasure in the trash.

Home Office

This is a business that can be run out of your home. We go to our clients and their houses become our marketplaces.

When we get a call, we visit the client, and, depending on the size of the house and the amount of merchandise we will be able to set up for sale, we establish our commission, which is between 10 and 25 percent. The larger the place, the lower our commission.

Dirty Job

After we take a job, we have to go through the entire house from attic to basement to clean, price, and put price tags on all of the merchandise. We look at every single item in the house, some of which haven't been touched for years. Often stuff lays around in moldy mounds where we occasionally find mice nesting. In fact, we once came across some snakes in a rarely used summer home. They were the interim, nonpaying tenants.

Often in the beginning, we would be sorry we took the job. But then we would find an old lamp on a garbage pile that we knew instantly was a genuine antique. This discovery part of the business makes it exciting. Even when we found a pair of dentures, we all cheered. We knew at that time with gold prices peaking, it was worth at least $700 for the precious metal alone.

Preparing the Sale

After we have cleaned, tagged, and inventoried the entire contents of the house, we are ready to set our sale date. Usually we allow about two weeks ahead in order to schedule our advertising and to get out a mailing to the long list of customers we have. At this point in our business, we have people who come back again and again as regular customers. Many are looking for certain items for their homes.

Also, we carefully place signs throughout the area directing people to the house. And, should there be an enormous turnout, we inform the local police department as it might like to assign an officer to direct traffic. If that doesn't happen, we will have one of the people working with us on these sales out there maintaining the car flow in an orderly manner.

Sale Day

The days of the sale are usually from a Friday to a Sunday, and often just Friday and Saturday as we have found that there is often a big drop-off of customers on Sunday.

We tape off rooms where there is nothing being sold and always have one security person in every room where there is merchandise on sale.

Most pesky are dealers who come early in the morning hoping to be the first in so they can find a costly valuable we have overlooked and priced for the secondhand market. The best way to control traffic is to give people numbers as they arrive and allow just about six in at a time. The in-home flow can be adjusted up or down depending on how quickly people are leaving to make room for newcomers.

We keep our cash box right at the door which is the checkout area.

For big items such as furniture, if we don't get our selling price, we take bids and telephone numbers. Usually we will get several for one piece. If it does not sell at our price by the end of the sale we call these people in order of the highest bidder. We generally get rid of everything. People are required to pick up their own pieces. We give buyers names of small truckers, if they do not know anybody.

The best part? Counting the cash at the end of the sale to see what our commission will be.

Trade Publications

Antique Trader Weekly
Box 1050
Dubuque, IA 52001
(319) 588-2073

Antiques
980 Madison Avenue
New York, NY 10021
(212) 734-9797

Collector's News
608 8 Street
Grundy Center, IA 50638
(319) 824-5456

25

Housecleaning Service

Throughout the United States, especially in suburban areas, house-cleaning services are much in demand with few available. Faced with personal problems and less than satisfactory jobs since she arrived in the United States from her native England in 1979, Jane Rowan started her Pride and Polish Housecleaning Service in Norwalk, Connecticut in 1985.

A college graduate who has held responsible positions in the business world both here and in England, Rowan took a pragmatic view of what business she would start. Realizing that there was a large market for a cleaning service in her town, she decided to do what would be profitable in the shortest period of time and require the least amount of financial investment.

Successful immediately and already growing, Rowan brings a traditional English dignity to what she is doing. Her customers recognize the pride her people put into their scrubbing and polishing. In fact, her clients talk about using her service as they might about owning an expensive, imported automobile.

Jane Rowan

I'm English and I've been here since 1979. I had my own business in England, and I wasn't allowed to work here until my husband got his working papers. I wanted to get back into the corporate world, but found it was difficult because of my very diverse background. Although I graduated college with a degree in art, I worked in banking, in government, with international corporations, and in the clothing trade.

I went to a headhunter who suggested I take a typing course. I took a course at Katharine Gibbs although in the jobs I had in England, I had my own secretary. I joined a company that went bankrupt three months afterwards. One of the investors had a wholesale travel company, and he asked me to work for him doing sales and marketing. I designed quality packages for American travelers.

Start-Up

I started Pride and Polish because I could no longer stand the anger and the frustration of having my ideas totally ignored, and six months later people coming to me saying if only we'd listened to what you had said. I knew I had to go out on my own because the only way I was going to make money and be successful was to be in charge.

I did a tremendous amount of research. The only way you can start any kind of business is to do your homework. I used every contact that I had to learn about this business. I'd go to company executives and pick their brains. I was so determined to be on my own that they gave me all the advice I needed.

I began in 1985. I was told I would need a minimum of $2000 and that was doing it on a shoestring. I did it for a lot less. The way I have set up the business we are totally professional, and, therefore, we supply the homeowner with everything. I had to buy machinery and materials, and I did it as I went along. You need vacuum cleaners. I had two household vacuum cleaners, and I used those for the first few weeks until I started making enough money to buy commercial equipment.

I've literally financed as I went along. All the money made was put back into the business. The more money the business made, the more money I'd spend on equipment and materials. I didn't draw any salary. My lifestyle changed. Instead of eating in the most expensive restaurants, we went to the local diner.

Growth

I've seen a lot of companies on both sides of the Atlantic go under from greed and mismanagement. Mismanagement is usually the bigger reason. I didn't draw a salary for at least three months. As the business expanded, more money was needed to buy extra equipment. I had to advertise in local newspapers. I had to take out extensive insurance. You have to protect yourself and the homeowners. If anything went wrong in a home, I was sure to be blamed. It's the American way—when in doubt, sue. As everyone knows, insurance is not cheap.

Employees

Employees have to be responsible and trustworthy. We go into some of the most expensive homes in Fairfield County. We hold keys to over 90 percent of our clients' houses. Although we're relatively new, 75 percent of the clients came to us because they were dissatisfied with their previous services. So good employees really matter.

We certainly are not the cheapest around; if anything, we are the most expensive. I have yet to go into two homes that are alike. We have a $60 minimum charge. That's where we start. Most homeowners use our service every other week.

At the moment, I have three women full-time and one working part-time. Two more start in a couple of weeks. My people work Tuesday to Friday along with me. Saturday and Sunday I reserve for doing estimates. We only work during daylight hours. A beginner gets $8 an hour. An experienced person between $12 and $14 an hour. I really enjoy it and when you enjoy it, you do a good job.

The projected benefits are going to be medical insurance, and we will eventually stop using our own cars, as I will have vans. I pay the girls traveling expenses. I have a projected business plan, and we've already had a staff meeting where we all sit down and I tell them of my plans and get feedback from them. I'm now starting to delegate authority.

You have to project reliability because these people are giving you the keys to their homes. They will probably never see the girls that are working for me.

I was recommended to a commercial bank that is very large and very well known. I opened up my business account. When I needed a loan to buy equipment, the bank turned me down. I'm a very small risk. I was very, very angry. They even suggested that I buy my equipment on Visa. I pointed out to them that the reason I had gone to the commercial bank was so I could start to borrow money to expand my business by buying a fleet of vans. I then called a savings bank in this area, and I spoke with the manager, and told him my problem. He granted me my loan over the telephone.

Commitment

A friend of mine who owns a restaurant and is thinking about a second said that when you have lived through it, you understand the pleasure of owning your own business. A person can get all kinds of helpful advice; then it is up to you to follow it. You need commitment and determination to do it.

The reason I started this business was that my husband and I divorced, and I didn't have his salary anymore. I'm not only on my own, but I'm carrying a very expensive house and paying all the bills. If I failed, I would have had to sell my home.

Security Problem

The only big mistake I made so far is locking a house up too well. I am a stickler for security, although we have some homeowners who insist on leaving their houses open. That worries me to death because we would have a big problem if that house was robbed.

I like this business as I get to meet some wonderful people. In fact, Pride and Polish has become a status symbol, like having a BMW in the driveway.

Trade Publications

Cleaning Management
17911-C Sky Park Boulevard
Irvine, CA 92114
(714) 261-7192

Services
8315 Lee Highway
Fairfax, VA 22031
(703) 698-8810

26

Interior Decorating

Although Martha Brown studied interior design at the New York School of Design and her partner is a graduate of the Parsons School of Design, she readily admits that many people in this profession do not have any special training.

Although anyone with a special feeling for decorating can get into the business at any time, it does require some awareness of furniture selection and knowledge of where to locate craftspeople and dealers who supply wallpaper and fabrics for various jobs.

While legislation regulating the profession is being considered by some states, it is still a business that is not licensed, and is open to anyone. As far as any legal controls of the profession are concerned, they are still a long way off. In most states, they will never be formalized.

After working for a furniture dealer as a sales person contacting office planners and architects, Brown opened her own business as an interior designer in 1984. She now has a partner and both are doing very well. Here are her guidelines for success.

Martha Brown

I worked for a contract furniture dealer before I went on my own. I originally did just residential as I was married and had children and wanted to work part-time. Later I took a full-time job with an office furniture dealer. It is profitable. It was a sales job. I'd call on architects and designers, showing them the different lines of furniture we had. It was basically selling, but it was lucrative. Also, I was contacting upbeat people who held administrative positions in major offices. It was more exciting than dealing just with women who want their homes furnished. It involves more selling of products that would fit into the space already designed by architects and space planners. Of course, I would make furniture recommendations. We would also be responsible for delivery and installation of the pieces ordered.

Back to Homes

Since 1984, I am back doing interior design as a full-time business with a partner. We do residential homes and some office work. We do it all, from the ordering to supervising the deliveries. I had a desk delivered to a client. It was very expensive. It was within one-quarter of an inch of getting through the door. So you tip the deliverymen substantially and they take the molding off. Meantime, they scratch the desk. So I call the guy who will hopefully come to do a very small repair. Finding the right person is the most important thing in this business. Nobody is going to come for a small job like that. But when I got a guy a $1500 job elsewhere, I did a trade-off. I had him agree to come to Armonk and do the small touch-up job for me, which I paid for. This sort of thing happens regularly.

Responsibilities

As a designer, I do the layout and then I call the dealer for what I want. Having worked for a dealer, I know the other end such as what their discounts are. I know when they tell me that they are adding freight that some don't charge anything. But they will try to bill you for the freight even though they haven't paid any. The guy I worked for in New York City used to charge clients horrendous amounts. Knowing these things, I can really get the best deal for my clients.

Getting Clients

Most successful designers work with people that are somewhat affluent. Your clients are usually people that you know, that you go to a club with, that you play tennis with, or golf with. A well-connected husband can help you make many new clients.

If you really want to do it, you can. But it's tough when you are divorced and self-supporting. I've been very lucky. My friends have been very supportive. I know a few people in real estate who provide me with leads. I still maintain my social situation, but I should be doing a lot more entertaining. However, it takes too much money. It's really a business investment. But it's a lot easier if you are married, or if you have a boyfriend, or if you are the type of woman who goes to a country club by yourself, or if you have a family, or if you have some sort of base.

To start in this business on your own you should have social connections. You have to have been around and continue to get around. Also, advertising in local papers and magazines can help. We've been very fortunate. We've done it from word of mouth. People who have seen our work contact us. And recommendations from satisfied clients are very helpful.

What we do is meet with prospects and then prepare proposals for them, which include pictures of our work. Then the person is shown my house and two more. It's tricky showing people houses. Show people who want a very contemporary house one that has a very country feel and they'll say I don't want that; then you have to convince them you can do any style and convince them you'll do what they want. You can show them the most magnificent house that everybody loves, but it isn't their style. It doesn't make much of an impression. Some of them want to be led, some don't. It depends on the person. Some people never go to look at furniture; others will spend weeks going to New York and will see everything there is. Others would rather be on the golf course.

We have turned down some jobs knowing we couldn't work with certain clients. I don't care about personality. It's when they are indecisive and have no awareness of what they want, or when they want everything, or when they'll never make up their mind. Their husbands have to make the decisions. You can almost tell sometimes when they'll say, oh I've worked with six designers and I can't find a thing. That can't be. All six designers can't be wrong. That's a clue they will be difficult.

Charges

We ask them what their budget is and how many rooms they want us to design. Also we ask what their time frame is, in order to fit it into our job schedule. We have to ask for a deposit because the manufacturers ask for one. Our fees are flexible.

Some people just consult with us and then they go out and do their own shopping themselves. That's only a design fee, depending on the size of the job. Sometimes we work on a percentage of what clients buy from the manufacturers, and sometimes we combine it with a design fee. We show them the design and then we go ahead and start doing the purchasing. Some want to pay on a time basis. Today, with so many women working, they want us to do all the buying, as well as the designing.

My partner and I both bring in a certain amount of clients developed from our contacts. We live in different communities. Also, it helps to have someone to bounce ideas off of because sometimes you must get yourself in a box. We get different ideas from each other. Also, when one of us goes shopping, the other is available to meet with our clients. It's a pleasant way to work, and this is a lonely kind of profession. You are usually alone, or you're talking to the client and dragging them to New York. But there are working women clients who can only see us on weekends or at night.

Working Lifestyle

If you work by yourself, it does get lonely. I make buying trips to Manhattan, usually alone. I talk to people at the places I visit, but showrooms generally have one manager who knows me and chats a little. I go from showroom to showroom and that's a little interesting. But many are very quiet. If there's one person in each showroom and it's very, very quiet, I feel alone. I spend a lot of time alone at home doing my paperwork. I have a lot of it, all the purchase orders, a lot of paperwork to do by myself. I spend a lot of time alone, and it does get to me. I'm not too social on the outside. If you don't like going alone to social functions, you just create more loneliness for yourself.

Preparation for Designer

Some people take a fine arts degree or a minor in art, or go to an art school. Clients don't ask to see your degrees. But efforts are being made to regulate the profession. However, it's still in the planning stage.

There isn't any real interior decorator school. I just took interior design. If you have no schooling in it, but you have a real flair for it and people trust you, you can do it. You could do it for a friend or two first, but it gets a little tricky. You could get a little fancy, and if you didn't know the difference between a Louis XV chair and a Louis XVI chair, someone might catch you. It pays to have some kind of training. Take some courses. You don't have to be an expert on antiques but you should know the different periods and know why you recommend one thing rather than another.

Most important is to know the resources, where to get what, and to know the tradespeople who will guarantee their work. This you learn by making a few mistakes. If you are in the community for a long time, you can inquire about the skilled people you will need. Other interior designers might give you some leads. Usually you will know where certain tradespeople are such as furniture refinishers. It's a dying craft as few people go into it and the good ones are really busy. It's expensive, too, and sometimes your clients will not understand that.

Time is Precious

It's hard to say how small a job is worth taking on. You could have someone who wants to cover two couches and wallpaper a hall. You buy beautiful wallpaper and do the two couches and your client is delighted. You could be rewarded with "Gee, that was wonderful," and a recommendation—"I told somebody about you and they want you to do their whole house." You have to decide whether it's worth chasing around because you think the person will do something for you, or if she's a good friend and you just want to do something for her.

The obvious bad jobs are from people who want a little chair covered for $100 with a fabric bought at a discount store. You can spend hours there discussing the piping in another color or the 100 chintzes you brought. Sometimes you get sucked into something in error. Avoid it. Your time is worth too much.

It's a fun job because it's creative. The hard part is the business end—the follow-up and the deliveries. It can get sticky as people don't understand why it takes 12 to 16 weeks for deliveries. And the manufacturers don't really know.

Investment Costs

You don't need any real money to start. Basically you just need a bank account to carry things for awhile. There isn't a tremendous start-up cost, especially if you are close to a city. You don't have to buy that many samples if you are near the manufacturers' showrooms. You do need money to put a small percentage down when you order, but your clients also give you an advance payment. If you work it right, your clients will pay on time and everything will be covered. Most manufacturers demand, on a small residential job, payment on delivery. You may have to shell out, but you try to get it from your client first until you can build a credit line with dealers.

You can show a profit in a year if you get good jobs to start with. You aren't in business until you have a client. If you can't start with people you know, you can open a shop. A lot of people start with wallpaper, fabrics, or accessories shops and offer a design service. Then you need capital. It's like opening any retail store. You really have to have contacts or money. Advertising could attract clients but I have never done that.

Working Schedule

You work a good 10 hour day. You can't slough off if you want to make a good living at it. You are almost better taking Monday and Tuesday off than the weekend. Many clients are only available on weekends.

It isn't a job with lots of time off. I think you can do it and still be a good wife, because your time is flexible. Expect to work Saturdays and Sundays and be off on Mondays and Tuesdays. But you do have flexibility in changing your schedule. You can arrange to be off many weekends.

Earnings

You could probably make $30,000 a year and more. You can deduct your house as an expense as your office; and your car because you drive a tremendous number of miles between houses and manufacturers and tradespeople and antique stores. Those are very legitimate expenses.

On a good residential job, say for a retired couple who moves to a nice condo, if they spend $40,000, you should be able to clear at least $10,000 to $12,000. If you have a few of those things running a year, you can do all right. Each job has a different time frame. Some people order one thing and wait before they order the next. If you can get a whole bunch of them rolling, then they overlap. If someone says to you, I want you to do it in six months, you really must push.

Much depends, too, on how quickly clients make up their minds. Very few people make decisions fast. Usually you have a few jobs going at once. It's fun if you get a nice client who makes decisions quickly. You show them everything, and they make the decisions quickly, and you can get the job done.

The part of the business I like best is the designing. I don't dislike the shopping, but I like getting it all together. It's satisfying, but you go on to the next thing. Generally the people are happy. I haven't had anyone who was really unhappy. Sometimes they don't envision what they are going to get, but I haven't had anyone unhappy.

Trade Publications

Interiors
1515 Broadway
New York, NY 10036
(212) 764-7522

Interior Design
475 Park Avenue South
New York, NY 10016
(212) 576-4182

Designer
114 East 32 Street
New York, NY 10016
(212) 689-4611

27

Investment Syndicate Thoroughbred Breeding

Leonard J. Messina, Chairman of the Board and Chief Executive Officer of AmeriGroup, Inc., Stamford, Connecticut, while still clutching his college degree, was determined to own a major national organization. He satisfied his entrepreneurial thrust by immediately becoming a partner in a real estate construction company but left that for further education.

It is a wise person who knows that he must still ripen and learn in the complex world of business. To further his business skills, Messina took a job in the pension planning department of a major insurance company. Along with pensions, he acquired an awareness of many other forms of investment planning.

When financial planners were permitted to incorporate, he started his own financial investment consulting firm. The operation wrote 150 pension plans during the first year and it became the springboard for his shift into the high finance area of thoroughbred breeding. In a sense it was related to investments, as this had tax shelter benefits for people with top income.

The swift and enormous success of his AmeriGroup Thoroughbred Syndicate has made Messina one of the most respected names in the breeding industry. This is how he did it.

Leonard J. Messina

I have had an entrepreneurial feeling, and, when I got out of college, I decided to go into business. Along with a couple of partners I got into real estate developing property in the beach area of the Hamptons on Long Island, New York. I did not like it, so I sold my interest.

What I felt I needed was some solid financial background in investments, so I took a job in the pension department of Mutual of New York. While I learned about pensions, I also got a solid education in general financial planning. By the end of the year, financial planners were allowed to incorporate, so I started my own investment planning company. We wrote about 150 pension plans during the first year, and that became the base for the thoroughbred breeding syndicate.

There was a growing demand by professional people in the high income brackets for more tax shelters during the 1970s. I then extended my financial product line to include life and health insurance, and equity investments. I still had another ambition and that was to have a truly national company.

Leasing Equipment

After exploring other types of businesses I went into equipment leasing. However, it took until 1981 for me to put together an equipment leasing syndicate. I had experimented with syndications in real estate, oil, and gas. Equipment leasing worked, and we now have clients from the Fortune 500 group. We lease high tech computer and communications equipment.

Thoroughbred Breeding

Before getting into the thoroughbred breeding, I found that this was an industry that had a continual upswing since World War II. Along with having certain tax shelter benefits that are attractive, I also discovered that most of the people already in this business were at the low end of racing, which made it harder for them to raise investment money.

I decided that our syndicate would only be involved with the top five percent of the breeding industry—the very best bloodstock available. Most people might be able to raise about one to two million dollars. Through our very first offer in 1983 we got $6.8 million and it has since appreciated about 40 percent. Our second offering in 1984 raised over nine million dollars and that has appreciated about 300 percent since.

Also, we are able to act as our own bankers through a security firm that we control. All of our operations are under the name AmeriGroup.

Management People

One of my major investments for AmeriGroup was to get key people. They provide operational strength. I have eight of the best managerial people in the business.

Our staff is constantly searching for quality thoroughbreds that are up to our breeding standards. They have to check pedigree such as Seattle Slew who won $1.2 million and then was syndicated for breeding rights for $12 million. Today, because of his success in the breeding shed, he has a value of $100 million. Clearly the capital appreciation end of the business is in the breeding and not the racing. That's why a top notch staff of executive people who totally understand the objectives of thoroughbred breeding is so vital to the growth and success of our operation.

Acquiring Stock

Mostly we buy privately. Actually, there are bloodstock agents just like real estate agents. They provide us with a list of horses that are at the top five percent level offered for sale. Then we look at their histories, who the sire is, and go back three generations on the mother's side, and make our analysis.

First year we bought 15 broodmares, stallion shares, which is a breeding investment in a horse someone else owns, and a quarter interest in a leading thoroughbred race horse. This was our acquisition for the $6.8 million we raised in 1983 that is worth well over $10 million at this moment. By the time your book comes out, the value of this first purchase will be considerably more. Our acquisitions for the $9.25 million we raised in 1984 has appreciated to over $24 million. You can see why investing with a thoroughbred breeding syndicate that is well-managed can be extremely profitable for investors.

In 1985 the investor monies amounting to $16 million that we received are now worth in excess of $20 million, just one year later. Also, our organization performs other services in the racing industry. We syndicated the rights to an owner's unborn foal crop. He had 20 of the finest broodmares that were impregnated by the best stallions in the world and wanted to acquire cash for them. What we did is to get him investment partners for the horses that were to be born.

Large Range of Services

We do offer a far-reaching range of services since our profits come from the appreciation of stock and breeding and not from racing. We are the suppliers of top bloodline stock that have the potential of winning the big stake races for people who race horses.

One of the important thrusts of our business is to educate the public to the profitable expectancy from investing in thoroughbred breeding. In fact, members of our management staff travel throughout the country to speak at seminars we arrange explaining this business to people who might never even have been at a racetrack.

Tax Revisions to Help

The prospective new tax law which is about to be passed will be a boom for thoroughbred breeding syndicates. Since the majority of our income comes from the sale of yearlings that have been taxed as ordinary income, under the new law it will be taxed at 27 percent. Now we will have more cash available. Before, if we sold $2 million worth of yearlings, we would keep $1 million and pay $1 million in taxes. Now we will pay $550,000 and keep $1.5 million.

Getting Clients

I go to Kentucky fairly often with prospective buyers and to meet clients for the various services we offer. One of the main reasons I go is to bring potential investors there to get a firsthand view of the breeding business.

Also, as a totally independent manager, we don't have the conflict of owning a farm and raising horses. We board our stock both in the United States and Europe. Also, we can select our boarding sites. We use top farms that give our valuable stock ample room, at least four acres compared to the usual two.

Look, we don't own a broodmare that is worth less than $1 million and our most expensive is worth $6.5 million. I prefer to keep them on a larger piece of land because they get hurt less and, as animals, they do like to run around.

Now this seems to help in another important area. The industry average for live foal birth is 72 percent. Our average is 92 percent. And that is why we choose the board farms very carefully. I bring in partners to share in the ownership of the stock and it is my responsibility to provide them with the best management possible.

This pays off with the kind of results that investors are looking for; we have never undertaken a transaction that has not made money—and a great deal of it, indeed.

Also, it is a fascinating business, especially since we are the only syndicate operating at the top five percent of the thoroughbred market. Today (1986), we have about 60 horses valued at $75 million.

My best recommendation for business success is a positive mental attitude. Mix that with hard work, and you can make things happen.

Trade Publications

Horsemen's Journal
6000 Executive Boulevard
Rockville, MD 20852
(301) 881-2266

Blood Horse
PO Box 4038
Lexington, KY 40544
(606) 278-2361

Backstretch
19363 Couzens Highway
Detroit, MI 48235

28

Kennel

When Tom Craighead made a career switch in 1970, he went from just earning a living to doing something he loved. After working for the telephone company for 15 years, Craighead joined the family business, which had become a kennel after mainly boarding and showing dogs for celebrities.

Craighead, a truly rugged individualist with a huge appetite for adventurous and often dangerous recreation, parachute jumping, is a daring pilot who survived a horrendous crash and is also a gentle person who cares deeply about animals.

Owner of the Craighead Kennels, Cross River, New York, he has agreed to become the first kennel in the country to be entirely enclosed. This agreement involved making a concession to a builder who put up a sprawling condominium complex next to his kennel and then tried to close down the operation that was established in 1931.

Prevailing through all the legal battles to close Craighead, the considerate owner accepted the proposal to become the first indoor kennel as a way of keeping the barking dogs from disturbing the residents of the condominiums.

Kennels, still very much in short supply around the country, can be developed into a profitable business, but only for people who can cope with the seven day a week care needed by animals. Craighead explains how to do it.

Tom Craighead

This place was owned by my mother and father. My father bought Craighead Kennels, which was at that time (1931) a farm, for $18,000. My father was a professional dog handler and became famous for showing dogs. He showed dogs for Gary Cooper, Tallulah Bankhead, and other celebrities. Over the years, many famous people boarded their dogs here such as Dustin Hoffman and Vivian Vance.

My father's primary business was showing dogs. It was lucrative then. Dog showing was the thing to do for people with money. It was very prestigious. Later the barn became a boarding kennel. He started by building dog runs and eventually kept expanding and expanding. In 1931 he started boarding. Eventually, the dog showing ended and Craighead became all boarding.

Beginning

Although I was born and raised with it, and knew the business very well, I worked for the phone company from 1955 to 1970. I came into the business when my father had a heart attack. My older brother also left the phone company and came into the business. In 1972 my mother died first, and then two and half months later my father died. My brother inherited the kennel, but when he died the place went to his wife. So, I had to buy my homestead back from his widow. Scottish people leave their estates to the oldest son. That's the way it goes. I bought it back in 1974 for $230,000. It's probably worth about $1 million right now.

After I took over, I doubled the business. I expanded and kept growing and growing and eventually took one of my kennel buildings and made it into an animal hospital. We are going to continue to grow. We can hold 120 dogs today.

Employees

I have six full-time employees. They are people who really love animals as well as the work. In recent years, it's more difficult to find this type of person. It seems that the American way is changing. People are not so interested in working anymore, but I have been lucky. I treat my employees well. They like it here. I'm not a difficult boss to work for. But, I am demanding where it counts. For instance, medication for the dogs, cleanliness of the kennels, and that sort of thing. I would rather have people who don't know anything about the boarding business but are dog lovers. It would be nice if they had some experience as a medical technician. That always helps. But, I like to train them my way. We have been very successful because we maintain standards that are very high.

Operating Routine

At 7:30 A.M. we go down to the kennel. We don't open the kennel until 8 A.M. because we need that half hour to get the dogs outside. Once we go downstairs, the dogs know we are there, and they want to get out and do their thing. We get them out as rapidly as possible. We have very long dog runs. Then we thoroughly clean the kennels. We have hot water hoses and disinfectants right at each stall.

Another thing we use that many kennels don't is bedding. At other places the dogs sleep on the bare concrete. We believe in bedding because a comfortable dog is a happy dog. In the winter time, because of the cold temperature the animals remain outside for a limited time and are let back inside again because most of these dogs are house pets.

During the warmer months, they stay outdoors all day. There are wooden platforms for them to rest on and their runs are long. They have shade and rain roofing. If it rains, we don't leave them out. But we have this roofing over the runs so that if it does rain, they can stay dry until we get them inside.

The dogs are all in their own separate runs. When people have two dogs in the same family, sometimes they want the dogs together inside, and we have stalls large enough to accommodate two dogs. The next routine is feeding and then giving medication to those requiring it. Then comes the grooming routine. The kennel is a very active place. When we leave the dogs outside, we have to bring the troublemakers in. There are just some dogs who like to stir up trouble. A very hyper dog would constitute a troublemaker, one that barks and runs and chases the other dogs. Once he's in, the place settles down.

Getting Started

A retired couple bought a kennel and then came to me to get advice on how to run it. I told them everything I possibly could, even if they were to compete with us. We need more kennels anyway in this country. In the busy season, we have to turn people away. Since both were animal lovers, they put a lot of money into their place and made it a beautiful kennel. A year later they had to sell it. The wife had had a nervous breakdown.

If you don't know the kennel business, you should work at a kennel to learn all the things that have to be known to run this business of dealing with live animals. You have to be able to detect whether something is wrong with a dog almost instantly. We know a dog's personality. When the personality changes, there's got to be a reason for that. A couple of dogs died at that kennel because they didn't know the symptoms and get them to a vet to be treated.

People who want to operate a kennel should take the time to work for one, not for the pay, but for the training. It would take a good six months facing many different situations to learn the business.

We are a seasonal business. We are full at Easter, Thanksgiving, Christmas, summer, and during the mid-winter and spring school breaks. Then it gets empty. Our income at peak times has to carry us through slow periods.

Location

It's very hard to find a good location. We are located right in the middle of a very affluent part of Westchester County. But to find a piece of ground where the residents would put up with the noise of a kennel would be very difficult. We were here long before most of these residents were. It is probably better to buy an existing one, one that was in operation before zoning took place to keep out kennels. Today, it's almost impossible to get around the zoning.

New Concept

We are introducing a whole new concept of boarding animals—an enclosed kennel. It will be very well ventilated through a controlled environment. An enclosed kennel with an exercise area can be built anywhere because you won't have that noise of barking dogs. It's a new concept and it evolved because of the condominium development built next door. The owners are paying for the whole thing. I have never heard of any other kennel built this way, and that's why I believe this will be the first one—possibly in the world.

Now this is the way to start a kennel from scratch. It's more expensive if you buy a kennel that is already established. For some reason or other, they are overpriced. You're just not going to make it if you pay too much. Your best bet is to find a piece of land where you can live and start your kennel building on the same piece of land, because you'll have to be there anyway. Set up with maybe a 30-kennel capacity. And then you start to grow gradually. You start small, and then you take some of your income and put it back into the business to keep expanding. The more you keep expanding, the more your income will increase until you reach a comfortable level. It will take three or four years. In any small business, if you own the land and are building the business, you can pay it off in 10 years while you are making a living from it. You can earn extra income from bathing, grooming, and clipping.

You can make a good living from 80 kennels. I have 120. That's my plateau. I wouldn't want to get any bigger because of employee problems. The dogs don't get the proper care. That's the important thing, care of the dogs and of the employees too. You can't overburden the employees on the job or they'll leave. You want them happy so they'll stay.

24-Hour Schedule

There must always be someone around on a 24-hour basis. We structure ourselves so that everyone works five days. Our employees can fit into a seven day week. Starting off, you're in jail until you have somebody to relieve you. You just don't go anywhere. The kennel business is a high pressure business. I always hire one more person than I actually need as a backup when someone gets sick, or is on vacation. I would rather do that and have a good, healthy enjoyable life myself rather than take on extra pressure just to make a few more dollars.

Customers

The animals that come here are fantastic, but many of the owners are not. We have about 3000 customers. When someone gives us a hard time, I ask them if the dog is healthy, in good condition, fine, and happy. But if I'm not happy with some customers, I tell them to take their dogs someplace else. As an example, we close at 5 P.M. People will call and say we'll be five minutes late, which always means a half hour. We'll put up with that.

We have a 3:00 checkup. If customers call about being late, we won't charge extra as long as they make it here by 4:00 or 5:00. Anyway, if people can make it in by 3:00, we give them extra time without charge.

When a dog is sick or gets hurt, we do everything to get it well. Everything is done to correct the situation, including taking the animal to a veterinarian. If my people let something go by that they shouldn't have, I get mad at them. I am easy to get along with except when dogs don't get their medication or are not bathed before they go home.

We have medication lists. A lady who had brought the exact number of pills her dog would need for its stay found two left over. She raised hell, and I don't blame her. Either she brought too many pills, or we skipped the medication. Somehow we missed it. This is when I get testy, and my employees know that. That's why they're careful.

Problems

We have never had a lawsuit. The customers understand that they leave their dogs here on risk. We have liability insurance for people, but not for the dogs. It's too expensive. If necessary, we would pay the medical bills or replace the dog.

The worst part of the business is when a dog dies. We have never had a dog die here because of kennel neglect. But there is a thing called bloat. There is no apparent medical reason for it or any known way to prevent it. We changed the dog food about six years ago and we have had only two cases since then. We used to have one a year. When it happens, we have an autopsy done, which we pay for. Now we have a medical explanation when the person comes back. If we have an emergency number, we call the owner. We do everything we can to find out why. The worst part of this job is to have to call somebody and tell them that their dog died at the kennel. That's my responsibility.

Trade Publications

Animal Nutrition & Health
Sandstone Building
Mount Morris, IL 61054
(815) 734-4171

Groom & Board
207 South Wabash Avenue
Chicago, IL 60604
(312) 663-4040

Pet Business
5400 North West 84 Street
Miami, FL 33166
(305) 591-1629

29

Kitchenware Store

The pleasant way to start a business is having the time to pick what you want to do as a balance to a life that has become somewhat boring. Betsy Barnett conceived the idea for her Consider The Cook Shop, Cross River, New York, to do something more than just being a mother and housewife.

Without knowing much about kitchenwares and concerned that a long course of study about this area of retailing would kill her enthusiasm to do something entrepreneurial, she took a chance and opened her store.

Starting it with the purpose of doing it only part-time, Barnett eventually ended up with six women partners. For seven years the partnership as well as their friendship has endured. A collective group of people survived one of the most troublesome areas of any business—working together. There is hope for commercial togetherness.

However, Barnett was not so lucky in her marriage. After her divorce, she realized that her shop was more than a joyful refuge from the chores of raising children and taking care of the house. It then became a welcome addition to the money she needed for her single parent home.

Here is Barnett's special formula for business success. It can work for you.

Betsy Barnett

Starting the store happened after my last child went off to school. I just wanted to do something. I had been to a kitchen store that I was intrigued with. Then I found the location, two old barns. The owner was expanding his antique store into kind of a shopping village, and I just thought it would be wonderful. I did not know anything about anything. If I had really conducted a great study someone else would have rented the space, so I just jumped right into it. I think if you want to start a business, and you got into studying it, it could drag on for months and months and ultimately you lose interest.

I had worked at Lord & Taylor for one year after college and then as a kindergarten teacher in New York for about five years, stopping about one week before my first child was born. I did nothing but be a mother and do volunteer work after that until my last child went into first grade. Hard to believe that this is our seventh year in business. I was 41 years old when I started in 1979.

Ours is a kitchen store, but it leans more to table top—people in the trade would understand that; it's sort of a more pleasant term than pots and pans. We sell a lot of pots and pans and we attract people for most things like placemats, flatware, decorative objects that can be used in a kitchen.

Merchandise and Costs

What makes it successful, I think, is that it's in two old barns, and it looks attractive the way we have it set up. It's not just a cut and dry store. It's sort of artfully displayed, you might say. And we carry no electrical items. That is different. I do not know of another kitchen store that does not carry electrics. This has been a good decision for us because originally we had intended to but Cuisinart did not want to do business with us because our store was too close to one the company was already supplying. That made us rethink everything, and we decided not to carry any electrics. Since people can get trade-ins on electrics, a lot of cut-rate appliances due to price wars—shoppers are better off getting these items at a discount store.

If I remember, the total cost investment (I have always been a little confused about the figure) was between $75,000 or $100,000. We had raised the total amount of money upfront ourselves by having six partners. We figured it out and decided we had enough to start the business. We did not borrow any money. We were very lucky that we did not have to borrow money. It would probably cost as much as $150,000 to start this business today.

Attracting Customers

To attract customers we advertised in the local papers. We did not do any mailings; it was a lot of word of mouth. We were lucky that a magazine, *Country Living*, did an article on us when we opened. It was really helpful. And other magazine editors started using our store for photos, and we would get credits.

We do advertise in the *New York Times* now, but as a group of shops, not just one store. Our shop is one of seven other businesses in a complex. There is an antique store, a flower shop, and a candy shop, none that compete with each other.

Earnings and Employees

We consider a profit anything over and above what we have spent. For the past year we have made between 5 and 10 percent. We have profited from the day we opened Consider The Cook. We have always made money over what we spent, but we do pay very low salaries, typical of the retail business. Salaries are low because it is a desirable type of occupation and we are able to be successful partly because of this. We don't pay unfair salaries, but our pay is low compared to other businesses. High school girls are hired through the year only working on weekends and occasionally at Christmas, and we pay them over minimum wage.

We're open from 10 A.M. to 6 P.M., six days a week, except for December when we're open seven days a week. We close Mondays when, if necessary, I go to New York and buy products for the business. Mondays are my longest workdays.

Problems

The worst nightmare you have is that the customers won't appear. There are other things that happen that can be bad. You never know what to expect on any given day. You can have a very easy day with no deliveries, and then you can have a day with six trucks piling up in front of the store. That's when we unpack right in the middle of the store.

We do face breakage and damaged goods, fighting with the truckers about the breakage and trying to get our money back from the company. Customers can be difficult. For example, they will bring back something broken that they swear they've never used and you know darn well that they broke it. In the retail business you have to bite your tongue and tell the customer that you will try to replace it and hopefully get the company to agree.

We will replace something with no questions for a good customer or if the piece looks like something freakish happened to it. A lot of people want special attention, special orders, and we have to race around. You don't want to disappoint anyone, especially a good customer. As far as I'm concerned, I can get swamped by special requests and sometimes it gets to be too much.

Appealing Products

People love to spend money on their houses, supplies. They will come in and see some new placemats or something that they really want—but do not need—but they want them. It gives them reasons to decorate their houses and a lot of it involves people doing things to make their house look better. This kind of product appeal generates sales.

People just like to come back again and again. They like our store because we are constantly getting in new things. We are always ordering and we have a lot of fresh merchandise. It is always being replenished. Our customers expect to see new things at all times. A lot of the business is from people doing their own houses and a lot of our sales are for presents.

Sales Incentives

The high season is right before Christmas. The worst month we have is usually September, and that is because we think that people are spending their money getting their kids outfitted to go back to school. We never offer special incentives to buy, but we hold two sales a year. One is in January and one is in July. I am concerned about conditioning our patrons to buy only when things are on sale. So far this has not happened to us. Our customers don't seem to mind paying the price if the item is good. If they want it, they'll buy it.

I think that the very big stores must constantly run sales. People in the retail business know that most times the consumer is not getting much of a bargain. The original price noted by department stores is often close to the sale prices in other stores, and that is what we sell our products for as soon as they are displayed. Technically, the large stores have to put an item on the floor for one day at the original price and from then on they can slash it and say whatever they want is the original price.

It's Enjoyable Extra Income

I enjoy the fun of buying the goods. I enjoy the fact we have been successful in maintaining our friendship—that goes for all the people working at Consider The Cook. We love to go to work and we have become like an extended family. It has just been a good thing for all of us. We have been lucky that we have not had to live on this business. Some of the partners are married and some are not. But no one is dependent on it for their livelihood. It's an extra.

We put a lot of money back into our inventory and pay a lot of rent. It's successful in a small way, but not enough to totally support six women.

Caution

I think one of the main things is if you can try to run a business without borrowing money. Other than that, I think you should be decisive about picking merchandise. There is a lot of stuff out

there to look at and if you're indecisive about it, you fall apart
when you see it all. There are too many choices.

Preparation

I did not have any special training. I worked at Lord & Taylor,
but I was not in the retail end of it. I was hired as a teacher for
a training program. And then I taught all the incoming people
from sales clerks to buyers the systems of the store. I took that
job as a teacher because I didn't have to work Saturdays. It was a
five day week, Monday to Friday, which was much better for my
social life. And I liked it.

Expansion?

Yes I did start a successful business and I love it, but if you read
these magazines like *Inc.*, everybody wants to start branch stores,
wants to make a bundle out of their businesses. The only way to
really make a bundle is to keep expanding, some people believe,
and that is the true spirit of it. We have considered having a second
location, and it has been a relief that we decided against it. We
felt it would, to some extent, take the fun out of the business for
us. It wouldn't be hard to do the buying. You just buy more of
the same items. But we would have to get loan money at this point,
mainly because of my divorce. We could get it, but it becomes too
involved. Also, we would have had to go farther away so that we
don't have another store in our backyard. That means commuting.

    We want to keep the partnership the way it is. We don't want
to bring more partners into it and carve up the pie more. It would
change the whole concept of the business. But worse, for me, it
would involve a lot of long-range planning. It would just be a
totally different thing. I can manage eyeballing the merchandise,
but not in two locations. One partner has a full-time teaching job
and another gives full-time voice lessons. We all work part-time
at this business. That is the fun.

I like the way my life is now. I can be home when my youngest child comes back from school. If I have to be home because of deliveries, I can do it. But it would be different if I were driving 40 miles to another location. I'm not saying that we will never do it. I know we could be a success someplace else, but many people have said to us during the years, suppliers and sales reps, watch out because when you try to spread yourself too thin, it could wreck your business. You could possibly drain the business of the profits you are making because you have to invest money.

We also considered doing mail order which seemed easy. You get a warehouse, you hire some people, and you ship the stuff. We knew it would be a big financial outlay to put this together. But it was much more of a financial outlay than we thought. To put a catalog together would cost at least $75,000 or more. And mail order is usually not successful for at least three years. People want credibility from a mail order business. They want to keep getting the catalogs and reading them before they order.

Mail order is a very tricky business. Many people thought it was a good way to make money fast, but now there's too many of them. Selling things through the mail is a whole different ball game. It's not selling things from displays, it's taking things item by item and making people focus on one item on a page.

Would you buy out any or all of your partners? I wouldn't want to do it. I would be very unhappy if this happened. For seven and a half years no one has moved away. If someone did move and wanted to sell, I couldn't even determine what the stock is worth. If anyone moved away, that could be the beginning of our branch store—wherever they went. If somebody wanted out of the business, I would rather join the remaining partners to buy that person's share of the business rather than bring another person into the business.

Maybe ultimately, something we never think about now, we might sell the business and retire. I don't know what we would get for it. Someone buying this business is buying a good store, and buying a fine reputation. I'm confident we could sell it if we wanted to. I don't know exactly what we could get for it, but I'm sure it would be more than the $75,000 that we put into it originally, easily well over $100,000.

Trade Publications

Kitchen & Bath Business
1515 Broadway
New York, NY 10036
(212) 869-1300

Kitchen & Bath Design News
University Plaza
Hackensack, NJ 07601
(201) 487-7800

Totally Housewares
21 Locust Avenue
New Canaan, CT 06840
(203) 966-9377

30

Limousine Service

At one time personal transportation service of any kind, especially to the airports, meant you would be driven to your destination in a large, oversized automobile. Not today. Standard cars are usually used to transport people distances not covered by a local taxi service.

Without the need for stretch type vehicles that can accommodate up to eight people, a limo service can be started with your own car and right from your home. Of course, certain licensing requirements must be met in every state.

Herb Sloan, a former engineer, started his Connecticut Limousine Service in East Norwalk, Connecticut, operating out of his house. Within three months, as the result of an active sales promotion campaign to solicit clients, Sloan needed help to handle the calls he was getting for personal transportation.

For this business capital investment is remarkably minimal. Immediate expansion can be handled by hiring drivers willing to use their own cars. When the cash flow is adequate, it then becomes more profitable to buy additional vehicles.

Limo service is an uncomplicated business, requiring little investment capital but demanding around the clock attention. However, with enough staff, part-time and full-time drivers, it can be organized into a civilized and highly profitable enterprise. Here's how Sloan did it.

Herb Sloan

I am an engineer and worked for several companies. I just got fed up with it in 1969 when we were in a recession. I thought at first that I could go out the next day and get another job, but it didn't work out that way. That's when I got into the transportation business.

Costs

When I first started in 1980 with one car, insurance was about $900 as compared to $3500 today. Start-up costs were less than $2000. I now have five cars, three full-time drivers, and three part-time drivers. I operate out of my home.

Promotion

I was in the black in about six weeks. I contacted people who used limousines. I sent out all kinds of notices. It was an insignificant cost. The first notices I typed with my two-finger system. After a while I got good at it. I sent these letters to people I knew when I was an engineer. I sent out five letters a day. The first month that I was in business, I did about six trips; the next one, 30. Then the phone never stopped ringing. It went from about 30 a month to 150 a month.

Getting Help

I could handle four trips a day myself. But if I got two trips at the same time, I needed help. At first I tried to find an owner/driver to take care of what driving I couldn't do. A friend who was looking to do something for the winter months when he couldn't do construction helped me.

Hours and Customers

The trouble with limousine work is that there are no set hours. You are on call all the time. It's 24 hours a day, seven days a week, in all kinds of weather. In winter when there's six inches of snow on the ground, people need the limo service to get to the airports. You have to gear yourself to the lifestyle.

About 90 percent of my work is airport transportation, mostly for companies. Anyone trying to survive on vacation customers will not make it. You need the corporate accounts, the people who travel regularly. However, all services around here will drop between July and September to about 30 percent of our normal trip load. At the holidays it slows down again. People generally stay home. It's not a strictly seasonal business like lawn mowing. There are times when nothing is going on and then all of a sudden all hell breaks loose.

Incentives

Whenever you ride with us, you get a voucher. When you get 18 vouchers, you get a free ride to the airport. I figured if you were going once a week, that's a frequent rider who should get a free ride. It's good customer relations for loyal customers. A customer generally will not switch unless you mess up. I mean you could have a breakdown, or miss a flight. Most people are reasonable. If a person is unreasonable, I don't want him. If there is a legitimate gripe, I take care of it.

Employees

I get my employees by advertising. The responses range from the dregs of humanity to people looking to supplement their incomes. That's the way you get part-time drivers. Most full-time drivers tend to follow the circuit. They will have worked for other limo services and just change. Some are prima donnas. You have to overlook a lot.

The things that aggravate employees are funny. It's usually something small. We only had one woman call up in response to an advertisement. She wanted a part-time job. I gave her a road test. Just because you have a driver's license doesn't mean you can drive well. I sent her out to get her public service license, which you need in Connecticut, and then she got transferred by her company.

Mistakes

The biggest mistake is to lease or finance cars for four or five years. At the end of three years, that vehicle is ready for the junk pile. It's shot, and you are left without the equity to purchase another one.

In this business people get into trouble at the two-year point when they have to replace their vehicles or get new ones and have no money to buy them. When we turn over cars they have approximately 160,000 miles on them. After driving one for two years, replace it.

Trade Publications

Passenger Transport
1225 Connecticut Avenue NW
Washington, DC 20036
(202) 828-2800

Commercial Carrier Journal
Chilton Way
Randor, PA 19089
(215) 964-4513

31

Liquor Store

Larry Kiss made the career transition from machinist to liquor store owner a successful one. His Banner Wine and Liquor Store in Norwalk, Connecticut, was opened in a section of the city usually bypassed by shoppers. For Kiss the location option, so vital in building a business, did not exist. This was all he could afford at the time.

Aggressive promotion, a friendly manner, and becoming a near expert on wines encouraged patrons to shop at his store. Business built up so well that he had to abandon his absentee management to take over the establishment on a full-time basis.

The building changes in his area was another act of benevolence that helped him. The need for residential space attracted builders who began to convert old apartment structures into condominiums. Kiss eventually expanded and is now a highly successful entrepreneur.

Taking a chance is what it is all about if you want to have a business of your own. Kiss overcame unfavorable circumstances and made it. Here's how.

Larry Kiss

Before I had a liquor store, I was a machinist. My aim was to start a business. My parents owned a winery in Hungary. They are still there. I came to this country when I was 19. I knew I could never raise the money to produce the wine, but I could sell it.

Start-Up

I opened in 1969. At that time, rentals here were cheap. I started up with a $20,000 investment. I recall exactly because they were asking for $7000 for the business, not including the stock, and at the time there were certain rules and regulations you had to go through. You had to be accepted by the Liquor Commission; you have to be licensed. The business had already been a liquor store. The style of the store was here, and I didn't change it.

The store has rough wood paneling with an English look. The ceiling is arched with white stucco and exposed beams. The selling area, where the registers are, is like an old fashioned cellar. One of the things I have done is to use spotlights effectively to highlight plants and sale items.

In time you have to deal with salespeople representing the wholesalers and the importers to determine who can guide you to the wine products that will sell best. Also, you must keep alert as to the products that are being given heavy television, magazine, and newspaper advertising support. This, of course, will develop sales traffic, and it's important to keep enough stock on hand for the demand.

In recent years wine coolers were introduced with heavy promotion. I had to get information from the wholesaler or importer on which ones would be promoted the most. There is no point stocking a brand that isn't being pushed to the public. Radio and TV advertising, I have found, produces more customers than ads in upbeat magazines like *Bon Appetit* and even in the *New York Times*.

Making Recommendations

When asked to make recommendations, I ask the customer what wines he or she likes. In this way I get some idea of their tastes and can make suitable recommendations. Also, I want to know how the customer is going to use the wine—as a dinner or dessert wine, or just for conversation. Even knowing what food is to be served guides me in making a recommendation.

Owners should know their stock. When customers come back and say they like the wine, they will often order more. Or if they tell me their guests loved it and asked where they could buy it, I have made new customers for my store. Mainly, if the customer is satisfied, it will mean repeat business.

Getting Good Guidance

I was lucky to have someone with me from the day I opened the store who knew wine and then taught me the differences between the products. While this elderly gentleman knew the business well, he was not a good salesperson to have representing me when I was still working as a machinist. I had counted on the handsome look of my shop and the ample parking to maintain a good competitive edge over the other stores that were situated not too far away from mine. However, I realized that just having a salesperson available was not enough. A store needs a person with a good customer personality, so I took over the business full-time.

Employees

Being on the premises, I realized that the way the store was laid out (very long and narrow with doors at both ends), I would need more employees to help people make their choices while browsing about. I then added the personnel necessary to give customers the kind of personal attention that brings them back.

As business continued to develop, I hired young people to help keep the shelves stocked and other pleasant sales personnel. But I was getting to the point where I needed a good manager. I advertised for one but got too many applicants who were more rough than gentle. Not what I wanted. I wanted a person interested in taking care of the customers.

I decided to manage the operation myself.

Promotions

I did a lot of promotions such as offering a discount on the wine of the month. Also, being located in a poor area, I made up fliers offering various bargains to try and attract new customers. I had to get people to come to this part of town to buy their liquor.

The promotions help bring people in, but, truthfully, during these lean build-up years I made a living but would have earned more as a machinist. But I was satisfied being my own boss and earning enough to cover all my needs for the family. I really liked the business very much.

Two things helped me to build up the business. For one, I became a sales outlet for the state lottery. That at least brought people to the store to see what a truly nice looking place I had compared to my competition.

Then the building I'm in was being converted into a condominium. I had to decide whether to buy my place or not. Meanwhile, the store next to me remained empty. People were not too anxious to come into this area. I decided to buy my store and the one next door and expand.

Appreciation of Store

Today I could sell my store for about $100,000 since the character of the neighborhood has changed and business is really very good.

Costs

For a liquor store, you do not have to pay for the stock you order for 30 days. This gives you a chance to build your cash flow before paying your bills.

I do extend credit, which, if not collected when billed, can affect me paying my bills. I give credit two ways—on a weekly basis for people, and on a monthly basis for companies.

Right now I make a very good living from my liquor store, and, most importantly, I still enjoy the business.

Trade Publications

Beverage Media
161 Sixth Avenue
New York, NY 10013
(212) 620-0100

Liquor Store Magazine
352 Park Avenue
New York, NY 10010
(212) 685-4848

Wine World
6308 Woodman Avenue
Van Nuys, CA 91401
(818) 785-6050

32

Mail Box Rental

The rental of private mail boxes is increasing throughout our country and is becoming a profitable business. In fact, it is growing so rapidly that Mail Boxes, Inc. is franchising rental stores nationally.

For former school teacher Marilyn Parkinson, who had no reservations about opening her own business, this unique retail service operation appealed to her most after investigating a number of other possibilities. Also, instead of opening up on her own she decided to buy a franchise that provided guidance, networking, and promotional support.

Parkinson offers some very interesting insights into what is involved in purchasing a franchise, the costs, and extra opportunities for income.

The mother of grown children, she now operates Mail Boxes, Inc., Hartsdale, New York. She is also the area representative for the company, which gives her a chance to increase her annual income.

Getting connected with a franchise is interesting and might be the way some people might like to get into other businesses that are run by franchise companies.

Marilyn Parkinson

Before getting into mail box rentals, I was a teacher. I taught in the secondary schools, and I was a high school special education teacher. Also, I was the spouse of a corporate executive. We moved quite a bit. I taught for seven or eight years. I think I always wanted to go into business since we got married, which was 17 years ago. We toyed with the idea. But my family came along, and that was my top priority.

As my family grew older, I started investigating going into my own business. For instance, out on the West Coast there is something called Pieshops. But that's a 24 hour a day business. You are dealing with a product and inventory that you have to get rid of right away, unlike a pen or pencil that can sit forever. I kept bringing ideas to my husband who was put in touch with the man who was very successful in the mail box rental business. My husband looked at the stores and said it was great. He tried to push me in this direction. I resisted as this is a business that can be understood best when people actually walk in the door. I was the same way.

In April 1984, I explored several stores. Between Los Angeles County and San Diego County, there are 30. I walked into one and then another and all of a sudden I thought that it was a great idea. I thought it would work. After going to the franchise corporate office, we decided that this was what we were going to do. I was at the point where I finished teaching, had married kids, and was now ready to take on a business project.

Start-Up

It's easier to acquire a franchise than to start something from scratch, especially for me. I went from education to business, which is a totally different world. I'm still making that transition. I still have problems.

The franchise fee was $12,500. For that, they help select the site, get you set up, and arrange for a grand opening. They give you continual ongoing support with advertising projects. You get the national advertising. You get group rates on all your equipment. You get a group discount on Emery Air, which is one of the shippers. You get more and more recognition as the concept grows.

Also, you have a network. I may have a franchise call me from Florida and say they have someone who wants to rent out a mail box with a New York address. Or vice versa, I will call someone else and tell them that I have a customer here that wants a Washington, D.C. address. Or someone will call and say that they want a box from us. They have found out about me by talking to my corporate office in California. We refer people to each other. We also do packaging and shipping. We have a facsimile and a telex machine that is hooked up to our stores. If you wanted to send a fax to someone in Los Angeles who didn't have one, he could pick it up at a Mail Boxes store in the city.

Terms

The franchise agreement must be renewed after several years, costing about $1000. You have to pay your royalties and your franchise fee. Your royalties are five percent of your gross, two percent of which goes to advertising. One percent is held in a fund and is available to you for local co-op advertising which means I pay only 50 percent of the ad. If you want to do a lot of advertising for Christmas, you have matching funds. So you do get that money back. Items that you don't make a 10 percent profit on are not added to your gross sales. Those earnings are all yours. Your mail boxes are your highest profit item. The basic service of the business is to provide private mail boxes to customers.

Costs

The franchise fee is now up to $15,000. That's just franchise fee. You pay for setting up your store. To put up one of these stores today would probably run between $50,000 and $60,000 to open the doors and keep you going for a couple of months. We all know that most businesses fail in the first year because they are undercapitalized. I would say you would need more than that $60,000 after a couple of months to keep you running.

I have been operating since February 1985. The biggest problem is the rent for retail space. It's supply and demand. You will pay an average of $20 a square foot. In less congested areas of the country, it gets cheaper. But the closer you are to big cities, the higher the rents. That is what has hurt us more than anything else. All merchants complain about the rent.

We have 236 mail boxes. We buy them from the suppliers. Most of them manufacture in the midwest and in California. They would be listed under mail boxes in the yellow pages. The mail box rentals range from $10 to $25 per month, depending on the size of the box. People have access to them 24 hours a day. I am doing well. Other stores have made profits even faster. We have a lot of space and a high rent.

Area Representative

I am an area franchisee. In addition to an exclusive territory, I bought the rights to become an area franchisee, which means that if someone else comes here and they want to put up a Mail Boxes, Etc. store in this county, which is my area, they have to come and see me. I help them do the site selection and get their store open. In other words, I am acting as a franchiser. I am the middle person. I can subfranchise these franchises out in this particular area. I am paid 40 percent of the franchise fee and two and a half percent of the royalties (two and a half percent of the five percent that goes to the franchisee).

The reason we need so large a space is because, as an area franchisee, we are going to start holding seminars here on Saturdays or one night a week to sell franchises. We'll be using this as a sales and training office. We train newcomers. We undertake the cost of arranging all of this.

New Ideas

We are always developing new profit centers. For example, the facsimile is new. That's only a year old. What will happen is someone will try a profit idea and then tell the corporate office about it and how much money it's bringing in. If the corporate office thinks it's a good idea, it tells the other franchisees. What I am doing now is looking into leasing equipment and seeing if we can make that a profit center. If that takes off, we would introduce it to the rest of the franchisees. We are developing that profit possibility. Just opening a small cubbyhole renting mail boxes alone would not be profitable. Out of the 236 mail boxes, we have 165 rented now. But mail boxes are the highest profit margin in this business.

Market for Rentals

People are tired of the post offices, their bad locations, the inconvenience, the terrible service. We serve the private sector now such as people doing sales promotion mailings. That type of thing. The people who need this service are often starting new businesses and can't afford office rents, or even a copy machine. They will rent here because they get a street address, not just a box number. If it comes to a point where we have a waiting list, we will knock out a wall and install more mail boxes. We have planned for expansion.

We try to keep the hours more convenient than the post office. So we are open at 8:30 in the morning until 7:00 at night. We are also open all day on Saturday. As you know, most post offices close at noon. We have had to kind of reorient the public, the customers, so that they would know about all our services. On Saturdays we are open from 9:30 to 5:30. At other times people can get to their boxes when they know the access code to our store lock. Yet we have no trouble with break-ins, possibly because thieves think we are part of the federal post office system.

Problems

Problems come from our shipping and packaging service. You have lost articles and must take the responsibility for settling claims. It's a pain. Some of the shippers can be difficult, not on a lost package but on a damage. So far we have not personally had to make up any payments. I have heard of instances with other franchises where they have gotten stuck.

Profit Differential

Each store has its own type of traffic. A store that is in an affluent residential-type setting generates most of its profit from shipping for local women. They don't want to go to the post office because it's a hassle. They don't want to go to the post office because it's a million miles away. That store will ship out 40 or 50 packages a day. In another store, in an area more like this, where you have thousands of residences and a lot of small businesses, we get our extra income from copying, telexing, facsimile, all business-related services. Each store takes on its own personality. This store is not located in a wealthy residential area.

Payment and Earnings

Payment is in advance each month for the mail boxes. We carry people for two months and then stop the service. For nonpayment, I send in a notice to the last known address and tell them that they have 15 days to pay us or we will change the locks. And we do it. All we really lose is a month's rent. Most of the bad debtors never come back. We just rerent the box. When we close the box, we take all the mail and return it to the sender and inform the customer by mail. By the time our termination notice goes out, they already owe for two months.

This operation is simple, it's clean, there's not much to it. This is an active investment. It's the kind of investment that's not passive. If you want a passive investment, do something else. You can't come in here and think you're going to make a lot of money overnight. Basically, you can gross about $300,000 a year in this business after about three years.

Trade Publications

Cashflow
1807 Glenview Road
Glenview, IL 60025

Business Advocate
1615 H Street NW
Washington, DC 20062
(202) 463-5833

In Business
PO Box 351
Emmaus, PA 18049
(215) 967-4135

33

Motel

Coming to the United States from Greece in 1965, Chris Hardrinos, part owner of the Norwalk Inn, a motel located in Norwalk, Connecticut, found the United States more than a land of opportunity. For Hardrinos, struggling with his new language and forced to work in a factory during his first years here, it is a place where a determined person can be his or her own boss.

Hardrinos, a man committed to making it, became an insurance agent and a real estate broker. Unhappy with spending a lifetime earning a living at blue collar jobs, which were all that he could get as an unskilled immigrant, he worked at eventually becoming an entrepreneur—the ultimate American freedom.

While still maintaining his insurance business, Hardrinos along with two partners bought the Norwalk Motel. Within a year, they expanded the operation so that it will eventually provide full-time living for all three who still can only give the place part-time attention.

Chris Hardrinos

I came to this country from Greece in 1965. I didn't know the language, and my education was limited. I had heard that this is the land of opportunity and that's what I came for. In the beginning I just worked in a factory. I went to school to learn how to read blueprints and then got a job in a machine shop as a machinist. I was always looking for an opportunity to get out of the factory. A friend suggested that I become an insurance agent or real estate broker. I went to school and got my license in insurance and real estate. I finally had something that I could earn a living from outside the factory. But language was and still is a problem for me. And my social background is very limited. It was obvious to me that I would have to forget real estate and insurance.

Start-Up

With the help of my nephew who is an attorney, we started exploring possibilities for investment. The hotel just happened to come along as a place for sale. My nephew, a friend, and I became partners and bought it.

The place is expanding to 70 rooms, with larger meeting facilities, banquet facilities, a restaurant, a cocktail lounge, and a bar. When we got involved we didn't know anything. We only saw the potential and decided to take a chance. The people here were losing money. Once we got involved, we realized this place was a gold mine.

There are no hotels in the area. We made our accommodations first rate in order to establish a reputation that would help us remain profitable even if some competition came into this area.

We had to borrow for everything. We showed our proposal to the bank along with our background. We had our problems but we were creative financially and got what we needed to meet the one month deadline we were given to meet the terms of the contract. We opened in June 1985.

At this point, we relied on income from guests. We didn't have any extra capital behind us. We maintained the same rates regardless of improvements. A double room is $49 for two people.

Of course we put our money and our lives into it. We had very little money when we found this place, but we were able to find a bank that backed us.

Our present renovation will be done by the end of the year, and we will be able to do much more business. We're making a profit now and paying off our mortgages.

I have established my own insurance business, as well as working here. We are here about 50 hours a week. We have about 15 to

20 employees at this time. Most of them were employees of the previous owner. We eliminated some positions but haven't made any major changes.

Seasons

Our high season is from June to November. We are hoping not to rely entirely on the rooms. We hope to have our banquet and meeting facilities going full blast. That is our objective. The steady income, however, does come from the rooms, but we feel the banquet room will bring in a lot of money, also. We are putting $1.5 million into the renovations. We will increase the room rates. We are completely refurnishing all the rooms. Outside we are doing landscaping to make the place look good. The pool will stay the same size but be updated to a modern one.

Employees

The present manager was the assistant manager under the previous owners. Our philosophy is that people have to be compensated for what they do. If you treat the employees well and pay them fairly, they will always do a good job. We find the right people by offering them good working conditions.

Problems

Things have not run as smoothly as we might have wanted. None of us can put 100 percent into this business because we all have our own jobs and businesses. We haven't discussed the possibility of one of us being here full-time.

This country gives you so many opportunities. Take a chance. When I first came here and I was talking to my first boss, he said that if you are an honest person, and a person with integrity, it will help you with institutions such as banks. And this is what we have capitalized on.

A mistake that we made is that we did not think bigger. In the past maybe that kept us from coming further along than we are now. If you think big, you can make it. If you have a wall in front of you, don't just beat your head against it, go around it.

No, I didn't have any special training. All I had was the opportunity.

Trade Publications

Hotel & Resort Industry
488 Madison Avenue
New York, NY 10022
(212) 888-1500

Lodging Hospitality
1111 Chester Avenue
Cleveland, OH 44114
(212) 696-7000

Lodging & Food Service
755 Boylston
Boston, MA 02116
(617) 267-9080

34

Natural Food Store

A health conscious America is responsible for the growth of health food stores across the country. For Douglas Dill, the young owner of the natural food store in Yorktown Heights, New York, it was a family business he took over.

With barely any experience in operating a health food establishment, Dill acquired the store from his brother, expanded it, and even opened a second one. He later sold number two at a considerable profit.

Knowing almost nothing about natural food, Dill hired people who did. This is a common practice, as disclosed by many of the entrepreneurs interviewed for this book, to get a business and then learn how to operate it. Not only do they acquire the skills but they succeed as well.

Here is the health food store story.

Douglas Dill

I worked out a deal financially for the store, a lump sum in the beginning and at the end, and monthly payments in between. I got started without having to deal with a bank at all. I dropped out of college to buy this natural food store. Owning a retail operation, I feel, is in my blood. My father had a lumber business. Retailing was discussed at the dinner table: how to make displays and how to deal with customers. I've been working in retailing since I was 14, at the lumber yards, in a book and record store for a while, and a pizzeria. Having my father in the lumber business gave me an entrepreneurial spirit. I didn't want to work for somebody else. That's what I meant about it being in my blood. Every male in my family is working for himself and has been for most of his life.

Operation

Since I bought the store in 1979, sales have doubled and the square footage of the store has doubled. The dramatic expansion took place about eight months after I took it over from my brother. It was a sink or swim situation. The first two years I was scraping by, living in the slummy part of Mohegan Lake. I was on my own. My brother, who went to Harvard to get his MBA, then needed income to pay his tuition. I paid him $1000 a month for four years, plus a lump sum of about $5000 in the beginning and $5000 at the end. Since he had it for two years, it was making a profit, but just enough for me to take a very, very small salary immediately. This is the advantage of buying an existing store.

All my employees were older than I was. The second week I was there, two of them confronted me demanding a raise, threatening to leave. I was getting lessons right from the beginning on how to run the store. I knew that this was the time to either make it or break it. I was putting in six to seven days a week, 8 to 10 hour days.

I had managed a natural food store for a summer when I was at college, and that did help. But this was a larger store. It was a learn as you go situation. I had a basic knowledge of how to purchase the foods and who the suppliers were.

Growth

During the seven years since I took it over, when I was 20, I doubled the entire shop. The profits have doubled. That's because as volume goes up, your expenses don't go up as much. The rent is still the same no matter how much the volume is. Right now I have six people working for me. I have three full-timers and three part-timers. All of our part-timers are either college or high school students. I think a great resource in this community of part-time workers are students. My manager at the store is a registered nurse, which comes in really handy. She has a background in nutrition. She is very good with customers.

Spoilage

In the vitamin line, there is not that much risk of spoilage. But breads go bad every three or four days. Grains can go bad. There is definitely spoilage. We need to constantly rotate our stock, and I think that is the advantage to having a larger store with high volume; we have constant turnover. We buy in bulk, 50 pound bags. There is a 400 pound minimum from one supplier and an $800 minimum from another supplier. There are different ways of ordering.

Ten years ago that's what the natural food industry was. Little stores just selling vitamin tablets. Then it graduated into food with the larger natural food stores selling a lot of bulk. We sell over 100 items loose. Ultimately, they all move, some more slowly than others. We are always trying new products. That also includes bulk honey and bulk peanut butter. When we have a slow mover, we usually put it on sale and try to liquidate that stock. And with a new product, we don't order a huge quantity to start with. We see how it sells first. For example, four months ago we got in three different granolas. The blueberry granola flew and the others went slowly. We can't return food. That's why we don't give credit in the store. You really can't return food, unless it's bad.

Competition

When I first got into the business, there was a dramatic increase during the first few years. Now it's sort of leveled off. There are a few different theories about why. But competition is one reason. Groceries have added natural food sections, and more pharmacies sell natural vitamins. The natural food industry has not gotten larger; it's encroached on by other retailers. Even the produce stands in New York City carry a lot of these products. The leveling off has become noticeable during the past two years.

There is still enough demand for someone to think about getting into the business. Location is critical. In retail, the three most important things are location, location, and location. It's still a solid business. I think that there will always be natural food stores. There will always be successful natural food stores and then there will always be so-so stores.

In the natural food industry a total approach is the critical factor. An owner should know nutrition and have a business background. It's not enough to just know business and not have nutrition background. You need both. However, if you have a very strong business background, hire people who have the nutritional background while you learn that part of the business. It can be done. During the time I have been in business my employees have been more knowledgeable than I have about nutrition.

Two Stores

My profits increased when I had two stores. But I was spreading myself thin. Also, having two managers and extra employees, costs were dramatically more. I sold the second store even though it was profitable. I didn't enjoy running the two places. When I devoted my time to the one store, my profit level dramatically increased. On-premise supervision is important. It's a five day week for me now but it started out as six to seven. The store is open seven days a week, on Sunday only to 3:00.

Customers

There are definitely customer problems. One woman wrote a nasty letter saying that there were mice droppings in the rice, and she thought that was disgusting. They weren't mice droppings at all.

The rice comes in very dirty. All of our dried beans and grains need to be washed and it turned out that what she thought were mice droppings were little rocks. We do not rinse and clean the grains, the customer does. She reported us to the Health Department which came to inspect the store. We get inspected all the time.

They agreed that there was no problem. We don't have any rodents, only mealy moths. They come in the summertime. Because these organic products are not sprayed or fumigated, the larva, which is microscopic, remains in the grains. That is the only problem. We have monthly exterminators.

Legally, we are not permitted to prescribe vitamins or special foods, but many customers ask for our advice. What is good for this or that? We will show them a book or an article, and they can read up on it. That's really a touchy situation when the customer wants your advice.

Professional Group

There are seminars and conventions twice a year held by the organization that I belong to, the Natural Food Association. They have very good conventions both here and on the West Coast. There are sessions on how to run the store, management, nutrition, every aspect of this business. When you are first getting started, they are fantastic. I went to them constantly. It has tapes that it will send you. When first getting started, I strongly recommend attending a convention. You make all the contacts for the business.

Costs

Start-up costs for me were between $60,000 and $75,000. That includes everything: lease, deposits, redoing the floors, cash register. Buying an existing store can be decided on the basis of two times profit, or 40 percent of gross sales. There are different ways of coming to a figure for buying. In the natural food industry, this is a common way of starting up.

Outlook

I was thinking of selling this store, and then realized that I really didn't want to. I am keeping it. However, I am going into real estate full-time and will be here at the store one day a week. This is an experiment for me. I think a store like this can be run in an absentee fashion after the owner has been there for four or five years and knows the business. I can come in and answer questions and deal with problems such as employee theft. In the last seven years I had to let two people go because of dishonesty.

Tips

I think the most important thing is the business end. You need to learn as much as possible about that aspect. Just because you are interested in having a healthy way of life is no reason to be in this business. That's motivation. Bottom line means profits. That's why the business end is much more important than the nutritional end. Having ample products in a clean store and dealing with customers are also important aspects. Having nutritional knowledge helps.

I think this business will continue to grow in the future.

Trade Publications

Health Foods Business
567 Morris Avenue
Elizabeth, NJ 07208
(201) 353-7373

Whole Foods
195 Main
Metuchen, NJ 08840
(201) 494-2889

Health Foods Retailing
390 Fifth Avenue
New York, NY 10019
(212) 613-9700

35

Newsletter

The public's passion for newsletters has never diminished. There are more newsletters covering a wide range of subjects being put out today than ever before. In fact, some subjects such as investment advice are on overload. It is hard to imagine that another newsletter can be added to the market and succeed. It depends on the subject.

Almost any subject has the potential for being converted into a newsletter format if enough fresh material can be assembled for each issue. How about pregnancy spawning a book and then a monthly newsletter for expectant mothers.

This is no Dr. Spock type publication, but one that tells ladies-in-waiting what services are available to them from hospital facilities to where to buy what. Also included is helpful information for the new mothers. It even includes the best places to exercise for nursing or infant-care mothers.

Journalist Helen Rosengren Freedman had questions to ask and services to find when she was pregnant. Her book *Big Apple Baby* then listed everything she found that could be helpful to expectant mothers living in Manhattan. Then came the newsletter for pregnant women, extended to serve parents until their children are seven years old.

This is how she did it.

Helen Rosengren Freedman

Writing is my profession as I was a newspaper reporter in Australia. I worked for five years as a newspaper reporter—general reporter and feature writer—and then I was transferred to the New York bureau of the newspaper group I was working for. That's how I came to New York. I came here in the beginning of 1976, and I continued to work as a correspondent for the *Melbourne Herald*, which is the largest evening daily in Australia.

After I decided I wanted to stay in the United States, I got a job on a trade magazine where I learned how to do magazine production, which I had never done before. So I wrote and did layouts. I then quit to freelance full-time, writing articles at home mainly for the foreign press. I did that for another couple of years. Then I got the contract to do the book listing magazine requirements for writers. That turned into a full-time job. This covered two volumes; one for nonfiction, the other for fiction. I decided that I really liked writing books as opposed to articles, especially since there was no one calling up asking where the article was. Also I enjoyed working at home.

Big Apple Baby Concept

After finishing the books, I became pregnant and spent time marketing my books. I had the baby in August 1983. It took several months before I got back to writing. I started thinking about the recent baby boom and all the information that would be helpful to pregnant women. There were so many things I discovered afterwards that would have made life easier. I then got the idea to write the *Big Apple Baby* book, a guide for expectant and new New York parents. I did a proposal, but first called my agent to tell her the idea. She felt it was too specialized and the market was too limited. I was very angry that my agent refused to read my proposal. In fact, I was so mad that I decided to publish the book myself. My husband agreed. As an author, I knew the problems of self-publishing. The biggest one is to get the book into the stores. However, since this book primarily would be for the New

York audience, I thought distribution would be manageable. Also, I saw it as a book that would be sold not just in book stores, but in baby shops and maternity stores and other outlets of this type. The book is divided into two parts: one covers the needs of pregnant women, and the other the services available after the child is born. The pregnancy part ranges from where to buy your baby furniture and maternity clothes to how to have your baby, how to find an obstetrician. It lists all the hospitals in the city, outlining their services from a consumer point of view and even discusses midwives for home births. And the second part deals with the time after the baby is born (when you're raising an infant in the city), from where to buy your baby clothes, to where to take your baby. If you're traveling around the city and you need to nurse or diaper your baby, where do you go? It's a very complete source book. When I was doing the book I thought, why hasn't anyone done this before? No one had. I was lucky that I had an idea and that no one else had done it.

The Newsletter

After spending much time on distribution and marketing, things were starting to slow down. My thoughts were now directed at how I was going to keep this going, what kind of publicity I needed. Is it a book that I will be revising and publishing every year? The best approach, I decided, was to publish a newsletter to provide updated information. I knew that although my book was printed in 10 days, six months later it was slightly out-of-date. It would be a year between new editions and a lot is happening, particularly in the area of childbirth, in New York City in between each new book. The timing was perfect for this. My newsletter would be current—filled with late news, interviews, and other happenings for expectant and new parents in the city. I found so much material that I would have more than enough for each issue. There is no shortage of information.

I thought initially that a newsletter would be simple, something I could put out every month myself, type it and sell subscriptions. I mentioned the idea to a friend who did the illustrations for the book. We talked about her doing illustrations for the newsletter and then decided to become partners. We soon discovered that advertising was needed to keep it going. It worked. We started out with an eight-page issue in November 1985. Now our monthly newsletter is up to 12 pages and profitable.

I had a list of people who bought my book and used this as my first mailing list. There were about 300 people. The response was about 60–70 percent, a huge response for mail order. They liked the idea of having a newsletter version of the book every month. Pregnant women want informative material as they have very special needs. An excellent market for this type of thing.

My friend agreed to sell ads and do the illustrations and I would do all the editing. After the first sales letter to subscribers, I got prospect lists from maternity stores. Mailing lists are available from commercial houses costing $50 per thousand names for a minimum order of 5000. After having babies, the parents still need information we provide for many years.

Within three months we had 500 paid subscribers. But we print 3000 copies each month. The additional 2500 are distributed free to parenting centers, stores, doctors' offices, and hospitals. People pick them up and become subscribers. We get about 100 new ones every month. A mention in the *New York Times* resulted in another 100 subscribers. I keep publicizing the *Big Apple Baby* newsletter all of the time.

Getting Advertisers

I thought originally that for the first few issues, we would give free ads to get it going. We got such a terrific reception that by the second issue it was all paid advertising. We have no trouble selling ads. Our rates are very low yet. We priced our ads to simply cover costs of production and mailing. For $100 an advertiser could get one-third of a page. We expanded to 12 pages due to our growing number of advertisers. One-third are repeat ads. After six months, we covered our costs.

To put out 12 pages, 3000 copies each month, costs $1000. We sell $1000 worth of ads. We still have out-of-pocket expenses of several hundred dollars a month. The business is presently part-time since we both have young children. We expect to cover all of our costs in another six months.

We don't want to turn this newsletter into a magazine for two reasons. There are several parenting magazines already out. We feel it won't be long before there are other magazines, newsletters, or papers on the subject. We decided that what we have to do is more sales promotion. While 3000 is very nice, it's not enough. We want people to see it and to see it every month. We worked out a plan to print 20,000 every month and to go to 16 pages. To do that we need $5000 per month for expenses. We, therefore, need to sell $5000 worth of ads.

Expansion

We worked out two business plans. One is to do it with investors, which we would need to do properly with an office and one extra staff person, all facilities, though not extravagant ones. To do it in the right way, we would need $200,000 per year. We need to find that kind of investment money. We are looking now to make big money.

We thought of changing the newsletter to a tabloid format, but we feel that the way it looks now is very unique. Once you go into a tabloid, you are talking newsprint, which is cheaper looking. Maybe in the future. We will keep the format the way it is and just add more pages. It still has a distinctive look to it. We don't intend to just stay where we are for the next year until we find investors. We plan to make use of resources now to increase the monthly run of the newsletter to 20,000 copies ourselves.

This means getting help from people who are willing to work from home. Mothers who want some part-time income to sell ads by phone. We have never visited any of our advertisers in person. Everything has been done by phone. We send our advertisers a page proof, so they see the ads before they appear in the newsletter. My partner does all the ad layouts at no cost.

My book is just for pregnancy and infancy; but the bulletin goes up through infants, toddlers, and pre-schoolers five years old. This is how we keep our subscribers. But we still need to expand our readership. Therefore, we will eventually expand our age group coverage, probably up to six, seven, and eight years old. When this happens, the *Big Apple Baby* newsletter, now mainly for pregnant women and for people who have just had babies, will become the *Big Apple Parent.*

Now it's sold only in Manhattan, but we plan to expand to the boroughs. We are doing that gradually. In one issue I did a story on choosing a childbirth teacher and for the first time I went out of Manhattan and talked to people in hospitals in the other boroughs about classes conducted there. Soon we will begin to distribute our bulletin in all the boroughs. It's a huge audience.

There are 108,000 babies born in the city every year, which of course is a phenomenal amount. That is not our primary market, because a lot of those people are low income families. But we would like to get subscribers from this group, too. That's why we devoted an entire issue telling parents all about poisons. This is very important information for families with young children, no matter where they live.

The more subscribers coming in, the more we could charge for our ads. We don't want to lose our subscribers when their children get to be four or five years old. We don't worry about the glossy magazines being competition. Most readers just don't have enough time to go through a whole magazine. Our bulletin comes to them in the mail once a month, they can sit down with it for a half an hour while taking a coffee break and read all of it. Also, our ads are interesting because they come from small neighborhood people.

Pricing Ads

It is not our aim to go off to Johnson & Johnson, or Procter & Gamble. There are enough local people to approach. Of course, with an increased circulation, our ad rates will go up. But we will offer a lower price rate for the small business person, the person who is giving childbirth classes, or providing other special services. If you are a store or a corporation, you will pay higher rates than if you are a one-person operation. That's how you keep your interesting ads.

We have a classified section. Interestingly enough, we have had a lot of trouble getting classified advertisers. I think it is because of the size of distribution. When we reach 20,000 it will work better. The 20,000 distribution will begin in the summer of 1986 as the *Big Apple Parent.*

Marketing

We do the marketing, and the printer sends out the finished product. Marketing includes calling people to subscribe to the newsletter, publicity and promotion to subscriber prospects. A newcomer to the newsletter business can put out a typewritten product. Good content will help it sell. Ours is very professionally produced. I wasn't sure this was necessary, but now I am. It's a plus. We do the layout and paste-up ourselves. Typesetting is done in Albany by a person who has a business in her basement. When you self-publish, you find all these people. You don't pay top dollar.

We use a post office box. My partner works out of her home in Forest Hills and I out of my Manhattan apartment. We do the paste-up together in Rosalie's home. You really have to be interested in the subject. This one is really dear to our hearts. We do it part-time. If someone could do it full-time, it would be very profitable.

We started out selling subscriptions for $5.00 for six issues. We recently raised it to $7.50 for six issues. We felt that $5.00 was too low. A lot of people have similar publications and distribute them free. I do not agree with that. I think that people appreciate what they're paying for, look for it every month, and take it more seriously.

Certainly it is our aim to make it a big money-maker. I see us eventually having an office and a staff, and even though it might not ever be a tabloid format, I see it as a working newspaper for parents. We change the color of every issue to make it more distinctive. It's easy to do. Every month, we learn as we go.

Trade Publications

Business Marketing
220 East 42 Street
New York, NY 10017
(212) 210-0187

Direct Marketing
224 7th Street
Garden City, NY 11530
(516) 746-6700

Marketing Communications
50 West 23 Street
New York, NY 10010
(212) 645-1000

36

Outplacement Service (Personnel)

Robert Pfann, who had endured the stress of surviving as a top level executive in the corporative world for 25 years, now heads his own outplacement consulting firm, Robert Pfann & Associates, in Greenwich, Connecticut. With mergers, acquisitions, and take-overs flourishing throughout the country, Pfann's business is brisk and profitable.

As a highly specialized form of job consulting and placement, Pfann has ample and continuing business fueled by the merger-acquisition-takeover thrust of industry that has become more intense in recent years. When two companies are joined, however it comes about, there is always an excess number of management people at all levels who are terminated.

Along with severance pay, another one of the perks given management people terminated because of the overload is help getting new positions. Sent to outplacement agencies such as Pfann's, they are guided through the process of finding new jobs.

After lengthy personal consultation, new resumes are prepared and job objectives are defined that fit these people's skills and the marketplace. Then the outplacement agency tries to place the job seekers into new positions.

The best part is that the corporations pay for this service.

Bob Pfann

The firm that I was last with in Connecticut was sold in late 1983. When my last job ended in 1983 after being in business or working for corporations, I decided to open my consulting firm. After a career of 25 years, I felt I was ready. I teamed up with an individual who handled the outplacements for my last firm.

Many corporations provide outplacement service for people terminated. The companies pay professional consultants to help them get new jobs. We then review all the basic elements: assess their strengths, their weaknesses, what they want to do next in their careers, prepare resumes, and go into the various nuances of a campaign strategy for the job market. We decide on the most effective ways of using their time to locate new positions so they don't waste energy pursuing unlikely objectives. Many people who have been employed for 15 to 20 years do not have any idea of how to write a resume, what's out there, or how to plan getting the right next position. Professional outplacement firms provide all the help and guidance needed.

We do get high level executives looking for new positions. Let's say one company acquired another and by consolidating obviously they will have more top people than are needed. They might have two financial vice presidents, two heads of data processing or accounting managers, four human resource managers—all basically doing the same thing. The company will determine which of those people would be the stronger to retain and let the others go. These high echelon extras are sent to us to help them find new positions.

Challenging Work

This type of involvement has always been exciting to me even though it's not the most financially rewarding. There's never a dull moment because each individual is different, having special, personal desires, and career aspirations. To be able to work with them, understand, and assist them to reach their goals in any way, shape, or form—through training, guidance, availability, whatever it takes—is the greatest satisfaction. I found my niche and I never want to leave it.

Being a consultant is very different from being an accountant. It is not like keeping a set of books, it's being involved with people. There is something new every day. It's challenging and enjoyable, especially after walking to someone else's drumbeat for 25 years. I'm on my own. Also, I have a service to sell to many small corporations that need my expertise. At the present time 65 to 70 percent of my consulting is done for small companies.

Expansion

When I started on my own I had a partner, and we were constantly approached by consultants who wanted to team up with us. Within nine months, we had 10 associates. We had temporary offices, and we decided to call a halt to the growth because we did not want to get too big. We wanted to stay small. Smallness has a market and it allows you to give the special attention. Our size has not changed, still one partner and 10 associates.

Anyone planning to go into a business should have enough capital to sustain for one year. Of course, the amount depends on the size of the business, the rental, the printing of stationery and such, promotional materials for prospective clients, telephone, travel expenses, and entertainment money. If you hold down your salary, for the first year, the total cost of a small consulting firm might be approximately $100,000 to $125,000. It might take over a year to actually make a profit.

In consulting you can make 10 sales in a week or not get any business for six months. Since you're filling a need, it depends when the need arises. As your own boss, there is no such thing as a set number of hours to work in a week. You work as needed until your business becomes profitable. When you reach that point, you will have recovered your investment.

The slowest season is late June, July, and August, and then the holiday season. The peak seasons are January to May, and September to November. In human resources services, it is really unpredictable. Our services include contract negotiating for the people we place, compensations, surveying competitors, and finding suitable job openings. We study employee relations programs to evaluate policies, practices, and their communications programs. Then we determine how the employees feel about the business, whether they are happy with the situation or not. Employees talk to us. As outsiders, we don't threaten people.

We have promotional material. One brochure with a classy cover has a pocket on the inside so we could insert specific materials for each client. We didn't really know, starting up, what our long-term blend of services was going to be.

Beginning

Starting out it took about 11 hours a day, five days a week including weekends, getting all the nitty gritty stuff done. Now the basic workday is about 9 to 10 hours. But even on weekends you don't leave it. I try to avoid that because I still have to have a lifestyle and a family. If you're so totally immersed, then it doesn't become fun anymore. It is fun if you make it fun.

Associations

We belong to several business related associations and chambers of commerce and are trying to get more involved with them, particularly personnel associations whose members are people who hold personnel jobs. They have negative feelings about consultants. They feel consultants are there for one purpose: to market and sell clients rather than to participate.

Tips

You've got to be capable of taking rejection. As a small business there is a lot of competition out there. If you don't know anyone internally the only way you're going to get to talk to him is by sending him an introductory letter, followed up with a phone call. Don't overkill with dialogue. It takes patience and time and a lot of stamina to really hang in there.

Everyone should get a good accounting background. You've got to keep your own books, or, if you hire an accountant, you have to know what he is doing. It's important to take business related courses that provide an understanding of how companies are organized. For young people, it's better to get a corporate position and learn from doing.

I started when I was 50. And I've talked to people who are 53, 54, 58 who are making career changes. You should never think that you are too old or too young to do anything.

I enjoy placement, seeing the person land the right job. That totally outweighs the financial rewards.

Trade Publications

Personnel
135 West 50 Street
New York, NY 10020
(212) 586-8100

Personnel Administrator
606 North Washington
Alexandria, VA 22314
(705) 548-3440

Personnel Journal
245 Fisher Avenue
Costa Mesa, CA 92626
(714) 751-1883

37

Pet Shop

The pet shop is a store teeming with life—puppies, kittens, birds, and tropical fish. For anyone who thrives on having a direct link with living nature, this is a wonderland. It is a type of shop that often has as many people visiting to be amused by the collective antics of the store's pet population as interested shoppers.

But these living, dependent creatures sold to people who want to add live nature to their homes, require continual in-store care and feeding. That's why it is a business that demands personal attention seven days a week.

Educating customers is one of the most delicate problems of this business. Easter bunnies bought as gifts for children might be tolerated for as long as a week at home. Full-time care is often more than a shopper bargained for when making the purchase. The obvious is overlooked. This kind of impulse buying of the cute kitten or the adorable puppy has troublesome consequences for pet shop owners.

While pet bounce back is one of the woes of the business, overall, it is a joyful way to make a living. Michael McCormick, owner of Pet Alley, Stamford, Connecticut, explains precisely how to handle this problem and others he has encountered operating his shop for almost 20 years. Does he enjoy it? Indeed he does.

Michael McCormick

Beginning

Before I started this business, I did the same thing—worked in pet shops. I eventually became manager of three. Then I moved to Connecticut from Long Island where I was living and worked for someone up here for about a year. Then I got a job in a pet shop in Norwalk where I worked for about six months. The lady who owned the place fired me and said I would never make it in the pet business. I am now going on my 19th year.

I think every person that wants to go into business wants to be independent. I was always independent. I was the manager of a pet shop at the very young age of 18. In a way, I really never had a boss. I really never worked directly for someone. I worked on my own as a manager. I ran the pet shops so I was really my own boss.

To go into this business, you need to have some experience. Actually, my first job as a very young person was on a farm. I really got to like animals. I even had horses at home and I found that I liked them.

Starting Up

I was lucky to get a loan from a bank through a relative which I paid back within the first year of business. My father-in-law cosigned a loan for me. It was $15,000 in 1968, which was a lot of money then. Today that would be about $50,000 with inflation through the past 18-19 years.

Let me explain how I was able to pay off my loan in a year. I didn't open up from scratch. I started with a business that was already successful. That business was showing a profit when I bought it, and I increased that profit to be able to pay the loan back in 12 months. The person who sold it was tired of running a seven-day-a-week business. Operating a pet shop is a lot of responsibility and it can be too much of a burden for some people.

When I first started, my wife worked for me for four weeks. What a horror. We were either going to get divorced or we would kill each other. So I hired a part-timer who worked for me after school for the first year. Then I was lucky to find a part-timer for the morning as well.

Earnings and Seasons

Actually in this business the profit mark-up should be about 100 percent. If you buy something for $1.00 you sell it for $2.00. So, if you spend $500 a week in supplies, you take in $1000 a week. You know you are making $500, and then you would have to subtract your expenses. Don't forget, I bought a business that had inventory and customers. I didn't have to open up and wait for customers to come in. I bought this business December 1, before Christmas, and I had a steady trade from the day I put the key in the door; I had customers waiting out on the sidewalk. Every retail store peaks before Christmas.

But there are low seasons. I find that May is slow because we would be in between selling tropical fish and dog supplies. Dog products sell best in the summertime and cat supplies in the wintertime. As far as puppies and kittens are concerned, they sell well all year round, but peak in the spring. People like to buy a puppy in the spring, because they can housebreak the dog easier and train it outdoors in the good weather.

Developing Store Traffic

We always advertise. Twelve months a year, especially in newspapers. We do a lot of coupon advertising. These are mailed directly to homes, and are a good type of sales promotion. Each coupon is good for 90 days. Of course, we can monitor the impact of coupon promotions easier than ads. Customers have to bring the coupons in to redeem whatever I'm advertising such as a penny sale for tropical fish, or a dog bone for 59 cents.

Work Demands

I'm a workaholic. I want to retire early. I have set up a schedule for myself. I'm 40 now, and when I'm 50 I'll be able to retire. But I do work seven days a week. One key thing is that I like it. I like working in the store and dealing with customers, except when buying pets for their kids. Also, I do have help, so the business is never a burden.

As an owner, I feel free to take time off whenever I like. After 19 years of being in business, I can comfortably leave the shop in the hands of my two full-time sales employees. In addition, I have a full-time dog groomer and I have two part-time boys who work after school. I can take off any time I want to, but as I said before, I am a workaholic. I do like to be here.

Customer Problems

There are many, many little problems and some of them are due to the lack of knowledge the customer has when buying certain things such as a fish tank setup. We do try to explain as much as possible. The trouble is that some people say that they do understand, but they don't. They'll go home and fill the fish tank up with water and make it too hot or too cold, and then plop in the fish. Then they all die, and they'll rant and rave at us.

Another problem could be when a person buys a puppy but cannot emotionally handle the dog at home—such as housebreaking, taking the dog out, feeding the dog on a decent schedule. An animal that is to become a pet requires an emotional investment. I can also predict trouble in advance. Take a mother who comes in with two or three kids and wants to buy a cute puppy for her children. It's not likely to work out, but I have to sell her the dog. Since she already has a problem handling her kids, how is she going to take care of the puppy, too? She can't.

My policy is not to take animals back, only because if I did, I'd be taking dogs, fish, and kittens back a week or two later when people find out that it's a job taking care of an animal.

I do explain how to take care of the dog, but I can't give the person the feeling of responsibility. I don't know their lifestyle at home, I don't know how they conduct their household. I don't know if the person is mentally equipped to bring a puppy into the house. Some people cannot take on a responsibility like that. I just don't know. I can only guess. I write out in black and white what they have to do at home. But most people don't read. They just go about doing what they want to.

Pet Association

There is an association being created to represent all the pet shops in the United States. It will fight against laws being passed in many states outlawing the sale of some exotic pets like turtles. Most of the people who pass these laws probably never owned a pet. They might have read about someone having trouble with this kind of pet at home. This is a growing problem in the pet industry—lack of knowledge by the legislature. New York State has a law prohibiting the sale of wild sport birds such as parrots from South America. We are trying to rescind that law now.

We have found out that there are poisoning problems on farms where the birds get sick because of diseases caught from chickens. A lot of people in the pet industry object. What could happen is that people who love birds one day might not be allowed to go to a pet shop and buy a canary or a parakeet.

Loans Require Security

For people who might be interested in starting up a pet business, loan money is available to anyone with some security. You will not get a loan unless you have security. Let's face it, it's 1986 and if you don't have collateral, you will not get a loan. But if a person needs a small business loan to expand, money is always available. But to start a business, if that person does not have security such as a house or bank account, I don't see how they can get a loan from a bank.

Observations

If someone came to me and said they would like to open a pet shop, I would say I think they're crazy. If they're serious and want to work seven days a week caring for thousands and thousands of tropical fish and tropical birds, fine. But they should know when the electricity goes out for two or three days due to a hurricane or heavy rainstorm, you lose all your fish. I am insured for business interruption, but that doesn't cover losses in livestock.

This business has paid me many, many personal dividends. I think that if a young or energetic person would want to open a pet store and is willing to work—that's the key—they could make a good living.

I do enjoy the pet shop, other than making a living. I've been here an awfully long time. I've dealt with young people coming in years ago, buying a fish tank for themselves, and now I'm dealing with them as parents bringing their children in to buy a fish tank. They remember me, and I think that is probably the most satisfying thing. I see adults now who came here first at the age of five or six and now they're walking in at 26 or 27. They're still in the area and still shopping here.

Getting Help

I don't advertise for employees. I see who comes into the store, people who are interested in tropical fish or interested in puppies, and I approach them to see if they need a job. I have to find someone who has a knack, number one, in tropical fish, who can set a tank up, who is successful in it, and who has a nice personality and can handle the customers. If you advertise, people read an ad and come down, not because they love animals or love the pet business, but because they need a job. And this is more than a job.

Trade Publications

Pet Dealer
567 Morris Avenue
Elizabeth, NJ 07208
(201) 353-7373

Pet Age
207 S. Wabash Avenue
Chicago, IL 60604
(312) 663-4040

Pet Business
5400 NW 84 Street
Miami, FL 33166
(305) 591-1629

38

Printing

Joe Foley, owner of Foley's Graphic Services, Yorktown Heights, New York, clearly details how a quick printing store can eventually mushroom into a full-fledged printing business. Also, there is as much demand for printing services in suburban areas as there is in the cities.

Foley, who runs a bustling business located in the corner of a modest mall, has even overcome an essential ingredient for retail business success: a good location. Driving into this shopping center, it is impossible to see Foley's shop. It is completely out of sight to shoppers.

Without the advantage of attracting customers from passing traffic, Foley had to build his business by establishing an admirable reputation for genial customer relations and quality service. If it is not done right, customers don't pay and Foley will do it over. In fact, he is more than gracious about redos for customers. And they keep coming back. This is how he did it.

Joe Foley

We started very small. To give you a brief history on my operation, my dad knew nothing about the printing business. What he did was he looked into the business, and while exploring, he found the National Association of Printers, which he immediately joined without even having a printing shop. Then he went to the first meeting, which was in Philadelphia in 1979. At that meeting, he met a lot of printers and got much valuable information. Luckily, from his other business he knew a supplier who set him up with equipment from a bankrupt operation.

Equipment

What is needed in a basic shop is a small offset press, a large copy duplicator, a large volume copier, a small paper cutter, a three-hole drill, a drill press, and a platemaker. A platemaker is something that shoots an original. It's like a camera. It's taking a picture of an original and being able to make a plate to be put on the press. That's the offset terminology. In commercial printing, you have to shoot a negative, you have to strip the negative up, and then burn a metal plate. It's a long process. In quick printing, you get a paper plate from the plate maker in seconds. It goes right to your press. You can go from a camera-ready original to a printed piece within 15 minutes and get good quality out of it. The offset press is the basis of your business.

What we did was my dad went to speak with a paper salesman from a large company. After discussing what kind of shop we were going to open, the salesman recommended what inventory should be stocked. It's important to find some competent people in the business to guide you before you start.

Start-Up

To start off, a printing operation today would cost between $50,000 to $75,000. Six years ago when we started, it was substantially less.

With owner's compensation, your salary, payroll, and other expenses, you should be able to come out with a 15 to 20 percent net profit.

I started out this Foley store with my stepsister who worked the afternoons after school. She worked from 2:00 to 5:00 or 3:00 to 6:00; and I worked 9:00 to 6:00, full-time. I had a pressman come in at night to run a lot of my work. That's the way the operation started. We kept building and building and my night pressman then became my full-time day pressman. He originally would come in 5:00 to 7:00, or 5:00 to 8:00 at night, and run my difficult work.

Through my dad's contacts, two guys who had a successful shop, I got a chance. I took a two-week cram course in their shop. I learned how to run a press, how to run a paper cutter; I learned how to do all the facets of a quick printing operation. When we opened our door up, I was prepared for the business.

I would suggest that anyone getting into this business get someone outside your competitive area to teach you. I would say, "Could I pay you a fee just to watch your operation for a week, two weeks, a month maybe? I'm out of your area. I'm not going to compete with you." Do everything the way I did. I cleaned their camera and I did a lot of maintenance. I think that it's important to learn all of the business. I also learned from my night moonlight person who was very knowledgeable. He wasn't just a regular pressman. He was a craftsman. Also, the printing supplier who sold me all the equipment knew all the printers and all the pressmen in the area. So he got me this moonlight guy at night and I paid him very well. Six years ago I paid him $10 an hour to come in and run a press for me at night. The knowledge I got from this guy was amazing.

Growing

In time, we developed more and more of a customer base. We grew equipment-wise and manpower-wise. We've added two self-service copiers in the front which take care of walk-in traffic when people want to make just adequate copies. We've added a larger paper cutter, and a complete darkroom facility so we now can do commercial printing. We grew in the commercial printing area because the people I employed knew a lot about commercial printing. The biggest plus for us was that we went into a town that had no competition. And that helped us dramatically because we were the only real printer in town, and we grew as the town grew. Yorktown has grown dramatically.

Quick printing accounts for about 50 to 60 percent of our business. When I say quick printing I mean the short run paper plate type thing. We have a large duplicating facility in the back of the shop, too, in which we do a lot of reports and manuals.

We started with an IBM; my dad, being an ex-IBM salesman, was partial to IBM. Kodak was not a factor in the copy business then. Three years later we got rid of the IBM because it was just outperformed by Kodak and Xerox. We went down and saw a demonstration of Xerox and Kodak one afternoon and decided on the Kodak. Xerox and Kodak are very comparable.

Employees

Good personnel is a very difficult thing to find in this business because you can't pay $10 an hour, and college graduates are overqualified. You have that end of the spectrum, but don't want to settle for an idiot. You have to find a happy medium as far as salary and smarts go in a person. We do get a lot of people that just don't work out. It's just a matter of weeding out. When you do get good people, you want to hold on to them, to take care of them as best you can within your budget.

Problems

The printing business is very competitive. It's a very high-pressure, deadline type of business. People need it yesterday and they have a lot of money riding on what you do for them. It's a very service-oriented business. It's not a nine to five type operation. It's also a very mistake-prone business. Making mistakes obviously costs you money. You are responsible. That's one of our biggest problems over the years. It's what we call redos, doing a job wrong and having to redo it at my expense.

If it's the customer's mistake, I'll give him a 20 or 30 percent discount on a rerun. Also, most of the time if there is a mistake, it has to be redone as quick as possible. That's another problem with this business, the fact that you have to rush a lot of work. And when you rush a lot of work, you make errors. Proofreaders are very important.

Background

I went to school for law enforcement. I have a BS from Bryan College, Smithfield, Rhode Island. I worked my way through four years of college as a store detective. After I graduated from college I worked in retail security and later became an investigator for a large department store that had 5000 employees. It had a lot of internal theft. While I was working, my dad had the ambition to start up another business. He already had one business going on at the time that my brother ran. But I did not feel like coming out of college and going into it. I wanted to be on my own for a while and work in the city. Two years in the city was enough. When he approached me with an offer to run a print shop, I accepted. I now have 15 employees.

Highly Competitive

It's a very competitive business in which people are very price conscious. A bit of philosophy that I give to my people is this: You've got three components to a printing job. You have a price, you have the quality, and you have the turnaround or time element. Customers can have two of the three. They cannot have all three. They can have very good price, and I can turn it around very quickly for them. They are going to sacrifice quality. If they want a real good quality job and they want it turned around real fast, they'll pay for it. We have a basic price structure. These are just basic philosophies.

I try not to hit anybody with a rush charge because we are a quick printer, and that's how we have become so successful. We try to do what the customer wants, but there is a lot of pressure from customers about deadlines and price from the large accounts. You have to pick up and deliver for them and you have to constantly service them. If they have a problem with any part of a job, with anything that they have, they will often request that I make a service call. I then go over and sit down and talk printing with them and discuss whatever they want. It's also disappointing when you price 20 jobs within the week and get only one.

There are people who price shop over the phone. They call six or seven printers with a job, and they go to the lowest bidder. I don't preach to be the cheapest in town, and I hope I'm not the cheapest in town. My philosophy is that I like to serve the customer, I like to be competitive in price, and I guarantee my work. If there is a problem with my work, I'll redo it, and I will rectify the problem. It has to be a give and take. I have to make a reasonable profit and a customer has to be satisfied with my work.

Tips

You should make about a 40 percent gross profit. After your administrative expenses, it gets down to about 15 percent. When you get more into the commercial end of the business, your profit margin decreases. I recommend staying out of commercial printing in the beginning until you have the expertise for this part of the business. It's much messier than the quick printing business.

I offered specials when I first came into business. It's advisable in the beginning. But after a while, specials work against you. A person is going to get those 100 copies regardless of whether you have a special or not. So, if you want to get people in the door in the beginning, you might want to offer a special, but after a while stop them.

In the beginning, six years ago, the yellow pages worked well. But now it is becoming expensive. It doesn't have the impact it used to as there are so many different types of advertising books out now. When we first got into business, it was God's word.

I've done some cold canvassing, going out and knocking on doors with flyers and introducing myself. That has been somewhat successful. Direct mail is important. Although I have not done too much of that, I plan to do more. Make phone calls. A lot of that type of marketing is good. We are lucky that we hit a good location. I am in the process right now of getting a billboard in town. I'll see what happens with that.

The associations are important. There is a convention every six months, a winter convention and a summer convention. At the summer one there is an expo showing all the new equipment. I usually go to one of the two shows. Most of the time, I go to the summer show to see the equipment and talk to printers to find out about what their problems are and successes. It's good mingling with people in your business. A lot of good things come out of it. It's very helpful to exchange ideas.

Trade Publications

American Printer
300 West Adams
Chicago, IL 60606
(312) 726-2802

Printing Journal
2401 Charleston Road
Mountain View, CA 94043
(415) 962-8976

Instant/Small Commercial Printer
Box 368
Northbrook, IL 60605
(312) 564-5940

39

Publishing an Advertising Booklet

A voluntary service for her local business association eventually became a career for Joan Silbersher, owner of the *Country Shopper*, Pound Ridge, New York. It is actually a smaller version of the *Pennysaver*, the franchised advertising-packed publication that is sent free to homes in different sections of the country.

It is a profitable business for towns where the local newspaper has little impact or carries just a few merchant ads. Retailers are eager to advertise in a publication that reaches all the homes in their town, as well as part of the surrounding area.

Silbersher first realized how well read these handouts are when she sold ads and collected the ad money for the local association flyer. She discovered that this advertising-only mailer produced shopper traffic for merchants.

The next step was to open her own business. Without any publisher training at all, she produced a four page flyer on her electric typewriter with practically no investment but time. Her four pager ultimately became an 80 page publication when advertising was at a peak. At the end of 10 years her personal business earnings soared from $8000 to $36,000 a year.

You can do it, too, Silbersher claims. Here's how.

Joan Silbersher

Before starting the paper I was a gym teacher and a real estate broker selling land only. I had my own office. The only thing I had done in publishing was that, while I had my own office selling land in Scotts Corners, New York, I became active in the local business association where I put out a flyer for the organization. I did it for a year voluntarily knowing nothing about publishing at all. The only thing this experience taught me was that the people would pay $40 for certain size ads. That's all. The flyer was just all ads.

Beginning

What led me to start the *Country Shopper* was simply money. I had been selling land and making sort of a living at it. But after I got divorced, the economy changed and it became impossible to sell property. A publisher in town who saw the flyer said that I ought to start a newspaper. It would be a nice little gossip newspaper. He kept insisting, month after month. When I found myself going broke trying to sell land, I started to think about it seriously. I had stopped doing the flyer for the association. The new gal wasn't very good at it. She was even worse at getting three months advance ad money the way I did. She wasn't collecting and the thing was getting smaller and smaller.

I called the association and said I'd do it again but as a private business. I would give 10 percent of the profits back to the business association. The president at the time said no way, we don't want to have anything to do with it. It's not a success the way it is. That's it. That's how I started.

I didn't like the idea about the gossip. I just did it with ads, sketches, and a classified section, not just shops but services, too, and cottage industries. Immediately it went to beyond Pound Ridge. The first issue was 5600 pieces. It was delivered by mail, third class.

Costs

I did almost no market research. I knew that the number of ads we got paid enough to break even. I wasn't very scientific about it when it began in 1976. I just said to myself, I can do it, I can sell that stuff, and if I can just double the size, go to eight pages, there'll be enough profit to generate the amount of money I needed to live on. I think I was looking to make, in those days, something like $8000 a year which, together with my alimony and the income from the tennis and paddle tennis lessons I was giving, would keep me going.

I had $68, my typewriter, and an office. I didn't need anything else then. I had to go around and get advertisers. I already had a good rapport with the local businesspeople. I could go to the Pound Ridge Travel at that time and say the ad is $40 but you have to pay up front. If they took three ads the fourth was free. Since they paid first, I had the money to pay my printer. When I had some extra money, I bought a better typewriter. When I earned more money, I bought more equipment.

I took a wonderful course once at American Women's Economic Development in the city. One of the guest lecturers spoke to the group and said you can't create a need for a business. Your job is to identify a need and fill it better than anybody else. I saw a need for a communications tool between the local businesses and the local residents, because at that time the *Pennysaver* was very weak up here. There was no other local paper. The advertisers were looking for a way to reach the residents. The residents were looking for information. I found that I could sell without much effort. I could fill a flyer with ads from one location. I saw that it was relatively easy. I'm sure that's why I did it. I had nothing to lose.

Earnings

I started making money right from the start. I was never in the red. I got money up front and did everything myself. I did the art work myself, I did the typing, the truck driving, the packing. Then when I used articles, I did all the reporting myself. When I added photographs, I took all the pictures. I wrote the special stories on antique shops and craftspeople in order to broaden, to get my paper more readership. I did all that. If I had paid anyone, I would have been in trouble. However, in a few years I hired a classified salesperson and a display person. They didn't cost me anything because they were on commission. Then I got help for production. For a long time, I was overburdened, and I still am. The last 10 days of the month we are in production because it is monthly. The first week of the month I don't do so much, but the last week I start at 7:00 in the morning, and I stop at 11:00 at night at home. I do my production here. There isn't room at the office and my downstairs is very big. I set up worktables for that period and have my typesetting equipment here. I'm either editing or sorting or typesetting or preparing stuff for the other people to do. The other weeks are just normally busy.

Location

If I sold my business and relocated somewhere else, could I start it up again? Yes. If I were well known I could. You have to be known and be in an area that is weak in newspaper coverage. You would have to be careful to pick a good spot where there are a lot of little shops and not a good newspaper.

If I had started as a stranger, the merchants might not have been so cooperative. I did it all in my office in the beginning. I slept on the floor at night when I had finished the paste-up. When all the ads were in, I'd be there with all the pieces to be pasted up. I put a chair in front of the door and put a cushion on the floor so people couldn't look in and see me there when I was sleeping.

I think it is bad to start in your own house. You need to be in the town and available to advertisers. It's too much a cottage industry in the home. I think people would resent it. They'd say she's asking me to pay for her mortgage. She's doing it out of her living room and not risking her money, very negative. I really struggled for a long time because as the money came in, I put it back in the business. I took as little out as possible. This is an expense-heavy operation between printing, commissions, and mailing.

Promotion and Expansion

To attract advertisers in the beginning I sent the paper to everyone who could possibly be an advertiser. I mailed the paper and rate sheets and I had special articles on different kinds of businesses just to get in the door. I'd do an article on shoe stores and include all of them. I'd take pictures and write about the specialty of each shop. That helped me broaden my base.

I have an anniversary sale once a year when I offer a 30 percent discount. I asked a lot of questions, took a bunch of different courses, went to trade conventions and equipment shows in the metropolitan area.

The first relatively expensive piece of equipment was only a Selectric with the different type styles. For headlines I used the special transfer lettering, and I would get them enlarged or reduced for about $300 per issue. Then I got an IBM composer for about $2000. That was a poor purchase since you couldn't correct on it. Then I bought a hand electronic composer and later got a second one. We still use it for all the body copy. They are about $4500 apiece. Then I went to a photo typesetter so I could get rid of the transfer lettering for heads, which was taking me too long, costing $4000. I outgrew that right away because that would do just one long line, so for two lines I had to cut and paste it by hand. I now have a headlining machine, a photo typesetter which does small type all the way up to headlines with centering and flush right or left. These are my main pieces of equipment. Then I have some small ones like a rapidograph pen and different kinds of papers.

The electronic equipment saves me money. I paid cash for them so I don't have any carrying costs. In my case, it would not have been feasible to get any better equipment since we only use it eight days out of the month. The paper got too big to do without electronic equipment, up to 80 pages. I bought used equipment. I am big on getting good second-hand buys.

Problems

The biggest problem to me is that I feel harassed and agitated. I have too much to do. I come in ready to work when the phone rings and a lady takes five minutes to tell me something that should take 60 seconds. The inefficiency of other people bothers me. We are on top of the nonpayers and the late payers.

When I have a person who will not pay, I do everything I can to get the money. We send an invoice, then we send a pink paper.

I read somewhere that pink paper is effective for delinquents, and then the next month I send another one and add a two dollar service charge each time. I don't care whether the law says that it's illegal to add interest. I don't say it's interest. I just say it's a service charge. I then send a demand letter saying pay me within 10 days and tell them I am going to take them to small claims court. I never do it, but I threaten it. I send it in a blank envelope because I found that those people I am dealing with throw it away when they know it's from me.

If they still don't pay, I have a very efficient system. I don't bother the town clerk. I type up a summons for each advertiser that is delinquent for 90 days. I send them to the town clerk, and she has the judge sign them all. I then make a photocopy of each one and mail them again in a blank envelope and usually that gets me my money. Usually the money starts pouring in then. If they still don't pay, I then call to be sure they aren't sick. I make allowances for illness. At this point, I go in and buy something from them, spending a little less than they owe me. Then I stop payment on the check at the bank and send them a letter—again in the blank envelope—and I state in it that I have stopped payment on the check and have instead credited them in full for the long delinquent payment of their account. I'm sorry to do business this way, but they have failed to respond to all of our efforts.

Commission Payment

I have a system regarding paying commissions for ads where I haven't been paid and I am just upgrading it. A former employee of the *Times* gave me an idea. I pay commissions within two weeks. At the same time I keep a running chart of those who haven't paid for their ads for 90 days, so I deduct for these people who haven't paid. I also pay the commissions when I recover bad debts.

I get about four calls a month from clients who say they don't like the ad. That's what I call harassment. If we have made a mistake, and sometimes we do, a typo or leave out something, what we do is offer to do a larger ad for the cost of the smaller size. If it is a full page ad, and the client insists, I give them a free ad.

If we have a problem with design, and I'm getting tough about this, my sales staff is not to come to me but take care of the customer complaint. Now when an advertiser doesn't like the type or the illustration, I tell my sales staff to handle it. I will not make an adjustment, and I don't want to hear about it. We are not an advertising agency. They can pay an agency to get the ad just the way they want it, but as long as they tell me what to do, and we do it, that's it.

A local study showed that the *Country Shopper* pulls better than any other local paper. I have been able to raise my rates every year without any problem. No fewer ads. My sales reps are always afraid it's going to be harder to sell but I've never had a problem. I don't know of anyone afraid to raise costs. All mine have gone up. My boxes of labels have gone from $13 to $23 in the last couple of years. We're all used to paying more.

Payroll

All my employees are paid by the hour or by commission, no salaries. I report only my commissions on W2 forms. I tell the freelancers, it's in my books, and if I'm ever audited, the IRS will see what I paid you, so you'd better pay taxes.

I don't have to pay perks such as withholding. I get employees by advertising in my paper, but more often by word of mouth. One girl told me last week she's moving to London for four years and she's got someone to replace her.

I am a member of the Independent Newspapers of America and the Advertising Clubs of Westchester and Fairfield.

I barter ads for services, especially for restaurants. I have never figured out what it costs me for the ads I take out in barter. Some of them I pay commission on to my sales people, if I ask to trade.

Viewpoints

I have been able to develop this paper because I have the strengths that are needed for this business. But I have my weaknesses: my brashness, impatience, short temper, frankness, and sloppy dress. That doesn't hurt me here. I am good at math, I am highly organized, and I have no problem saying to a customer, I'm sorry, I made a mistake, even when I know I didn't. I'm very happy to lie to keep that customer. I'm a very practical, reasonable person with good business judgment and I'm good at planning. I have always liked to figure out a system. I was terrible at memorizing things, but good at logic, and that is very important in this business. I know how to figure out how many pages we are going to fill. When I take on a new territory, I figure out how much we need to sell there to justify the additional cost of publishing and distributing.

I expect to do this until I am around 60. However, it's not exciting anymore. It's routine, boring, smooth, and predictable. I've got a little more time this year. Now I can work at home a few days a week, which I like. It isn't really challenging anymore but it's gratifying. I am proud of being a publisher. I wasn't proud of being a gym teacher. Now when I say I'm a publisher, people react. There's more respect.

Trade Publications

Editor & Publisher
11 West 19 Street
New York, NY 10027
(212) 675-4380

Publishers' Auxiliary
1627 K Street
Washington, DC 20006
(202) 466-7200

Publishing Trade
464 Central Avenue
Northfield, IL 60093

40

Real Estate Agency

Selling real estate has always been a sound business. With the huge demand for housing expected to continue right into the twenty-first century, it is certain real estate will remain a profitable business. However, it is a sensitive business that can be slowed by high interest rates no matter how many buyers and sellers there are in the market.

Spencer Markatos, owner of the Chris Markatos Real Estate Agency, one of the oldest and biggest in Yorktown Heights, New York, and the surrounding Westchester County area, points out that despite the demand for homes, and, in recent years, condominiums, sales are not always easy to conclude. Matching a buyer to the right house does take experience and skill.

In New York State, only a licensed broker can open a real estate agency. It takes a year of selling before a person can take the broker's exam. During this time, a person is required to take a 45 hour course about the business. Other states have similar requirements.

It is not difficult to get into and fulfill the requirements for becoming a licensed broker. Markatos tells you what it will be like to run your own agency.

Spencer Markatos

I went to American University in Washington, D.C. and got a business degree with a major in real estate. I think I always had it in the back of my mind to work in the business which was started by my family about 31 years ago. It was something that was begun in the kitchen of our home, so I grew up with it. I've been doing this for 16 years.

Licensing

Each state has its own licensing requirements. In New York you have to have been a salesperson for at least one year before applying for your broker's license examination. You fill out a lengthy form listing all the transactions you've been involved with and closings. We encourage our staff to get their broker's license.

There is a certain status involved with being a real estate broker as opposed to being a salesperson. It shows that you have the experience and have furthered your education enough to pass the exam. In the last several years the state has tightened its requirements even for salespeople. As of April 1986, the salesperson has to take a course prior to taking the exam for a broker's license. It's a 45-hour course.

After two or three years in the business, we find that people usually go for their broker's license. The test is a written test. Only licensed brokers or salespeople can legally be paid by a seller. Also, only a licensed person can be a partner in a real estate agency.

Employees

Our profession, from the standpoint of personnel, is probably like any other. Good employees are the absolute backbone of our business. Finding motivated individuals is very difficult. There's not a tremendous amount of turnover. We interview pretty well for the positions here.

Start-Up

Much depends on how you're going to start. If you're going to go out and rent an office, buy furniture, hire a staff of two or three people, be prepared to pay between $40,000 to $50,000. Part of that money is to get your advertising started. The problem with our business is that you can make a sale the first day, but it takes 90 days to get paid. So you need something to fall back on.

I think geography plays a big role in what people expect you to be. In this area if you work out of your home, you won't attract the staff. In Westchester County things are more sophisticated.

You can spend a fortune advertising in the papers and other media each week, but unless you have the staff to handle the inquiries, it's wasted. The most important part of this business is the product, and the product is houses. You can't sell apples from an empty cart. Getting the people to list their house with you keeps the agency going.

We started exclusive listings in this town in 1970. It's good for the broker. If there is a sale of the house from any source, the broker gets part of the fee. It also allows the broker to promote or advertise the house, knowing that at some point he or she will be compensated.

In a nonexclusive listing, an owner will call a number of brokers and say I want to list my house, and the first one that sells it gets the commission. It also means the seller can sell it on his own. The basic commission is the same in both cases.

The Operation

We have about 75 or 100 listings right now. If you want to be in this business you're going to have to make a commitment. It takes up a major part of your life, and the advantage of that is that hopefully you'll be successful and have the money to improve your family's lifestyle.

We have 20 people on staff. That's a huge overhead which is almost fixed. It means almost selling a house a day to meet the overhead. It's a type of business that is controlled by outside conditions. We're tied 100 percent to the cost of money. Right now things are great because the interest rates are about 10 percent. When they're 13, 14, 15, or 16 percent it's tough, and we have no control over that. So you have to try and change your marketing techniques.

There is a buyer for every home. For some houses there are fewer buyers. But eventually everything sells. It depends on size, location, condition. In a normal market, we use historical data to price a house. We'll run a computer printout on houses similar to the one we're looking at in order to determine a realistic, comparable selling price. And then we sit down with the owner and go over the statistical data. Like everyone, if it's your car or your house, yours is always better and it's worth more. Human nature. Setting an appropriate selling price is subject to the emotions of the sellers and those we anticipate from buyers.

Fees are totally negotiable when a sale is involved. We are running now into a shortage so we have a high demand, low supply situation. Consequently prices are increasing dramatically.

Dealing with a seller, there are many things that can happen which we try to avoid. Doors can be left open, lights left on, lack of activity. It's a very stressful situation because your house is literally open to the public. Anxious sellers will call at 9:00 A.M., sometimes daily, demanding that more people be shown the house.

I have a sales manager that handles the deals very well. My asset here is the people who work for me. So trying to keep them happy is a big part of my job.

Hard Work

A lot of people are under the impression that it's an easy business and that you can make a tremendous amount of money with very little effort or expense. Nothing is further from the truth. You have to wear two hats. You're working for the seller, but, at the same time, you're trying to satisfy the buyer.

It's really nice to get a call from somebody after the sale who says gee thanks, we love the house we're in. That's worth a tremendous amount. At the closing, we have happy people. This compensates for the pressure and concern that went into making the deal. But you can't rely on yesterday's business.

Trade Publications

Real Estate Today
430 North Michigan Avenue
Chicago, IL 60611
(312) 329-8268

Real Estate Weekly
One Madison Avenue
New York, NY 10010
(212) 329-8268

Real Estate Magazine
415 North State Street
Chicago, IL 60610
(312) 644-7800

41

Real Estate Investments

Not only is there a boom in the sale of residential housing throughout the country, but there is a growing demand by people for real estate properties they can acquire purely for investment purposes.

Shelley Richman, formerly an instructor of English at a community college, when ready for an entrepreneurial venture became a real estate investment coordinator.

While she operates out of her home in Scarsdale, New York, she does have access to her attorney husband's real estate office when needed.

A business that will surely grow substantially in the future is this one—finding properties for interested investors. Actually, this business has also developed from the search for ways to make savings earn more than keeping them in a money market fund.

Buying a condominium or a house and reselling it a few years later for a big profit is attracting an increasing number of people. Here's how it is done.

Shelley Richman

I was in academia for 12 years. I did it part-time because I had children. I could teach and also be home with my children. I have a BA and an MA in English with a specialty in American literature. I like teaching literature.

I left academia to go into business. I shifted because I got bored. After a while, it's boring. I was teaching the same things. I think there is a similarity between academia and selling. When you teach, you are selling. You are selling a concept. You are selling an idea.

Starting

A friend of mine that had a clothing store selling very expensive goods asked me if I would like to sell one day a week. I did and I liked it. It didn't make any difference what I was selling. I could sell. I sold at this place one day a week for one season. And then they wanted me to come full-time. I did not want to do anything full-time. When you are a parent and you have two teenagers and a husband that make demands on you, it is difficult. You are torn between your children, your husband, and what you would like to do.

Then I started a dating service which was conducted by appointment only. This little business grew so much that it became too much for us to handle. It became a full-time business. We sold it after a year. But, I learned about accounting and advertising. I learned about working with clients and how to handle paperwork. If I had gone to school to learn how to initiate a business, I could not have gotten this hands-on education. I learned much more than I ever suspected.

Confidence

Most important, I learned what is needed to go into any sales oriented business, whether it is selling a gross of pencils or selling six months worth of dates. You have to understand how to handle people and to close a deal. No matter how much information you have, and no matter how congenial you are with people, unless you know when to close, you'll never make a sale. And I found that education, learning how to close, the most fascinating part of business.

What came next was that my husband asked me to work in his real estate business. Real estate was a booming business and expected to remain that way indefinitely. Also, I was not going to sell homes but to find profitable properties for people who wanted to invest.

I took a 12-week course in real estate where I met lots of people in the business. You can learn a lot from them. At the end of the course, I passed the test and became a licensed real estate agent.

Investment Real Estate

As I work with investors, I concentrate on areas where the real estate is going up in leaps. The people who come into the office are in this for short term. That is for about five years or less. I look for good investments in the newspapers and in the *Multiple Listing Service* book. Through the business, I have met a lot of people. And I call people to get leads. Brokers have properties and I have the clients. Whenever a good property came up for sale that I considered a good investment, I bought it with a good faith check. If the property costs $50,000, I put up $500. The check is made out to the broker. It's never cashed. It says that the buyer is very sincere. I move quickly.

Evaluation

I have certain criteria that I look for. The location of the property is the most important. It should be near transportation or a parkway. People buying apartments, condominiums, and co-ops want a good location. They don't want to travel 20 minutes to get to a parkway. So, location, meaning accessible transportation, is very important.

Also, the properties I acquire for my investors are usually in luxury buildings, with a 24-hour doorman. Other pluses are: indoor garages, balconies, and good views. For my investors to make the maximum profit when selling a $150,000 or $200,000 apartment, the buyer should have a parking space in a garage. There should be a doorman to take packages and to announce visitors. That's security. You have to look for specific things because as the property goes up in value, the amenities become essential. They're not extras. They are basics because your investor client expects this property to appreciate substantially.

I sell mainly condos and co-ops, not houses. I could buy houses that I thought were good investments. However, my clients are modest investors who want to walk away and forget about the property they own until they sell it. In a co-op, the maintenance is provided. You pay common charges. In a condo, you basically pay your own way. But in many condos, especially if the condo is within a building, there are people who work there who can maintain it.

Clients

I have a list of clients who want me to call them as soon as I get something suitable. Usually about 30 people. When I get a property, I make it available to everybody. I call them up, because good properties sell immediately and you don't find them usually advertised in newspapers. It's word of mouth. Good stuff never gets into the public domain. Recently I got a property from a broker on a Monday and sold it by Wednesday. By the time her ads were in the paper, it was gone. I sold it in one day.

Most of my buyers are first time investors. I know their financial situations, sometimes more than their spouses know. I must know exactly the cash they have to put up and what their income level is. These are really committed investors who believe in us because my husband and I are also personally buying and selling properties. We explain from personal experience as well what has to be done and what to expect. Often we can tell a client that we own an apartment in the building where he will be acquiring his investment condo. This has tremendous impact upon creating client confidence.

Client Concerns

The hardest part is doing it the first time. People are scared. All they can think about is putting up this cash and getting a tenant that will cover the mortgage and maintenance. I never put my clients into properties that cannot be rented. It takes from 8 to 10 weeks to rent the property. It depends upon the property. If it remains empty, it is refurbished during this period of time. I try to find properties that need almost no work. The rent basically covers maintenance and the mortgage. The investor might have to pay an additional amount that qualifies as a tax write-off. This might change with the proposed tax revisions.

Some people want to sell after six months and a day. I had a young client, 28, who had $15,000. I told him I would never find him anything. As it turned out, I located a studio apartment for $65,000. On a $65,000 investment, he had to put up about $13,000, which is the minimum of 20 percent, plus closing costs. He bought the property for $65,000 and said to me immediately, sell this in six months and a day. Meanwhile, I rented it for him for $700 a month. I told him I could sell it, and he would make $15,000. He told me he was going to hold on to it. He has not sold the property. I had just sold a similar property for $82,000. But he knew that by waiting he'd make much more money.

Every property I have sold has increased substantially. I dare not put anybody into speculative properties. Because eventually I want my clients to come back to me to sell their properties. I think timing is everything. The market right now is very good. My real forte is that I'm fast and I can zero in on the property that will give a higher yield, but the investor will have to do the least amount of work.

Tips

You have to build a relationship of credibility with people. This develops into trust. Someone who has been in real estate for many years and has built a following is an ideal candidate for this kind of business. You have to genuinely enjoy working with people. And you have to believe in what you're selling. The toughest thing is convincing a client to buy quickly. Investment property is grabbed up. People don't realize how much money there is out there for investment. I have had too many misses, because people would say "next week." Next week would come and the property was gone.

I would definitely say I will remain in this business for the next 10 years, at least. According to what I have read, this boom market will continue until the year 2000. And, remember, my success is not based on financial earnings. My success is that I was able to go from one field successfully into another. I am dealing with modest investors who really want someone to lead them by the hand, and I do that. Anyone that wants to go into business and not have to punch a clock should consider investment real estate. Also, the earnings are great.

Trade Publications

Apartment Owner/Builder
3220 East Willow
Long Beach, CA 90806
(213) 424-8674

National Real Estate Investor
6255 Barfield Road
Atlanta, GA 30228
(404) 256-9800

Real Estate Today
430 North Michigan Avenue
Chicago, IL 60611
(312) 329-8268

42

Restaurant

This is without question one of the highest risk businesses in the country. The failure rate is horrendous. But there are successes, substantial ones and those who triumph more modestly. However, this is not a venture for an inexperienced person who loves food and the public and thinks he or she can acquire all the skills needed just by owning a dining establishment.

Dieter Schramm learned every aspect of restaurant management starting in his native Germany where food service is a demanding and respected skill. After he came to the United States he worked at every level of the restaurant business from waiter to captain. In between, he learned how to cook as well, and that was one reason he survived in his own business and succeeded.

For those who want a modest establishment in the city or suburbs, Schramm's how-he-did-it story is not just inspirational, it is highly informative. From portion control to employees, he explains exactly what to expect in the restaurant business.

Owner of Lakeside Rest, Yorktown Heights, New York, he tells how he converted a run-down, diner-type place into an elegant German-American restaurant.

Dieter Schramm

I got my restaurant training in Germany. It was not something I wanted to do as a young person. I had no choice at the time. My father was a general contractor and wanted me to be a mason. After World War II there were few opportunities in Germany. I did it all, from bartender to manager. I really learned all parts of the business, including being a waiter, for over 20 years before I started my own business.

However, when I left my last job, I had no intention of going into business for myself. I always thought it was too much of a headache and didn't really want to risk my savings on a restaurant. Let someone else take the risk. But then a situation came along that seemed favorable and affordable that I could build up myself. I decided to take a chance.

The restaurant was known as a kind of a diner when the previous owner ran it. It was very much neglected. Maintenance was postponed for 15 years. I did a lot of the work myself such as renovating the kitchen and converting it into an upbeat, elegant restaurant.

Costs

The bank will not give you any money for a restaurant because of the high risk. After the first year 80 percent fail. Most of the remaining 20 percent close within the next five years. There is really not much of a success ratio. One reason is that people overpay, especially when they don't buy the property. They might have a lease that calls for $100,000 up front for the business, plus a rental of perhaps $2,000 to $3,000 depending on the square footage. Then when there is not enough business to generate enough cash flow to cover all expenses, you go out of business.

There's nothing else. If you buy the property, at least you have it to sell. I just bought the property. There are sources that specialize in restaurant financing. They can be found in the trade publication *The Restaurant Exchange News*. I took over the financing that existed already. There were a couple of mortgages on it and I took out another private mortgage—not through the bank. I knew you can only get more from a bank after you are in business for a while, once they know you are safe and don't need them anymore. The vice president of the Bank of New York walked in here and said, you're doing a great job, and then asked if I needed some operating capital. I told him not anymore.

The seating capacity is about 50. On hectic days about 55 to 60. Most of the reconstruction was done myself and it saved me a tremendous amount of money. I opened the refurbished restaurant in 1980.

Promotion

About 80 percent of our business is through recommendations, word of mouth, and, of course, repeaters. Advertising I do selectively. Right now I advertise just to remind people to come in. It runs a lot better once you are established than when you are trying to convince people you are worth trying. For example, I have Sunday specials such as roast leg of lamb and roast pork. That will bring in about 20 to 30 extra people on a Sunday afternoon when it is normally slow. Specials are very helpful. Blackboard specials are important whether they are on the menu or the waitress is reciting them to customers. When you have a lot of regulars, they like to see something different once in a while. Also, it's psychological with people. They believe if you have a special, it must be something better. If you have an item on the menu that is a slow mover, and then offer it as a special, it will take off.

I offered a free bottle of wine for a dinner for two and it was amazing how many people came in for that bottle of wine. Again, when we opened up, it was slow. Advertising doesn't do too much if people don't know you. Then you need dining incentives—a glass of wine, beer, or a free dessert. Once you get busy, you drop it. There's no point in giving things away. So gradually you change the advertising. Of course, the local paper is the most economical advertising medium. Once you have a good reputation, you don't have these special offers. In fact, I feel it cheapens your image. People feel that there must be something wrong with your place if you have a special for $6.95.

Employees

It was only myself and my wife for the first six months. I cooked and my wife was the waitress. We had another waitress on the weekends and someone for dishwashing and cleaning up as well.

We employ young people to work in the back. Some do a little cooking such as the potato pancakes to learn a marketable trade. Also, they prepare appetizers, salads, desserts. I advertise to get personnel, but there isn't much response. It's hard to get help for the lower paying jobs in the restaurant business. If you go to a shopping center, you will see help wanted signs. This is for youngsters without high school diplomas. Kids are usually not too interested in working. One big hamburger chain offers about $5.00 per hour and still has about 300 percent labor turnover a year. I pay $5.00 an hour, but they want to work here because it's more of a personal atmosphere than a place where they have to wear a uniform and work in a hectic environment. Here, it is more flexible. The cold kitchen gets busy, and the dishwasher turns around and runs over there and helps out with desserts, whatever is necessary. It's more interesting than just doing burgers and french fries.

I have no problem getting high school students. On occasion, I get college students. But they only stay for the summer and I have to hire and train again. I have one boy who has worked here for three years. He lives across the street. The others are here for about a year. We train them ourselves. And of course, the critical person is the chef. The cooking is, of course, a major factor in a restaurant. We had a problem with one and let him go. A lot of people will not complain, they will simply say today things aren't up to standard. They can easily go to a different restaurant and not come back. When I had the problem with the chef who was drinking, I lost customers. It was advanced alcoholism. I put him in the hospital several times. He actually cooked rotten fish without realizing it. He'd make a pot of soup, and three weeks later put it on the stove and start serving it. I had to do the cooking until I found the right chef. As owner, it's good if you can do the basics such as preparing your menu. In an emergency, I can do the cooking. The Chef's Association and the Restaurant Association can be called to get a chef.

Training

A lot of restaurants will take people in to learn without pay. If someone wants to hang around the kitchen to see what a chef does all day long, they don't mind. Many people work for nothing for a few weeks just to get some hands-on experience. You don't do the cooking, but you do get an idea of what it is all about. Chefs don't mind people doing that as long as they don't interfere.

I get flyers in the mail about courses given by very experienced people. Every little bit can help. You need to know food costs, calculations, payroll, things like that. I took business administration in college, but not because I thought it was necessary for the restaurant. Actually, the GI bill paid for it.

Food Supplies and Costs

The key is getting the right supplies because you want quality. The price is important too, but generally you have to pay for quality. To get a bargain is not worth it. Cutting corners will show up in your preparation and quality of meats and fish. The basic law is to rotate your food, whether it's lettuce or anything else. Whenever you get a new shipment in, you put the oldest up front. You are responsible for all of the food you are putting out.

Your portion size is strictly a food cost control. Your food costs should be around 30 percent. If you can keep it lower, fine, but the portion itself in a good restaurant should not outweigh the fact that people have to be satisfied with the meal. If you want to bring your food costs down to 20 percent by serving a five ounce steak, the customer will be very dissatisfied. My restaurant is 30 percent as is the industry average. Labor costs shouldn't exceed 40 percent. You now have 30 percent left for your other costs which are rent, insurance, and, then, hopefully a profit.

Bar Sales

When you run a dinner restaurant, your bar sales are about 20 to 25 percent of your total sales. With the crackdown on drunk driving, a lot of groups will select a driver who might drink only Coke or some other alcohol-free beverage. There is an increasing sense of responsibility by the public. I don't feel that I've been hurt at all because my sales didn't decrease. They are still the same percentage in relationship to the food. A lot of places have declined in bar sales. The ones that got hurt were the places with heavy emphasis on drinking.

Bar sales are important because your profit margin is better. First of all, the labor cost is not there; there is one person making the drinks. You don't need a chef, you don't need a dishwasher, you just run the glasses through the machine. The profit margin is about 200 to 300 percent. Your bar runs around 25 percent. The best profit item is wine which has become very popular. Industry-wise, liquor has dropped back, whereas imported beers and wines have increased. The consumer has become more aware of the fact that a good bottle of wine with dinner is a delight. With wine, you rarely have any intoxicated people. When you have the wine with dinner, the absorption of the food slows down the alcohol impact, very different from someone who has two or three drinks.

Growth

We were profitable from the very beginning. That is because our labor costs were practically nonexistent. It was a family thing. We gradually built it up without any loan money. We had the cash flow that we created ourselves. I only needed to break even at about 80 dinners a week. Naturally, as your payroll increases, you hire a chef and another assistant and another employee. You need more volume. Today we have reached 250 dinners a week. Of course, the profit picture looks much better. In the first year we averaged about 120. We are now pretty much at our limit because most days we are filled up, Saturdays especially. We have to turn away people.

Seasons

In the winter, January and February, business drops about 15 percent. If we have a major snowstorm, we will be knocked out for the day or maybe even two days if the roads are not cleared. It's not as seasonal as the New Jersey shore might be. It depends on your location. We are basically a year-round business. We are in the middle of a lot of suburban towns. On the average, we get people within a radius of 15 to 20 miles. Some weekends, we even get people from New York City. Usually they come here through word of mouth. Some people have weekend homes up here. We are running pretty much up to maximum.

Insurance

The liquor liability insurance tripled in one year and they cut the coverage in half. The fire insurance and product liability went up about a little more than double in one year. Not only that, some of the insurance companies go broke. For example, I had just paid my premium for the full year and two weeks later I got a letter from New York State that my insurance company had been ordered to liquidate. I was then on a waiting list to try to get my premium back. I had to hurry and try to get another company.

We use an independent broker because he has more choices. There again, it pays to shop around. At that time, I didn't have the time to shop around, and I probably could have gotten a better deal if I did. Because so many restaurants go up in flames, this is a high risk business to insure. I am insured for $100,000 in fire insurance, even though I could never replace this building for twice the amount. That is all they would give me. In fact, it's really only $80,000 because they only cover 80 percent. That insurance, plus the liability, costs about $8000 a year. It actually adds one dollar to every dinner. My overall insurance costs are close to $10,000.

Since I started six years ago, the insurance costs have gone up four times more. One reason that the company went broke was that they used to write policies for three years which kept the premiums low. Now they have such big losses that the New York State Insurance Commission which oversees those troubled companies forces the ones in the red to merge or liquidate. I never got my premium back. I'm not holding my breath either.

Routine

I love the business. If you don't love it, you have to get out of it. It's crazy hours. Your weekends are shot. Your family gets neglected. That's the reason that we have labor problems. People don't want to work in this business. They would rather do something with regular hours.

If I opened for lunch, I would have to increase my payroll. Being that I employ mostly kids here, it would be difficult except in the summer, which is not a good lunch period anyway. I would most likely hire some South Americans or illegal aliens. They are around by the hordes. All they want is room and board, which I can't provide. I prefer not to, because then I would have to lock everything up.

Another reason I hesitate is that I have limited parking. Most of the lunch crowd is made up of singles. To get 40 people in, I would have 40 cars. I only have room for 22. The profit margin for lunch is not that high. I just don't want to put in the time anymore. I make my living and I would rather spend a few hours with my daughter. If it were a necessity, I would do it.

You can't predict this business. You might not have anyone until 7:30 and suddenly the dining room fills up. Weekdays it's busy from 6:30 on and weekends from 7:00 on. People like to sit around more on Sundays, but not that much on Fridays or Saturdays.

Trade Publications

Restaurant Exchange News
PO Box 473
New City, NY 10956
(914) 638-1108

Restaurant Business
633 Third Avenue
New York, NY 10017
(212) 986-4800

Nation's Restaurant News
425 Park Avenue
New York, NY 10022
(212) 371-9400

43

Sign Painting

Breck Morgan, owner of the Morgan Sign Company, Norwalk, Connecticut, is a sensitive man with all the vision and ambition of a talented artist. But skill and desire to create magnificent paintings are not the substance of survival. The realistic needs of living make dreams vanish swiftly.

Fresh out of art school, Morgan had a brief encounter with the heady world of art. A gallery in New York City provided him with commissions to paint murals. It spawned a new direction for his craft. Doing large size art work fascinated and satisfied him. He decided that to earn a steady living and not rely on mural commissions, the big picture appealed to him.

In 1974, Morgan started his sign company in a small room over a pizza parlor. While it was an aromatic beginning, it did indeed turn out to be a very successful future.

Now more administrator than sign painter, having several employees on staff, Morgan enthusiastically points out the special joy of sign painting. "As an artist, you know that more people will see your outdoor work in one day than would ever come to a showing at an art gallery."

This is his story—one that can be duplicated by people with comparable ability.

Breck Morgan

Before starting up my sign company, I had been trained as an artist. I was going to be the next great abstract expressionist. Of course, when I got out of school I quickly discovered how difficult it was just to get a job. At any rate, I took construction jobs, worked on oyster boats, cut trees, and various other things. I finally got assignments from some advertising agencies that were related to my skills.

After that, there was a period of about a year and a half when I was painting murals down in New York. I did have a gallery connection for a while and they provided me with a number of different mural commissions. I thoroughly enjoyed it. This was one of the things that I was most interested in doing when I was in school. Painting murals was something that I always wanted to do.

Beginning

I started my business in 1976 in a small room that I rented over a pizza parlor. I had a telephone, a bench, and some brushes. Incidentally, I had worked for a sign company for about two years after painting murals, and truthfully, it was the first job I really enjoyed. It was a combination of the physical and artistic. You had to cut, prime, and paint wood, know three-dimensional objects, decorate and letter them. It was not as two-dimensional as design work in an art studio.

There is also a quality about sign painting that I feel very strongly about: it is very much like an outdoor art gallery. This is the kind of feeling I have about painting, and it shows in the pieces that I make now. It's something that thousands of people a week will see. It's probably the highest amount of visibility you can get as a commercial artist.

Start-Up Costs

The approximate start-up cost was about $300. The deposit I had to put down on the studio was about $150, and then another $100 for materials and a telephone. The reason it was a modest start-up amount was due to the machinery I had already owned such as a small jigsaw, hammers, several hand tools, and a small skillsaw.

Promotion

The first thing I did was have a bunch of business cards printed that I distributed personally to everybody on North Main Street. In this way I picked up a small amount of work that kept me going for a while. I continued to distribute my business cards and work came in. I would drive around in the afternoons, and every time I saw a store that was opening up, I would stop and leave business cards.

I also called customers that I had done work for at other sign companies to see if they needed anything. It was basically business cards and walking around to see merchants. I made up a banner that I had hung over the sidewalk promoting my business. The first two or three months was a very anxious period of time because I had never been without a steady paycheck. Now I was an entrepreneur who needed customers. That paycheck at the end of each week—I never realized how much security that meant. The simple equation is clients mean income now. It was always a surprise to me when people would call on the phone and want something done. I was surprised when people would walk through the door. I was always amazed that there were customers needing work done who would come to me. Each one, in the beginning, was a very special gift.

Building Business

I made a profit on pretty much the first job. That was not much of a concern. There was always enough profit, at least in terms of making as much or more money than I did when I was working for other people. I never made less than I earned when I was employed.

But, I had to first cover my overhead. I realized quickly that I had to do this by improving the quality of my work so that I could be competitive with any other sign painter in the area. To some extent, it required tools, but it mostly required skill. Sign painting, sign lettering, specifically, which is what I developed and became very good at, was a skill that requires a number of years of concentrated effort to achieve. It was a matter of just doing it over and over again until finally I could spell the word "school" with both Os looking the same; all of the block letters standing up exactly right; and the strokes flowing perfectly out of the brush.

Up until then, you are constantly struggling. I know a lot of people who never get beyond that. They work with it up to a year, a year and a half sometimes, but they are always struggling. They finally make the decision that it's not worth it because it never becomes easy for them. There are a lot of sign painters who never get beyond that frustration stage. It's really exhilarating when you master something. It's one of the few things in my life that I feel I have genuinely mastered. It's very exciting. It took about three years before I felt I could do anything comfortably, from show cards to paper signs, boats, window lettering, to gold leaf. I'm still not a master at gold leaf. But I'll get there.

Outlook

I was 29 years old when I started, hesitant and uncertain but hopeful. My feeling is that if you have the right attitude, do it. It's 100 percent attitude. You can succeed and fulfill your ambition. You will survive if you focus all of your energies on your objective.

You have to learn how to adjust and balance yourself to be able to provide things that are needed in the situation that you expect to stay in. At this point, I'm sure that with $500, someone could find a room someplace. They could open the door and start developing a clientele. Sign painting is the kind of business that is a skilled service. I have a feeling that everybody needs it, sometime. There are continuing clients and a lot of businesses that come and go. Even when going out of business, a sign is needed. And a new business usually needs several storefront signs.

Building Business

I did place a couple of small ads in the *Norwalk Hour* newspaper. I got a few customers amounting to over a week's work. It wasn't worth it for me because I was trying to keep the expenses down to a minimum. I started acquiring more business from word of mouth, so that the ad wasn't necessary a second time.

The slack periods in this particular business come in January and February. I have found that if I start telling customers in November or December that if they can give me projects during the slow times, I could give them a price break. Some are willing to wait up to three months if they can save $200 or $300. This incentive has usually carried me through the slack periods. Also, this is catch-up time for me. It gives us a chance to take a deep breath and to organize tools, replace those that are getting old, do repairs, or projects like shelf building.

Location

I moved into my present location five years ago. I realized after five years on North Main Street that the neighborhood was changing. It is being upgraded all the time, and I felt this was going to force me to move as I am in a building that is becoming more valuable as office space.

Fortunately, I moved in here five years ago having a lease with the option to buy. That made the first two years hard. Every week there was money put aside for the payments on the building. Within two years I managed to save the down payment and bought the building. It then took about two years to recover from the expenses of the purchase. It was only last summer that I became financially able to put the offices in and start upgrading.

Staff

I had five employees five years ago that included a secretary, a designer/pattern maker, and a full-time letterer. Among the 14 employees today, 2 people work the shop; 1 is primarily involved with cutting, priming and painting, and doing the woodworking; the others handle the installations, the physical construction of the signs, the lettering, and other chores.

I have two people in the office, and a designer who is also the general manager; several people work in the graphics department that produces computer graphics and patterns from a graphics computer. The computer saved me an enormous amount of time and increased business volume. I get employees through advertising in local newspapers and recommendations from friends. Some from art school. Some were people I knew from the neighborhood. Now, most of the staff is hired from ads.

Problems

The hardest problem of all, I think, is lack of communication. It's all a matter of not clearly understanding either what the client wanted, or not listening well enough. That's our job—to give customers exactly what they want. The advertising agency taught me a lot about graphic design, type selection—a whole understanding of visual impact. That was something that it provided. Doing it right the first time is something that I learned in the process of providing signs that had the wrong color or background. I never wanted to make that mistake again because you redo the entire job for nothing.

You need a clear understanding of the price from the start, and should learn how to deal with the business aspect of this kind of artistry. You should have written specifications, a contract, and a deposit. You must have certain standard business forms. There's a routine you go through that guarantees both people are fully aware of what the exchange is about. How much are they going to get? How much are they going to pay for it? And in what stages in the process? You'll learn after making a lot of mistakes over a period of time. Even today, there are still jobs that are new, that are a little larger than something I've handled before, so you set up as many of the forms as you can and try to make things clear. In the process of doing that, there are always little things you might miss and so you wind up negotiating the grey areas.

The ultimate goal is always to make sure that the client is happy when the transaction is completed. There are certain clients who are more difficult to please than others, and my option the second or third time around, if it continues to be unpleasant, is to drop them or to raise the prices to a point where it's worth the extra time. But, from the beginning everyone goes in with a full amount of trust, assuming that everything is going to work out right.

Outlook

My business is still small enough to feel family-like. If it gets very large, it will get fragmented. I won't like that. I've read about businesses which go beyond a certain level, and they start losing the family feeling because they don't have the time to know everybody or to understand what the people around them are like. At that point many sell the business or do something else since they want to have an intimate business and not necessarily be running a major corporation. I'm not interested in building a business empire. I want something comfortable. If I add another five employees, and feel it's still manageable, then we'll stay at that level. It's all a matter of continuing to enjoy our work.

Professional Associations

There is no national association, but there is a Connecticut Sign Association that I belong to. To be honest, I haven't been going to the meetings. I went to five or six a number of years ago when I first joined. It's unfortunate because I hear they're doing some much more interesting things now than they were then. They are having more demonstrations of new techniques and new products. They're also more involved in some of the techniques of craftsmanship.

One of the things that tends to happen is that there are so many different kinds of sign companies. It's almost like printers who have big machines or small machines, one-man operations, or monster shops that can produce the *New York Times*—too many levels. It's the same in the sign industry. There are one-man shops with very high quality craftspeople, and there are companies with 50 or 100 people working for them that do very large construction projects. Then the association expands into outdoor advertising, which is a separate thing altogether. It's just classified under signs. It's up to the individual to decide if joining any association is helpful.

Hours

I work about 10 or 12 hours a day on pretty much a 5½-day week. When I first started, I was putting in 16 to 18 hours a day, and it was almost 7 days a week for years. I would occasionally take a Sunday off and sometimes a weekend, which was a major luxury. The shop closes for a week at the end of August, and I usually take my vacation then. I've been extending that now to about a week and a half, sometimes two weeks.

Tips

There is almost no way to predict what to avoid. If it hurts, figure it out and don't do it twice. The most important thing is to not worry about what to avoid because there are endless lists of those things that you discover automatically by being in the business. The most important thing is to actually take the first step and start. There are more people that I know, friends, who continually talk about the possibility of opening up their own place and setting up their own shop and becoming a cabinetmaker, or a freelance graphic artist, because they're tired of doing paste-ups for a large company. And it's scary. It's a very anxious period of time. I think that the benefits are well worth it.

A lot of people don't have the temperament to want to work that hard to make it. And there are responsiilities. The responsibility of meeting the payroll the minute you have an employee is there. You may be able to get by during rough times with creditors who will let you go for a month and a half, even though that's not a good idea because you need your suppliers, but employees have to be paid without fail. There are no excuses.

I learned this by having a guy I knew very well start coming in full-time. He became my first employee. He had been working freelance a little bit here and there and it got to a point where he really needed a full-time job. I told him that I would provide that. I got involved with the taxes and the payroll and the employer identification number and all of the bookkeeping. That's all part of the process. A friend of mine had an accountant, and I felt it was time to get someone professional looking at my books.

What tends to happen is that if you do jump in the way I did, and you're alone in the beginning, things are still small and don't affect a lot of people. Your mistakes are still small. It's a fascinating process. I believe that when you need something it will be there.

When I needed an accountant, I asked someone and got one. When I outgrew him, I found someone else. There were a lot of pieces of information, parts of the puzzle, that came together almost automatically. You will see solutions to almost everything.

Pleasures

What I enjoyed most is the achievement of mastering lettering. That was a major feeling of accomplishment. I've gotten beyond the point of doing the work myself. Now most of my work is involved with administration. Right now it's something that I'm determined to master. It's difficult because it involves a whole different set of ideas and operational procedures. I have to start thinking in more abstract, functional terms. I have to start organizing in a way that I never before have been forced to do.

Thinking in terms of procedures, getting from one point to another so that I can figure out how a job is supposed to be produced, and then give a blueprint, a layout, and a plan and program so that someone else can actually produce a piece of work. There is an enormous amount of time spent figuring out what is the best way of accomplishing each task. It's a challenge that I have to perform. I am learning to enjoy it as I become more skilled at it. I'm faced with the same frustration at times that I had when I was trying to letter. It seemed then that lettering was as far away as being the great abstract expressionist that I wanted to be. But I'm getting administration under control.

I feel that at some point I'm going to have to go back to painting, with a little more discipline than what I had. The art school that I went to was extremely good in basics and setting up ways of approaching ideas, but it did not provide the day to day discipline on how to actually make a physical product. I'm still figuring out a mental approach. At some point, I'm going back to pure art. Right now, I must function on a financial level that is capable of supporting my children and family.

Approval

Feedback from the public is what I am most proud of. My brother is an entertainer; he's a songwriter and he said that there is an urge in our family that is probably different from others that really need large crowds to approve. In that sense, I think that one of the things I'm proud of is that the company has produced some pieces that are improvements for the neighborhood, that people are happy with, that they feel good about. There is a dialogue, an engagement, a feeling that we are, as a group, trying to produce the highest quality work we can. That, I think, was also something that was missing when working in a studio. There wasn't that contact or feedback. It was a very solitary kind of existence. I was not connecting on a wider sphere. I need that.

Trade Publications

Signs of the Times
407 Gilbert Avenue
Cincinnati, OH 45202
(513) 421-2050

Communication Arts
Box 10300
Palo Alto, CA 94303
(415) 326-6040

Specialty Advertising Business
1404 Walnut Hill Lane
Irving, TX 75038
(214) 258-0404

44

Stationery Store

While stationery stores do nearly half of their business with walk-in customers, the rest of their revenue comes from providing office supplies to commercial establishments.

The story of Sol Kreitman, who owns Westco Stationery Store, Yorktown Heights, New York, provides just as much guidance about the "don'ts" as well as the "dos" to succeed.

A business where there is a choice of over 200,000 items to place in stock that must be paid for within 30 to 90 days, depending on the credit you are given, requires substantial capitalization. Also, as Kreitman points out, if you don't get out into the marketplace to prospect for new accounts, which he and his partner rarely did, you can still earn a living but never really build a very profitable business. Here are Sol Kreitman's mistakes and guidelines.

Sol Kreitman

I started as a typewriter cleaner working for a large office supply and service company in New York City in 1946 when I was 18 years old. I washed and overhauled the typewriters.

Later I was promoted to office supply salesman. After being with the company for 22 years, I moved my family out of the city to the suburbs and decided to open a stationery store with a friend of mine. In 1968 we found a failing candy store that would be easily converted into an office supply store and bought it.

Start-Up

We started the business badly undercapitalized, something I do not recommend anybody ever consider doing. We paid $4000 cash for the store and got notes for the balance of the purchase for 10 years. This, too, was unheard of, as normally notes run from three to five years. In fact, when the attorney for the seller heard about the 10 year note arrangement, he told his client to forget the deal. But the store owner wanted out.

What helped us overcome our lack of capital was that we had New York City clients as salesmen that remained with us when we converted the store into stationery and office supplies. Also, since we knew suppliers from our association with the large office supply company, we were given a generous amount of time to pay for our inventory, sometimes as much as 190 days.

We were able to earn a living from the business, but with the payments on the notes it never really increased to much more than that for two people. Keep in mind, we have a large store and a huge basement for our stock and that means rental of about $30,000 a year. Since my partner retired in September 1985, I have been able to take more out of the business.

Making It

In order for us to survive, we worked seven days a week, which still is the policy of the store, to open every day of the week. We needed the cash flow that came from the walk-in people who buy everything from envelopes to typewriter ribbons. Adequate capitalization in this business is critical. It has been estimated that a stationery store has to choose from over 200,000 items to stock for its customers. Money is needed to keep a substantial inventory of supplies so you don't ever have to tell a customer you don't have what he wants.

Anyone getting into the business today must allocate about $70,000 to keep the right amount of inventory on hand for customers. For example, when I order paper, it has to be in six or eight different colors. There is also, as people know, a whole range of various typewriter ribbons that we must carry fitting just about any machine sold today, as well as the old ones. Lack of capitalization meant loss of discount buying, and not being able to pay bills promptly meant a certain amount of savings quick bill payers can get was lost.

Business Development

We have always advertised in the *Pennysaver* publication and still do. This is the best medium for us. We have tried radio and local newspapers.

We do rely heavily on passing traffic as people come in for ledgers, typing paper, and other items of this kind. Here's where we have our cash flow business that has helped us survive our poor capital situation.

We did go out and get several company accounts in the area as it began to build up with discount stores, travel agencies, personnel agencies, and lots of new shops. However, I still go into the city where I service accounts that I have had for nearly 25 years. They remained with me although I'm in the suburbs. It doesn't matter to them as long as they get what they want right after it is ordered. In fact, from the day Westco was started our in-city clients kept us in business.

Costs

Rents are high in the newer locations in this area of Westchester County. In the places just built, rents range from $30 a square foot and up. At my place it goes for about $25 a square foot. However, my lease is up next year, just when my business is really getting underway in a profitable sense.

Actually, this business turned around when my partner retired last September. Up to then we made a living but were not really a truly profitable operation. It's better now and should continue in the future since I am the sole proprietor.

This certainly could be a good business for someone who is aggressive and goes out and gets accounts. We just were not strong on selling although it's a must. Accounts are lost and must be replaced. We just did not have the drive to increase the commercial business.

Operation

Westco is opened every day of the year except one, and that is on the Jewish high holy day.

I have two full-time employees and usually have three part-time, mostly students. I even hired a salesman to open new accounts, but he ended up going into business for himself.

The new stores are competition rather than sources of new business. The discount places like Caldor carry stationery supplies that I have and even some of the larger drug stores have envelopes, pads and pens, and other stationery items.

Of course, we have charge accounts for our commercial clients and for individuals who buy a minimum of $150 a month. I've had no problem collecting. In 22 years I might have lost about $1000 to nonpayers.

Outlook

I feel the business will be better without a partner as I work my way. I have cut my inventory down and I know what to discount and what moves and doesn't. I don't have to guess anymore. A partner might have to be convinced to do what is best for the business. Different points of view.

Tips

Watch out when buying electronic equipment that soon will be outdated or produced for less money through advanced technology. I've been stuck with calculators that I have bought for $30 and within a year were selling at the discount stores for $10 below my cost. One large calculator I bought for $150 is selling for about one-third the price today.

However, the business itself is a good investment. If I were to sell this place I would get six figures for it. A bit more than what we paid for the store 18 years ago.

Trade Publications

Geyer's Office Dealer
51 Madison Avenue
New York, NY 10010
(212) 689-4411

Office World News
645 Stewart Avenue
Garden City, NY 11530
(516) 222-2500

Office Products Dealer
Hitchcock Boulevard
Wheaton, IL 60187
(312) 665-1000

45

Talent Manager (Children)

There are no union guidelines or legal requirements for a person who wants to function as a talent manager. That is why only agents who meet certain requirements can become franchised by the Screen Actors Guild, the American Federation of Radio and Television Artists or Actors Equity. People functioning as managers cannot.

Managers cannot solicit work for performers in television commercials, TV series, or movies. It has to be done through a licensed agent. Then what is the purpose of a talent manager?

To cope with the enormous demand for children in show business, especially for TV commercials. Managers serve as a supplemental resource for agents. When a call comes to an agent's office for a child with precise specifications in size and appearance, the agent searches first through his or her files to locate a suitable child. If, for various reasons, none is available, a call is made to talent managers.

If the child from the manager's office gets the commercial, the agent receives a 10 percent commission and the manager 15 percent.

Sandra Firestone, owner of Studio V. Management, Inc., New York City, for over 10 years, explains how it is done.

Sandra Firestone

Before I started Studio V., from the time I got out of college, I had a number of office jobs, got married and had two children.

When I was ready to go back to work (after my divorce it became a necessity), I decided that since there was a chance that I would be working the rest of my life I'd better be doing something that I liked.

I was trained in business administration. I had jobs such as coordinating escorted European tours and later as assistant business manager of the Goodman Theatre in Chicago. I also worked for a brief period of time for a travel agent in New York, but found the business was too cutthroat and decided to go with theatre work.

I explored jobs in casting, working with agents, but they were all entry-level positions which I could not afford to take.

The idea to become a talent manager is a result of my son's work in commercials, on Broadway, and in a film. Being a mother of a young, successful performer, I learned a great deal about the business and felt confident that I could be a theatrical manager. In fact, most managers of children, which is exactly what I do, are former stage mothers. A lot of them will operate from their kitchens or from spare rooms in their homes. I felt that in order to have credibility, I must have an office.

The Beginning

Getting an office was a good decision but acquiring a partner was not too wise. At least not for me. The partnership lasted about three weeks. We just were not compatible. I replaced this person with someone who used to work for my son's manager. For the first three years, he was enormously helpful in getting me started because he had contacts. We never became formal partners but just shared office space and profits.

To develop business I began in 1975 by approaching a few people with children whom I thought had the right look and ability for show business. I sent out press releases to 200 newspapers within a 50 mile radius of New York and got a fairly high percentage of them printed, which brought people in. I started in November but spent three months developing a good client file. It is a must before you start approaching agents. February 1, a letter went out to the agents with a client list stating that Studio V. was open for business. I had about 30 people, some of whom had experience.

There are many more mothers today that are interested in getting their children into show business than there were years ago. Also, there are many more managers who represent children. Finding interested parents is not difficult. One way to recruit in this market is to hold seminars. I conduct sessions on "How to get your Child into Show Business" periodically. However, one of the best ways of getting new children is by referrals from mothers of the children you already represent. Children I add to my client list must have a strong potential for making it in this business. I operate a highly professional managerial agency and I am very fussy about whom I take on. For example, while many managers have 300 to 400 clients, I represent only 40 to 50 of the best kids I can get.

Overhead Costs

It took almost one year to get to the point of breaking even. In fact, I started business in 1975, and had my first income check several months later. At that time overhead costs were not high. Office rents then were low, so expenses were not tremendous. Other monies were spent for advertising, entertainment, and office equipment. If you are renting office space now in New York, you have to estimate the cost at a minimum of $1000 per month. In renting, you are also paying one month's rent in advance and two months security. Phone installation minimally is $400 to $500, depending on how many extra lines you need, added to the basic overhead of running an office—stationery, supplies, postage, and so on. Actually, this is a business that can be run from a home or apartment.

There are more and more people coming into the business today as far as agents and managers. Why? According to an article in *New York* magazine there is a bigger demand for kids today. Of course, kids have always been an integral part of this business. In my opinion, overall there are fewer commercials being made. When I first started in the business there were constant bookings for test commercials. If they didn't like them, they threw them out. They don't do that now.

More Competition

Production costs are much too high. Now, they don't throw out commercials because they don't like them. Sometimes a product will test for 21 months, which is the length of a commercial contract, some longer. If it doesn't do well, they will drop it in a shorter amount of time. But since the recession, business has never gotten back to where it was. The advertising agencies are much more cautious with their money. A lot of that has to do with production costs escalating. Costs of producing and playing a television commercial have gone up astronomically. Yet, the budgets for talent are at the bottom of the list of expenses, unless you hire a superstar. For the average television commercial, your talent costs are about two percent. Payments have gone up through the years, but not in any way near the proportion of everything else that has escalated. The market has become diluted due to the increased number of agents and managers.

Down Times

The jobs go from $75 an hour for modeling to $50,000 for a national commercial. It is hard to say how many placements must be made in a given time to make the business profitable. If four network commercials could be done per month, an agency would be doing very well. But you never know how long a commercial might be used. It's very "iffy." They don't always tell you, and they're supposed to, whether or not it is a test run. It may run forever or it may only run for three to six months.

The first quarter of 1986 has been dreadful. In January there were more old commercials brought out that hadn't been seen in years. That, too, can be profitable because the spots are renegotiated. There is little control over negotiations. Unless the child is known or asked for, he or she works at scale. As you know, one of my children appeared in the award-winning "Mean Joe Green" Coca Cola commercial. I generated a lot of interest in him for TV shows and films. Unfortunately nothing panned out. But I was able to get him work after the Coke commercial for more than scale.

Losing Clients

What I like least about the business is when clients that I have worked with for a long time leave. It hurts a lot. I get an initial contract for a period of three years, but working with children, the contract can be broken at any time. A contract signed by a parent for a child is not legally binding. It does, however, represent a written commitment most people honor. There is no way of binding a child to you unless the contract is signed by a legal guardian. A parent is not a legal guardian. It really doesn't make that much difference, though. What are you going to do? If someone wants out, you let him go. A manager's contract, in a sense, could be written on one piece of paper in a few paragraphs, basically giving the manager power of attorney to sign checks and contracts guaranteeing exclusive representation of the child. Commercial contracts guarantee product exclusivity. That means a kid appearing in a commercial for Wonder Bread cannot make one for the Arnold company.

Manager's Payment

The biggest drawback for talent represented by a manager is that the client is paying a double commission. It is 15 percent and sometimes 20 percent to the manager and 10 percent to the agent. Some print agents are charging as high as 25 percent. You have to decide whether it's worthwhile to pay a double commission or to sign the child strictly with an agent who might not get as many audition calls. A manager deals with a wide range of agents who are getting calls for kids from casting directors.

It would be very simple for me to become an agent at this time. I have thought about it. This is a selling business. From my point of view, I can sell someone that I have a lot of faith in and I work very hard at it. But as a manager, I sell my kids to 12 to 15 agents. If I was an agent, I would deal with at least 100 casting people. Also, there are certain union regulations for agents that do not apply to managers. For example, I share an office space with another manager. If I were a franchised agent, I could not share space with anyone in a related field. I could not have a couch in my office. I would have to be a certain distance from the bathroom.

I would have to pay a franchise fee. There is a much greater sense of freedom in being a manager. And that's important to my lifestyle.

Working Operation

I have never had what I consider a full range of clients—that to me is four of each sex in each age category who are somewhat different physically. There have been times when I have had a lot of 6 to 10 year old girls. Right now I have a lot of boys in the 8 to 10 range. To get more kids, I send out press releases and sometimes advertise in the trade publications like *Back Stage*.

The number of new children I interview each week varies. Some weeks five or six, other times one or two. I need kids who not only look right, but speak well. Today, more and more agents are getting into print work. It can be very lucrative. I do very little in the area of modeling as the commissions are not regulated by any union, nor is the time period in which payment must be made. Most charge 20 percent on top of which there is a 15 percent service charge from the client. I now have about 40 children under contract and freelance with others—with the understanding that I have them exclusively in all areas except print. Many freelance children who do print are registered with many agencies. Many mothers are leery about signing a contract. In that case I am perfectly willing to work freelance for a while with them if they are good show business prospects.

I am not only selective about the kids, but also selective about the parents. If a father comes in with the child, I am especially careful. Stage fathers are worse than stage mothers. It is interesting that the biggest problem I have with my two top working kids is that their parents are very insistent that they get top grades. I can't argue with that, but at times it's hard to get those kids out for a job. Also, I have more trouble with teenagers than with mothers. Mothers seem to bow out when kids become teens and the teens are in a world of their own and much less dependable. I have comparatively little trouble with mothers. You must be assertive in the business but not overdo it.

Starting Up

This is a business that takes almost nothing to start if you work from your home. There is no inventory. There is more than one mother who decided that she didn't want to pay her manager and so she became the manager of her child. Many of these people really don't understand the business and some are almost "spoon fed" by those agents willing to do so. Many don't last too long.

I had a sound business background when I started. Also, I am a quick learner. I attended seminars on talent payments and takes, and when I started my business I knew what I was doing. I was organized and aware. Union contracts are renegotiated every three years and I keep on top of changes. You had better be as it's not as easy as it looks. The business is fairly complicated.

Payment from agents is usually not a problem. It is union regulated. Some agents are prompt, some are a little slower. Checks are sent to the agents who deduct their 10 percent, send me a check, and I, in turn, take out my commission and then pay the client. It is fundamentally simple but you must keep good records and be on top of everything; otherwise, you will get hurt and so will your client. When I see a commercial aired, I make a note of the day and time. If the check comes in and that particular airing is not noted, I get right on top of it.

Do I enjoy it? Mostly, yes. You find yourself dealing with a fascinating profession. But in the end, like any business, it's the bottom line that matters.

Trade Publications

Variety
154 West 46 Street
New York, NY 10036
(212) 869-5700

Back Stage
330 West 42 Street
New York, NY 10036
(212) 941-0020

Show Business
1501 Broadway
New York, NY 10036
(212) 354-7600

46

Tutoring Service

Jerry Belickis, president of Strategic Learning, Inc., Granite Springs, New York, is a former school teacher who has been tutoring since he was in high school. His organization provides private tutoring and diagnostic testing for students from kindergarten through college.

In addition, Belickis provides assistance to people attending college later in life and others preparing for civil service and other exams.

A thoroughly dedicated professional, his business is still not profitable after five years. However, Belickis demands high quality performance from his staff of teachers, mostly active ones. He gets the best and in that way he expects to have a tutoring service that will eventually be recognized as the finest and, therefore, be a highly profitable one.

Belickis knows that often what is needed before success is the will to sustain in order to prevail.

Jerry Belickis

Primarily, we offer tutoring backed up by diagnostic work and educational consulting. We work with parents to determine what type of learning difficulties their children have, and then develop appropriate remedial programs. Whenever possible, we work with the school system, coordinating our programs with the classroom instructors. The scope of academics covered ranges from kindergarten through high school, including special education. On the college level, we tutor individuals who have gone back to college. And, we work with adults taking what's called a GED equivalency program in order to get a high school diploma. We work with people out of school for a while who are taking civil service exams.

Start-Up

I started in 1981, and I am sole owner of this agency. My staff is made up of about 150 part-time tutors. I acquired the staff through advertising, word of mouth, and by placing notices in schools.

Tutors

My tutors must have at least a BA in education or a related field such as counseling, psychology, or social work. Of course, all tutors have a minimum of two years teaching experience. I do not take anyone right out of college. Recruiting tutors is not easy. It does take time. My requirements for tutors are so strict that many choose not to make a commitment to my guidelines. All applicants are required to read a statement and agree to all terms relative to professional behavior and procedures.

Earnings

It took almost two years from the time I started to acquire clients on a regular basis. I still have not met the salary that I was making before I got into the business. I could be approximating that salary at this point but I am continually building the business. I spend money on sales promotion and advertising to attract clients. Last year we spent about $8000. You definitely have to advertise to make your name known to the public. When I ask people how they heard about us, they tell me that they have seen our name around for many years. Expansion is a slow process because I must have personnel available in the new areas I plan to service.

Operation

My office is in my home so there is no rental overhead. But after the school year is over business comes to a crashing halt. When final exams for summer school are over in the second week of August, nearly everyone takes vacations. Anybody remaining prefers to start again after Labor Day.

A few people may start a week or two before school begins in September because they want to make sure their kids get some early preparation. Then it starts picking up slowly. Some parents maintain this service for their children on a continual basis.

Mathematics from the elementary to high school level is the subject we tutor the most. Special education also ranks high. I do have two degrees in that area and a lot of my teachers have training in special education. Science is also a big subject at the high school level, and language arts for elementary school students. The lowest demand is for help in foreign languages. That is primarily because it has been an elective subject. Since it is a subject of choice, children having difficulty with it just drop the course.

Costs

Costs range between $20 and $30 an hour. What the tutor gets also varies. Usually in the mid- to high-teens. There are two conditions that determine what the tutors are paid and how much clients are charged. One is a supply and demand. If I charge too much, the demand is going to drop. As far as tutors are concerned, if I am willing to pay $7 or $8 an hour I will get a good supply of tutors, but not good ones. A very high percentage of my 150 tutors have MAs. They are excellent teachers who have met my very demanding standards. That's why I give away about three quarters of what I make to keep high quality people.

Client Volume

Volume is really very important. Within the course of a year I get about 250 students. For the business to be really profitable I would need between 500 and 700. To sustain until I reach a profitable volume in the summer I do some consulting. My wife works full-time year-round. I would not be able to do this if not for the fact that my wife has been very supportive. To do this and to get something started like this and depend on this initially as a main source of income would not happen. Even after five years I could not support my family based on my earnings from this business alone. Perhaps in three years I will be able to support my family and my wife would not have to work anymore. The growth rate has been approximately 150 to 170 percent a year.

The most agreeable part of this business is I enjoy it. I am really dedicated to tutoring. What's upsetting is to get calls from individuals who really need tutoring. You know they need it; you can feel it in your heart, but there is nothing you can do as they cannot pay for it. But for those people we are able to serve, we really make a difference in their lives.

Trade Publications

Business Education World
1221 Sixth Avenue
New York, NY 10020
(212) 512-2168

Exceptional Children
1920 Association Drive
Reston, VA 22091

Instructor
757 Third Avenue
New York, NY 10017
(212) 503-2828

47

Typing and Word Processing Service

This is another service for which there is endless need and little availability. Also, it is a business that can be started and operated from a home or apartment and succeed with relative ease in the suburbs, as well as the cities.

While caring for her young daughter and operating from her home located in a rural section of Yorktown Heights, New York, Lauren Schnitzer launched her Wordsmith Typing & Word Processing Service and within a year was grossing a five-figure income.

The client mix that keeps her working steadily at her word processor is made up of companies farming out excess typing, the enormous number of people who operate small businesses, special publishers that use outside services to type their manuscripts, entrepreneurs who work out of their homes, and writers. College students are a fairly basic source of business which she has nearly outgrown.

Business has grown to a point that Schnitzer is looking for outside help to handle her own work overloads. Admittedly she has found it difficult to find typists who can meet her qualitative performance demands. This has limited her growth but she is considering opening a storefront operation where she can employ skilled, full-time help.

Lauren Schnitzer

I started in May 1984. I used to be employed full-time as a computer programmer/analyst, but I wanted to spend more time with my daughter, who at the time was two years old. I left the job to take up something that I could do at home. Also, I wanted to be my own boss. After finishing college where I majored in foreign languages, I had a few administrative assistant jobs. Being attracted to languages, I decided to try computer languages. I took one evening course in COBOL computer language, which I found fascinating. Not long after that I got a job as a computer programmer, and I remained in that field for seven years.

I learned to type on an old typewriter at home at the age of seven, and took typing in high school. During my last year of high school and all throughout college I did typing for other people. Through my administrative assistant positions I picked up such skills as how to prepare business documents and academic papers.

Start-Up

I planned Wordsmith for about six months before I actually began. It involved deciding on the equipment I would need, the kind of advertising I would do, the audience I wanted to reach, the rates I would charge, developing artwork, brochures, and a letterhead. The equipment I got was an IBM personal computer and a letter-quality printer. You certainly need something more sophisticated than a typewriter if you are going to go into word processing. I spent weeks researching the word processing software I would use, and had several packages demonstrated to me in the computer stores.

Promotion

I put ads in the *Pennysaver* first. I used a display ad that included my business card, logo, and a description of all the different services I offered. I put the ad in for several weeks in a row, and did not get much of a response. At the same time, I drew up flyers that had tear-off tabs on them with my phone number. I went to six or seven local colleges and I stuck them up on the bulletin boards. That brought business. I knew college students always have papers to type, and that this could be the bread and butter of my work until I could get commercial clients. Student papers are usually short pieces. You don't make much money from those.

It was expensive to advertise, so I put ads in the *Pennysaver* only occasionally. I also put flyers in some local businesses, especially photocopy shops. But basically I depended on the *Pennysaver* ads. I didn't use any local newspaper ads.

The business built by word of mouth. That was best. I did some work for lawyers and professors who told some of their clients and colleagues, and I got calls through them, referrals. When I got to a lull in my work, I advertised again. It didn't produce anything spectacular. Maybe three calls. But people kept the ads. When I didn't run an ad for a few months, I would get calls from people telling me they got my name from the *Pennysaver*.

I donated my services in situations where I could get free advertising in return. As an example, I type up all the monthly notes, recital programs, class lists, and brochures for the nursery school my daughter attends. My ad is featured on all of this printed material. By keeping the business name and logo out there, someone will be more likely to remember it when they need my services.

I had a steady flow of work after about six months. But I didn't consider myself profitable until I recouped the cost of my equipment and my start-up expenses, and that took about a year. Once you do that, it's a profitable business.

Costs

The personal computer at the time cost me about $3500, and the printer was about $700. You still need a typewriter on hand for filling in forms, invoices or envelopes, as this can be cumbersome on a word processor. But I already owned an electric typewriter. Letterhead and stationery and brochures and artwork—that was probably another $500. Then I had to stock up on bond paper, envelopes, mailing envelopes, labels, printer ribbons, diskettes— about $200 for my initial supply. And, of course, I replenish that all the time. I also bought an answering machine and a good dictionary.

One very important start-up expense is the word processing software that you will be running on your computer. There are about 10 or 12 strong ones out on the market which cost about $500. That's top dollar. You can get the same software through a magazine such as *PC Magazine* or *Byte* where it's advertised by various mail-order houses for less than half retail price. I got my software this way, at a low rate.

The total start-up figure was about $5500. I have to add, though, that it is even less expensive now as the prices of personal computers have dropped 20 to 25 percent. Someone could start up the same business now with comparable equipment for something like $4500.

Pricing

I got the price lists from several different local word processing services and a friend of mine obtained price lists and brochures for me from some word processing services in Manhattan. I collected all these price lists, and I noted the prices from ads I saw in the newspaper and *Pennysaver*. Then I came up with my own prices, trying to be competitive but still among the least expensive. I also studied the statements of policy from these brochures, and drew up my own.

Problems

To establish responsibility for errors in manuscripts I have disclaimers printed in my brochure. It will say something like "I will correct, free of charge, any error that is my fault, but errors due to poor handwriting or errors that existed in the original manuscript I will charge to do over." I also have a policy of free delivery and pick-up for orders over $50 within a five-mile radius.

Having people you don't know come to your house can be uncomfortable, especially if you're home alone. I've considered having a storefront operation, but that would be expensive and I would need a lot of business. I'm still considering it, though. With a storefront in town I would get walk-in business, since I would be visible to the public.

Work Schedule

I put in about 25 hours a week. If I were to do it full-time, I would advertise a lot more to generate the business. There will be times without any work at all. Then there are weeks where I can't handle all the work I have. It's a feast or famine kind of business. It's hard to control the flow of work because people have their own deadline. And you can't push aside deadlines, especially when it's a rush job. That's one drawback. Your time is not really your own sometimes. If you get two manuscripts at the same time and they are both due next Monday, you are going to be up until the wee hours every night until they're done.

I have considered hiring people for my overload. But I realized that when the people who are the spinoffs make errors, it reflects badly on my reputation. Your customers don't know that you had someone else type their work. If it came back sloppy, you could wind up doing the whole job over again. It's a big risk there, but it could be done if you had someone you could really trust and know is a strong word processor.

I would like to begin networking with other word processing services in the area, which means establishing with them an agreement where if they are overloaded, they will send customers to me, and I in turn would recommend customers to them when I am too busy to take the work. The way I see it, I would lose that customer anyway because I cannot accept their job, but this way I can possibly get new customers from my competitors.

By putting in a maximum of 25 hours a week, I was able to earn $12,500 the first year. It's kind of leveling at that because I'm doing other work. I'm not giving 100 percent to this business right now because I do have other interests.

I have an office in my house and I enjoy working at home. It's terrific. I am there to answer the phone and get my mail and packages. If I have enough energy at night and I want to stay up until two in the morning, I can. I can be comfortable. I don't mind that at all. I don't find the discipline a problem either. I am always willing to make the time to do my work, and my family is very supportive of this.

Lifestyle

The pressure can get to you. It can invade your family life and your personal life. At times I can't even eat dinner without thinking about the manuscripts I have sitting in my office. Also, I try to work when my child is in school. If you have a young baby, you'd have to work around nap times or work only at night.

Payment

Until I establish a business relationship with someone, I require cash payment on delivery of the work. Students especially must pay me immediately. Sometimes they have tried to avoid paying me, saying they forgot to bring the check. No pay, no paper. Sometimes they'll write a check and then call me and ask me not to cash the check for a week because it's going to bounce otherwise. I had a bad check only once. Eventually I got paid. I have trouble with the big corporate client that I have. They're very slow, even lost some of my invoices. I had to send them out again and again. I've always gotten paid though.

If someone makes me uneasy, or if they are reluctant to drive all the way to my house, I will arrange to meet them at either the post office or the library. I have sometimes met people for a cup of coffee where I can discuss the job with them. There is no fee for my consultation. Fortunately, most people who arrange to meet me somewhere keep the appointments. Many clients send me their work in the mail, so I bought a bigger mailbox to handle the bulky manuscripts and this works out fine.

I don't want the small jobs. It's just too much hassle to get my gears in motion for one page. A lot of students and authors with their theses and manuscripts have need for repeated changes, and that's where the word processor is so important. A resume will keep forever on my disk, so that a year later if a person needs a change, all I have to do is insert the new information. I get many repeats on resumes. The word processor is also great for handling the repetitive letter mailings, where the letter is automatically merged with the list of addresses and the effort on my part is minimal.

When I was first planning the business, it was kind of a letdown for me ego-wise because here I am, a senior programmer analyst for a major corporation, and I am going to be basically a typist. I thought it would be drudgery just sitting there pounding on the keys. But it can be stimulating. I am typing people's research and creative work. It's interesting, and I get a lot of reading done. I really read when I'm typing. I'm also pleased with the time I can spend with my family and the respect I get from my clients.

Trade Publications

PC World
555 De Haro
San Francisco, CA 94107
(415) 861-3661

Popular Computing
70 Main Street
Peterborough, NH 03458
(609) 924-9281

Software News
5 Kane Industrial Drive
Hudson, MA 01749
(617) 562-9308

48

Variety Store

Few people are as committed to taking the plunge into their own businesses as Dorothy Olson. A licensed practical nurse who had become weary of being buffeted by authoritative supervisors, she embarked on a plan to go out on her own.

She and her husband started by spending several years selling at flea markets in the Westchester County, New York area. Both learned from this table top retail selling about how to handle customers, how to order merchandise, what items moved or sold poorly, and other subtleties of merchant sales.

While learning, they were also successful. Selling most of what they brought to flea markets in the back of their car, they graduated to a van which permitted them to carry all the inventory needed for a full day selling at the market place. Their retail operation expanded to selling items at home, as buyers asked about where they could be reached to reorder what they wanted.

Finally, it was time for a store. The entrepreneurial plunge. Today, Olson is the full-time proprietor of Olson's Variety Store, Carmel, New York, where her husband still helps out on Saturdays.

Dorothy Olson

Anybody that goes into business and thinks that they're going to make money overnight is sadly mistaken. It takes at least three years, I really believe. Even though we have been in business before, this is an entirely new operation. We started June 15, 1985. This was after being in business at our home for 11 years. We have always been in business in one way or another, mainly selling at flea markets. We did start out with used items because that was all flea market vendors sold years ago. Gradually it changed over to new items, and we adjusted to the change.

Getting into new merchandise gave us the desire to be in business for ourselves. Flea market selling, going from place to place every weekend, was profitable. But it became very competitive, and the profit margin dropped when we were competing with so many other vendors. People go to a flea market with the thought in mind that they are going to buy dirt cheap. You deal with a different type of person who goes to a flea market than a person who walks into your store.

Peddling

Job stress I had as a licensed practical nurse prompted me to make a change. I took a three-month leave of absence to try my hand at various forms of selling. I got a peddler's license and I went out on the road to sell. Getting a peddler's license is a very difficult thing to do because many towns do not issue them. They do not like peddlers in their town so you have to get it from the county. It costs $50 for the license, which has your picture on it. It's only good for three months. It has a lot of restrictions. You can only be in one spot for 10 minutes and then you have to move. You just can't move 1000 feet, you have to move a few miles, so there's a lot entailed. I was selling the same new merchandise—underwear and socks. I would ride around but I got bored with that. There weren't enough customers. Then I went door to door. I didn't like that at all. I feel that people feel it's a big intrusion on their privacy, and they object to it. People that are ordinarily very nice are completely different when you go up to their door and bother them during the day.

Start-Up

I always wanted to get a store. I had looked at a few different places. None of them suited us. I happened to pass this store and it had a "For Rent" sign up. I stopped, inquired about it, liked it. I unfortunately acted too quickly, but I was in business. I already had the merchandise. People should be very careful. The minute they get the idea of going into business, they should take a course on how to operate a retail business. This is something I am going to be doing now. I should have done this before.

Getting Customers

At one time, people came to my home to buy. At a flea market you have crowds of people. They are always going by. You've got them there. But the minute you are located anywhere, you don't have those crowds of people. You have to think about how to get these people into your store. All these cars go by. How do I get them to stop? It's not as simple.

Location is very important. Parking is very important. The man next door does a million dollar business. Unfortunately, I have to ask his customers to park elsewhere because they are parking in my area. That's one important reason why we plan to relocate. Size is important for us, for what we carry. We have a variety of new, used, and antique items.

You have to be tremendously interested in what you are going to sell. If you don't like what you're selling, you are not going to sell it. A housewife who is very creative might decide that she might want to open up a craft shop, and she might be very good at it. I may go into it and be very poor at it. So, what they choose is important. It should be given a lot of thought. And, never copy the guy down the street. We had gone into trophies and people think there is a tremendous amount of profit in them. There isn't. Every person who walks through that door has a budget, and they want you to stick within it. We started with apparel and related items. But we wanted to get into the sports line. The sports line took us into the trophy line. It more or less goes together. We did get more sales of other items by people coming in for trophies.

You should have at least $20,000 and establish credit. Most manufacturers and distributors will deal with you only on a cash basis unless you establish credit. You have to be in business for a while until they trust you. Until then, it's strictly UPS COD. I can remember years when it was only UPS COD. It was a continual cash flow out, which is a very tough way to be in business. People should get business accounts for themselves. That helps, because you can say I have a business account and you give them the bank number. You can establish yourself with Dun & Bradstreet, which we did. This is very important to the small business owner because they think you have to be a tremendously big person to be in Dun & Bradstreet. You don't. It's a big help, and just to throw that out is prestigious.

Outlook

When we are in business three years, we will start realizing enough profit to excite me. Right now it's hard, hard work. I don't feel at this point that we are making money. We are still doing flea markets to earn money. But I feel we are going in the right direction. It's just a question of time. Being in any kind of a business, you are competing with all of your shopping centers. We are at a point where we are covering all of our expenses.

This isn't a seasonal business. We have a tremendous month and next month it could be just the other way. Or it could be mediocre. You don't know. It goes in spurts. We are not in a good location, but if you have a lot of cars parked in front, like we do, you lose your window space. No one can see our display merchandise. A good location would really increase our business. We have the ingredients here. We're certainly not lacking in salesmanship. If people were walking in I could sell to them.

Sales Spurts

Everything sells in spurts. You can't say that one item sells better than another. We had picture frames that sold tremendously during Christmas. They flew off the wall. Now, of course, they're sitting there. Trophies will sit for a while because they are seasonal. Everything that we sell here is paid for. Nothing is taken on consignment. Customers have been increasing since we started, and the big thrill is that they bring a friend back.

Advertising

Advertising is everything. The problem is that when you start a business, all of your money is tied up. It's tied up in the computer, the key press, the cat press, the merchandise. But it's so important to leave some budget for advertising. We do not advertise continually. We are going to be in 1986-1987 *The Guide*, which will help. We advertise in the local weekly paper. We have a regular ad in it. It comes out every Sunday. I advertise a lot in a Connecticut daily. We are almost on the border of New York and Connecticut. I can put an ad in today and tomorrow I will start getting calls. It's that fast. It's a tremendous paper for us.

Merchandise

We get used items at auctions, search the papers for used items being sold. The problem is that you have to know what to pay for old items. It's very, very competitive again because you're up against experts. There is a lot of running around and a tremendous amount of time involved acquiring merchandise. We sometimes go to private people to see if they have anything to sell. We don't just sit here and wait for them to bring things to us.

Hours

Right now our hours are Monday through Friday, 10 to 5. We had been opening on Saturdays. But people have so much to do themselves on weekends that they just aren't in this part of town. That's a location problem.

Long hours don't bother us as we love this business. I love selling. I love having people walk in the door and being able to respond to their needs. And sometimes it's not just something they want to purchase. We may have to be creative, too, when they are undecided. If they are looking for a particular gift and they don't know what to buy, or they have a piece of furniture that they're looking for, maybe we have something else they can use. We explain how they can use one thing instead of another. People sometimes leave their names with us so if we come across what they're looking for, we can call them. You can't just let people walk out if you don't have what they want. We try to redirect them.

Computer Engraving

The computer is good for engraving names on plaques. If I have 50 plaques, it would take a tremendous amount of time to do. The computer programs the whole job. It cost us close to $5000 and was purchased on a pay-out plan. Let's say we had to make up 18 plaques. To do it by hand would take hours. To do it by machine would take a few seconds.

Tips

We have some specials. People love them, anything where they feel that they are going to get a break.

Timing in business is very important. People go into business and then they feel that they don't want to be there themselves. They hire a kid and forget that he or she is not going to have the same interest as the owner. If you are going to be in a small business yourself, you have to be committed. If you want an eight hour day, forget it. Not when you're in business. If people give us an order that's substantial, like furniture or trophies, I visit their homes to discuss it. I encourage them to call me and ask that we stay until 6:00 or 7:00 if they can't make it in before that. We try to be very accommodating. If necessary, we will deliver. You have to think of your customers.

Trade Publications

Merchant Magazine
4500 Campus Drive
Newport Beach, CA 92660
(714) 752-1990

Accessories Magazine
22 South Smith Street
East Norwalk, CT 06855
(203) 853-6015

Casual Living
370 Lexington Avenue
New York, NY 10164
(212) 532-9290

49

Video Rental

Video cassette recorders, making it possible for people to enjoy watching movies in the privacy of their homes without coping with the theater annoyances of munching popcorn eaters and the babble of talky patrons, have spawned the growth of the video cassette rental business.

Dave Fleming of the small Yorktown Video rental store in Yorktown Heights, New York, has always operated at a profit even with two other competitors in the relatively small town. He plans to move to larger quarters as soon as his lease is up.

With ample opportunities for people to open this business anywhere in the United States and expect to do well, Fleming offers precise details on how to start and grow.

Dave Fleming

I still have my job with General Motors in Tarrytown, New York. I work off the line making shock towers; that's what holds the shock on the car. I've been doing that for nine years. Before that I did mostly construction work.

I thought video was a good side, full-time business. I wanted to do it badly but it took me four years to convince my wife. When I got laid off from General Motors, and I saw an ad in the *Pennysaver* for a video store that needed help, I called and the owner gave me a job. I worked there for three months and learned as much as I could about the business. He needed a partner and wanted to open up a second store in another location so I went into the partnership with him. But the partnership didn't work out.

Costs

Costs were very minimal. We started out with only about 250 tapes. This is really unheard of now; you need much more today. I have about 1100 tapes now. My store is 560 square feet and costs $880 a month rent. Initially, I had to buy a television set and a VCR, plus the 250 tapes, and employ three people, including my wife.

I would be able to make a living just running the store because I wouldn't need the two other people working here. I would eliminate one of them and the other would work part-time. He would work nights, and I would work the days.

I opened in April 1985, and started making money after the second month. We couldn't buy as many tapes in the beginning but now I buy 10 or 11 copies of the new releases, where in the beginning I bought only one or two. The suppliers sometimes give you a special if you buy three copies. You get an extra five percent off, but it's not much. Tapes range from $29 to $79.

When I bought my partner out, I paid him off in four months. I only had to pay him $10,000, and the store was all mine. In the beginning, I used my profits to increase the number of titles in the store.

To start out, a person should have 600 or 700 tapes. Because if people come in and you only have 300 tapes, they're not likely to get what they want. These customers don't come back.

Promotion

I never joined anyone's club, because I didn't want to be stuck just going to one place. But I had people coming in asking when am I going to start a club. People are always looking for a bargain. Finally, I did and I have 219 members who get rentals at discount.

I advertised in the *Pennysaver*. I have copies made of the ad and I have someone put them on car windshields in the Yorktown area, except around the other stores. I don't want to put them on cars in the parking lots where there are other merchants.

You can play a tape about 500 times but many don't last that long because people don't clean their machines, or the machines damage the tape. If I find it, I charge customers for the tape. Some people say okay I'll pay, and never come back. It happens about two times a month.

Problems

You've got to call people all the time to try and get the tapes back. I rent out about 900 tapes on an average week. There are about six a month that aren't returned. If I don't get them back after calling I send these customers registered letters. If I still don't get them back, I take them to court. But it's not worth all the time because I don't get anything back anyway. What happens is they don't show up in court, I get the judgment, then try to collect it. You can't. A video store owner in Carmel and I talk to each other every week and we tell each other who the problem people are so we can watch out for them.

About a third of the space is reserved for x-rated tapes. I do about one-third of my business in that area, more during the week than on weekends. Customers for pornographic tapes are of all ages, men and women. You can't be too moral about this as it produces good revenue.

We're open seven days a week. Most stores are.

Expansion

I plan to get about 2500 tapes in here. When I get to that, I think that will be enough for this store. When my lease runs out I'm going to look for a larger store in town. People come in and are impressed by the number of tapes you have.

Location and good parking are important. Many people don't know that the parking lot is across the street. Everyone wants to pull up to the door. When I expand it will be in a place where there's lots of parking room. Also, competition is increasing all of the time. I will have to find a spot where nobody's opened up yet.

Right now I'm competing with two other stores in town. My expansion plans include getting a computer. It will help with the paperwork and inventory. It will be easy to determine what's out and how many times a tape is rented.

My wife, who has a full-time job, takes care of all the paperwork and the books. She tells me what's renting and what's not moving, and what to get rid of. The computer will do this. If something is just going to sit on the shelf for two months I'm not going to keep it. I bring tapes I want to get rid of to video brokers where I can trade directly for other tapes or get a credit toward buying new ones.

Even with a three year old son, we're a working family. For me and my wife, who is a manager of labor relations at the Nestle company, this is just a side venture for us. It's going very well and can be a pleasant, profitable full-time business for anyone.

Trade Publications

Video Business
345 Park Avenue South
New York, NY 10010
(212) 686-7744

Video Store
Box 19531
Irvine, CA 92713
(714) 250-8060

Video Movies
3841 West Oakton
Skokie, IL 60076
(312) 676-3470

50

Weekly Newspaper

Owning a weekly newspaper is one of the entrepreneurial American dreams. In the congested warrens of the advertising agencies and the high pressure publicity mills, many stressful executives fantasize about getting off on their own, living in the country, and surviving by publishing a friendly weekly newspaper. It appears to be a civilized refuge.

Also, for people interested in writing, putting out a weekly paper has always been an appealing business. To encourage anyone who would like to consider such a venture, the story of Arthur Pedersen, the immigrant Norwegian who publishes the *Community Current*, Putnam Valley, New York (Current is the right spelling) is truly an encouraging one.

Pedersen has never been a writer but a printer. His publication is assembled each week with the use of press releases sent to the paper by merchants and organizations in his town. For a small fee, he is able to get young writers to do columns for the paper or cover various meetings.

The weekly newspaper—you do not have to be a writer to put one out.

Arthur Pedersen

I have a commercial print shop with everything you can think of for business. I learned the trade at my father's place in Norway.

In 1953 my wife and three children came to this country. Since my wife and I wanted to be in the country, we wound up living in Putnam Valley, New York.

As I had a card from the Norwegian typographic union, I got a job with the *Reporter Dispatch* newspaper in White Plains, New York, and I worked there for three years. I was a linotype operator and what you would call a typographer. I laid out ads for the big stores that advertised in the paper. Then I started my own print shop in Putnam Valley in 1956.

In 1958, we put out a phone book and sent it to all the homes in Putnam Valley once a year. We got the advertisers for this Putnam Valley's only phone book. We got our mailing list from the regular Westchester phone directory. We updated our mailing list of Putnam Valley residents every year. We were the first to put out supplemental town phone books. Now there are several others. In these small books it's so easy to find your neighbors' phone numbers.

Nine years ago, we felt that the community was big enough for a weekly newspaper. I thought that the newspaper was just going to be a sideline of the printing business. But the paper took off in such a big way that it takes us seven days a week to get each one out. However, we found that the Peekskill daily paper rarely covered our area. If there was a crime, it would send a photographer and a reporter. We felt that there were so many good things in this town, why only come here when something like this has happened?

Without advertising, you can't survive, of course. Nine years ago, the economy countrywide started to go bad. We found that after a while merchants who promised us advertising on the basis of a year began to fail. And we just started publishing. It was a tough time.

Subsidized the Weekly

For the first five years, I took the money from the print shop to pay for the paper we called the *Community Current*. That's right, it's *Current*. We were lucky in the sense that my wife and I had worked in printing and we did not have to hire anyone. We did everything ourselves. My wife does layouts for the paper and advertising. Of course, she also does all the paste-up. When we have 20 pages, that is a lot of production. She also proofreads the whole paper. It's a big job.

Start-Up

We had a little over 3000 homes, meaning families, living here when we started. When a town gets over 2500 homes or families, then it is really ready for a small weekly. We intended to print our paper but found the cost of newsprint, and paper which comes from Canada, too costly for a small weekly. I found that small papers don't do their own printing. There is a company that buys truckloads of paper from Canada. It does the printing for small weeklies. We produce the paper here, making the plate. It is called a mechanical. This special company then prints the paper from the plate. The procedure is so specialized that four different newspapers are printed at the same time. It's all done on a time schedule. In one and a half hours, we have our complete paper which today is 16 to 20 pages a week. We started out only with eight pages.

The Operation

I don't have full-time employees, only three part-timers for a day or two. A full-time, five-day-a-week staff is needed for a 32-page paper. To make a living from a weekly a person would have to put out a 32-page paper since the basic balance is 60 percent advertising and 40 percent news. This is a profitable ratio.

Expansion

The business community in Peekskill asked us to cover the city when the *Peekskill Star* was sold to a newspaper chain. They were looking for a paper to cover weekly events, social, and general news. We tripled our circulation. We might even consider expanding to other communities.

Costs

The printing costs for the basic 16 pages are about $500 for 5600 copies. The papers are mailed second class mailing as that is the most reasonable way. It costs me around 3.2 cents to mail a copy. I mail 1400 copies and the rest go to stores. We take in roughly $1600 to $1700 a week. It costs roughly $900 for everything. But if you go outside to have the mechanical made, figure another $800 for an eight page issue.

Legal Advertising

Each town designates a paper to be used for legal announcements. I stick to designation from each township. These ads run for three weeks and are very profitable. If you have the only newspaper in your town, you have to be assigned this legal advertising. At times two or three papers are designated when they meet the requirements. You do not then have to be the only paper in town.

When Profitable

It takes five years to be profitable. A good five years. That's why a person must be financially able to build the business. You have to find your own way. Just in our area, the same week as we started this paper, there were five other publications that began. One was *The Elephant* in Somers. It stayed in business one year. Couldn't make it. If you need to hire people to do everything at the beginning, it's too costly. If you know how to do things yourself, you have no problem.

Trade Publications

Publishing Trade
464 Central Avenue
Northfield, IL 60093
(312) 441-7488

Small Press
205 East 42 Street
New York, NY 10017
(212) 916-1887

51

Writing Service

Ellen Roddick started her business of teaching executives how to write more clearly and effectively with impressive credentials. Roddick, the dynamic president of Roddick Communications, Ltd., Bodega Bay, California, formerly the diet columnist for *Cosmopolitan* magazine, is also the author of two novels and the nonfiction book *Writing that Means Business*.

Prompted by a mix of cabin fever and the desire to develop a source of income that would be more dependable than royalties, she was advised to consider conducting seminars for top level management people on thinking and writing clearly. The premise for understandable communications begins by the process of selective thinking.

Totally immersed in the world of creative writing, Roddick entered the commercial world literally as an infant entrepreneur. She admits that even when she met with her first prospective client, she still did not know what a "presentation" was.

As a determined and committed woman, Roddick learned fast, accepted guidance from knowledgeable friends, and is now operating a successful business. Roddick tells how she did it.

Ellen Roddick

Having two novels and a nonfiction book published and writing a diet column for *Cosmopolitan* for six years with a young child at home, I had been in a fairly confined lifestyle for a while. I wanted to do something that would take me out and meet people. Also, I wanted a steadier income because with books it all comes in a lump sum and then there's nothing. I thought it would be nice to have the checks coming in on a more regular basis.

I went to a career counselor in Mount Kisco, New York, and I brought my books and some samples of my *Cosmo* columns. I dropped them on her desk and asked, "Am I worth anything on the open market?" She said I have two choices: "You could go into a corporation right now and write reports and make about $30,000 a year, two weeks vacation, and be there from nine to five. But I don't think from talking to you that it would suit your personality." Since I was not under any financial pressure, the career counselor suggested that I should write a book about improving executive writing skills. Then I could become a consultant for corporations, giving seminars and workshops teaching executives how to write more clearly. She said when this was done she would help me with the next step in my new career.

Starting

If I had had any idea of all the things I would have had to learn, I would probably not have started. Ignorance was bliss in this case. So I wrote *Writing that Means Business*. I took a year off and researched it and interviewed a number of successful people because I wanted it to be a practical guide.

I found that while doing the research for the book I kept falling asleep. I took more naps than any other time except when I was pregnant. I didn't want to write a book that would put people to sleep. I got the views of people in business who face this flow of garbled writing every day. I then focused the book on the problems they were having and the standards they wished people would achieve to establish clear, understandable communications in the corporative world. The practical, not the academic or theoretical.

My agent sold it to Macmillan, which was the first publisher that she sent it to. Then I began working on the consultant part of it. I joined the American Society for Training and Development (ASTD), which was a wonderful help. They have terrific seminars.

I joined their independent consultant special interest group. I subscribed to *Training and Development* magazine and that is how I learned training for the most part. I really learned through ASTD services.

I started putting together the kind of workshops I wanted to do and approached companies before I was fully ready. I learned that there is a big gap between the time a seminar is sold to when it is scheduled. I was preparing sales promotion material for mailings and to be used when I made my sales calls.

I really wasn't ready for my first meeting. I couldn't sell anything. When a man said to me, "Before you begin your presentation," I didn't know what a presentation was.

Promotion

I made lists of companies in this area and got the names of the vice presidents of human resources of each company. They would then pass me along to other people and then I would start making follow-up phone calls. Most people would say no. They usually do to a cold call. Once you begin to get clients then you get recommendations.

Before I made my first follow-up phone call I sat in my office and thought, I can't do this. It took me about a half hour, psyching myself up for it. I took rejection very hard. People at ASTD would tell us you can't take it personally.

Then my first client. The woman whom I met with asked me to design a two-day seminar specifically for her people. I did that and I didn't hear from her for a while and then I got an invitation to a luncheon the company was giving for all their outside consultants. And she told me that I had the job.

In the beginning I did prepare what people wanted. Now I have such a good sense of what people need that they are satisfied with what I have to suggest.

The next big step came when a senior vice president asked me to plan a seminar for his people and then to consult privately with each one to discuss samples of their writing. Basically I give the seminar and meet privately with the staff. People like my format and have used it successfully.

I gave my first seminar in May 1984, but I had been marketing for about a year before that. You need to establish identity for yourself in the market where you can perform best. I can deal with 15 people in three days from all different parts of the corporation and adjust immediately to the kinds of writing they're doing. I recognize the problems and obstacles they're having and help them overcome them to be able to write with greater clarity—and even to write less and still cover all of their ideas. Also, companies send me samples of writing to edit. My restructured writing sets a pattern to be followed in the future. I usually spend about two hours on each one, and my fee is $100 an hour. Then I go to the office and work another two hours with each person. These are very successful people I'm asked to see.

It should be understood that I never write for my clients. My major thrust is to help them figure out what problems they're having writing. It's almost always organizing their thoughts.

Visibility

I go out and meet a lot of people now. I go to luncheons and dinners held by professional groups. Expanding the number of people in business I know is one of the best ways to get new clients. I've gone to many meetings of women business owners both in New York and Westchester. I've just joined the International Association of Business Communicators also. These are all important sources of new business potential.

I'm still sending out letters and following up with phone calls. I also have sent out press kits, because I learned from talking to other professional people that visibility helps you to get accounts. I did get a job as a result of an article that appeared in the *New York Times*. Somebody who saw the article tracked me down and hired me.

I've worked with about 10 different companies. I show them my worksheets and give a copy of my book to the person who's interviewing me. I show them the important diagrams that I use and an outline or agenda. I also discuss with them the possibility of my working in my office on samples of the writing, and working in their office with the individuals and not doing a seminar.

Speeches

I also found that I was asked to make speeches. While I give speeches within a corporation, it occurred to me that I should register with the Speakers Bureau. I don't have the time to book speeches in addition to everything else.

Still Learning

The difficulties were that I had so much to learn. People did help a lot in fields that I didn't know much about such as doing public relations, publicity, and advertising. I had to learn that teaching and training are different. Teaching is conveying information to people. Training is changing behavior. Adults do not want to sit and listen to someone instruct them. To change their behavior and to have them enjoy and respect what you're doing, you have to be neutral. They want to participate a lot, so I had to design training materials that would allow them to be very active.

I have worked in situations where the people have substantial authority such as department heads. That is hard because they are extremely defensive and you spend the first hour or more dealing with frazzled egos. They want the group to know they are there as the control person. Very often they don't know why they are attending my seminar. They were just told to be there. One group was told to be in the room we were using at a certain time, nothing else.

Most of the people I've worked with want help. They are very open and receptive as they feel they can get something out of it. There are people who are responsive and easy to work with.

Problems

In any kind of seminar there are going to be some people who will argue with me about certain points. I think that makes it more interesting for everybody. If they give me too hard a time, I tell them that we obviously are not going to agree about this. If the way you're doing it is working for you—fine. One angry woman who had signed up for my seminar expected something different. Usually people discuss their feelings with me afterwards. Ten percent of the people in any group are incapable of learning anyway. I think there are sometimes people whom I can't reach. Other trainers have had that experience, as well. Luckily most people, and this is the rewarding part of it, seem to be able to take what you give them and run with it.

Outlook

I love it. I want to start speaking more. I'm working on my mind map diagrams showing how to organize thoughts to make them very simple to understand. I think it's a great tool for everybody who writes from teenagers to senior executives. I'm planning to use "stick-on notes" in the future. I show people how to write one idea on each "stick-on note" and then paste them on a flip chart and be able to arrange their thoughts by moving the notes around. In other words, I'm trying to find ways of expanding my business.

American business can lose a billion dollars a year through foggy writing and companies are taking that very seriously. They can lose clients. That figure comes from an estimate made by a magazine in 1982.

Preparation

In the development of my business I went to the School of Entrepreneurs in Tarrytown for two weekends. They taught me how to do a business plan which is very important when you are starting out. It's good to find some kind of course for small businesses and take it because there are things you need to know that you are not going to learn from going only to meetings or seminars. Even though it was just two weekends, it was enormously helpful. They were the ones who told me to focus my business on the one-on-one consultations because it's something I'm good at and I enjoy.

There's an organization called the American Women's Economic Development Corporation which is funded by banks. It has a business management course for women in the evenings. They offer very helpful consultations which I took. There are similar help groups in every part of the country.

Trade Publications

Executive Educator
1680 Duke Street
Alexandria, VA 22314
(703) 838-6722

Educational Leadership
225 North Washington
Alexandria, VA 22314
(703) 549-9110

Journal of Business Education
4000 Albermarble Street
Washington, DC 20016
(202) 362-6445

52

Epilogue

When I resigned my position as public relations director of a large corporation in New York City, the meticulously attired, affable marketing manager wished me luck saying, "Get it out of your system."

From his discouraging prospective, a common one for people who can never conquer their salary dependency, becoming an entrepreneur is the remedy for occupational constipation. He had already concluded that I would be back on some payroll soon.

Since that day, nearly 20 years ago, I have never worked for anyone again.

The most essential ingredient for succeeding in your own business is to become your own boss not as an act of desperation, but to fulfill a strong personal need for independence. You must honestly want to shed the suffocating day by day authority, continual accountability to others, serving body time having to check in at 9:00 in the morning and out at 5:00 in the afternoon for the satisfaction of making it on your own.

Becoming an entrepreneur is not a casual alternative to dropping out of the work force when you cannot find a suitable new job. This is not an advisable compromise for people conditioned to paycheck security. It merely heightens the risk of failure as most businesses require a certain amount of durability to succeed. Impatience and lack of adequate capitalization are two reasons many new ventures collapse.

It appears that for the people who sustain and survive, they earn more being their own bosses than they ever did working for others. By expanding, adding new retail outlets, the earning potential from a business aggressively managed is almost unlimited.

For many entrepreneurs, the revenue is not the major satisfaction. They are invigorated by doing something they like, working at a pace that satisfies their lifestyles, and are delighted to have that special sense of freedom. No boss.

If you make it on your own, and with proper advance planning you can, it will be one of the most important and rewarding experiences of your life.

INDEX